Complete Poems

Complete
Poems

Andrew Young

Arranged and
introduced by
Leonard Clark

Secker & Warburg · London

This edition first published
in England 1974 by
Martin Secker & Warburg Limited
14 Carlisle Street, London W1V 6NN

Designed by Philip Mann

436 59240 1 (hardcover)
436 59241 X (paperback)

PR6047
046 A17
.974
1

Printed in Great Britain by
Cox & Wyman Limited
London, Fakenham and Reading

Contents

INTRODUCTION

Andrew Young, priest, poet, topographer and naturalist, died on 25 November 1971. Born at Elgin on 29 April 1885, he was the youngest of the three children of Andrew and Maria Young. He was brought up in a good middle-class, and what he used to call an 'unliterary' Scots home. Yet he recalled seeing *Pilgrim's Progress, Paradise Lost,* and *A Household Shakespeare,* in that home. At five he wrote his first poem, about the battle of Bannockburn, as complete in incident and atmosphere as anything one could wish for. Its closing lines were:—

They fell, they fell—
Till there were few to tell
How the great battle was ended.

There was a Highland hero, too, one Fergus, whose exploits thrilled him so much that the writing of a poetic drama about this character was seriously contemplated. But not a word of it ever appeared on paper. Andrew Young also discovered at a very early age that not all of Shakespeare's lines rhymed.

The family moved to Edinburgh in 1887, setting up house in the Morningside district. Andrew first went to school at Gillespie's, long since disappeared; from there he won a scholarship to the Royal High School, where 'I ceased to do any work of any kind'. He never forgot the roaring voice and raging temper of John Marshall, the Head Master, nor how he played truant on several occasions. While enjoying the free air on Arthur's Seat on, probably, the last of these occasions, he was unfortunately picked out by the chance telescope of one of the masters. He was nearly expelled for this escapade, and had to forfeit his scholarship. He soon gained another and stayed on long enough to win fame by becoming the school's champion runner.

After taking his leaving certificate he went on, at eighteen, to Edinburgh University, to read Latin, Greek, English, Physics, Moral Philosophy, Metaphysics and Fine Art for his Master's degree. He became so interested in Fine Art that, before leaving university, he went with a scholarship to Paris, living a life almost of penury in the Latin Quarter. With what he once called his 'barrister's memory and the faculty of learning-up' he took a good degree and left the university, at twenty-three, to become a theological student at New College, Edinburgh.

In March 1910 his father paid for the publication of *Songs of Night,* Andrew Young's first book of poems. Inscribed to his mother, it was an attractive little volume for its day and age. One of its reviewers said of it, 'Mr Young has admirable powers of imagery and an enviable delicacy of expression. His poetic outlook on life seems tinged with a perpetual dust of melancholy, and the little verses in this collection are full of a twilight beauty and glamour.'

After four years at New College, Andrew Young was ordained a minister of the United Free Church of Scotland. His first call was to the Wallace Green Presbyterian Church, Berwick-on-Tweed, where, as Assistant Minister, he remained for a year. At this time he became engaged to Janet Green, a lecturer at Jordanhill Teachers' Training College.

He was then invited to take charge of Temple Church in Midlothian, where he became Pastor of a flock of not more than a hundred and fifty. He married Janet Green in Glasgow in September 1914, and soon after went to France to work, for six months at a time, with the YMCA. He made a reputation for himself with the troops by constructing short detective problems, in which he would give all the facts before inviting his listeners to make guesses as to the solution of the problem. When they failed, as they invariably did, he enlightened them.

The war over, he returned to Temple, but he had already decided to leave Scotland. John Baillie, the theologian, and a fellow-student of Andrew's at New College, described the Manse at Temple as 'modest enough, but whose interior was a carefully considered harmony of form and colour, the old Sheraton or Hepplewhite furniture blending admirably with the blue-and-white china, the rugs, the hangings and the wallpapers. But in the little piece of ground behind the house there was a pig—introduced to keep them down to earth.'

Andrew and Janet Young then moved to Hove, in Sussex, where he took charge of the English Presbyterian Church (now St Cuthbert's). His son, Anthony, had been born at Temple in

1915, and his daughter, Alison, was born at Hove in 1922.

The Youngs were avid readers and Andrew himself had a scholar's knowledge and appreciation of the classical languages, literature, theology, topography, painting and architecture. They spent many of their holidays at this time studying the Gothic architecture of England; later on, Andrew was to visit France to see the Gothic churches there. He was soon as familiar with the acres of the South country as he had been with his well-loved Highlands.

Now began the association with the bookseller, J. G. Wilson, who published Andrew Young's poems in slender books in 1920, 1921, 1922, 1923, 1926 and 1931. The editions were so small that the books attracted little attention but, as a result of them, he became friendly with John Freeman, Robin Flower, Henry Salt, and Viola and Francis Meynell. It was Meynell's Nonesuch Press which published Andrew Young's *Winter Harvest* in 1933, the book being described as 'not the work of a "new" poet, but the work of one surprisingly unknown outside a comparatively small circle'. Andrew Young's first *Collected Poems* appeared in 1936, and *Nicodemus*, a mystery play, was broadcast in 1937, with incidental music by Imogen Holst. The play was also performed in a Sussex church, and has been staged on a number of occasions since.

A year later Andrew Young met George Bell, the Bishop of Chichester, at the unveiling of the Edward Thomas Memorial at Petersfield. Soon afterwards he joined the Church of England. It was also about this time that he became friendly with F. A. Voigt, who greatly admired *Collected Poems* and gave Andrew warm support and much good advice.

After a few months at Wells Theological College, he was ordained by Bishop Bell in 1939, and went as curate to Plaistow in West Sussex, a small chapel-of-ease. He became Vicar of Stonegate in 1941, and remained there until his retirement in 1959. He was installed as Prebendary of Sutton, in Chichester Cathedral, by Bishop Bell in 1947; Edinburgh conferred its LLD on him in 1951, and he was awarded the Queen's Medal for Poetry in 1952.

In 1950, a second volume of *Collected Poems* appeared, and ten years later, a third volume of *Collected Poems:* this consisted of 209 poems, together with the verse-play *Nicodemus*. His long eschatological poem, (made up of the two poems 'Into Hades' [1952] and 'A Traveller in Time') called *Out of the World and Back* was published in 1958.

While at Stonegate he also wrote books about wild flowers and his travels in search of them. These were *A Prospect of Flowers* (1945), *A Retrospect of Flowers* (1950) and *A Prospect of Britain* (1956). These books display his scholarship, dry humour and exquisite prose style and should be regarded as complementary to his poetry.

Having retired from Stonegate, he went to live at Yapton, near Arundel, where he published *The Poet in the Landscape* (1962), consisting of a series of portraits of English pastoral poets as seen in their own rural settings, *The New Poly-Olbion* (1967), which he described as 'a gentle, lyrical guide to pastoral Britain', and *The Poetic Jesus*, his last book, which was published a few weeks after his death.

Mrs Young died on 12 March 1969, and Andrew Young was greatly affected by her death. His debt to her was enormous, for she scrutinised and criticised all his work from the earlier stages to its final form.

Mrs Young had suffered from a series of strokes, the first in 1965, each leaving her weaker until the final fatal one. In 1967 she fell and broke her hip, an accident almost identical to that which her husband had later. This left her an invalid. During all this time Andrew nursed her most devotedly, not an easy task, and the strain of this gradually took the toll of his strength and, incidentally, left him less freedom for writing. His visits to the London Library gradually ceased as it became more difficult for him to leave his wife. He greatly missed these trips where he had always made a point of calling on a few friends of long standing. John Arlott has written: '[The trips] last no longer than is necessary for that purpose. His small case full, he takes the next train back to Stonegate. He dislikes the values of London.' And he missed his visits to Scotland where it had long been his custom to travel for an annual holiday, always with his wife, to climb mountains and to observe wild flowers, especially the rarer varieties.

Although suffering from arthritis, and incommoded by a hernia which he refused to take seriously, Andrew Young remained in robust health and belied his years. He continued with his walks, and his reading which was largely concentrated on theology, mysticism and traditional poetry. In the last year of his life he compiled an anthology of religious poetry, with comments on each of the poems chosen, written in his typical pawky manner: the fount of his own poetry had by now dried up.

He enjoyed the visits of his family and friends, although these visits he preferred kept short. His neighbour, Mrs Muirhead, was a very special friend, as were Leslie and Kitty Norris, who drove him regularly to where he wanted to go, and watched over him with devotion. Many other poets, too, young and old, came to pay their respects to him at Yapton. However, he was often lonely during these latter years and did not enjoy living by himself. On the other hand, he had never relished social gatherings and chose solitude to company which was not of his selecting and, until severely incapacitated, preferred living alone to the idea of living with his family or with a housekeeper.

Had it not been for Mrs Muirhead he would have been much lonelier; he depended a great deal on her companionship, cheerfulness and liveliness of mind. He spent a great deal of time watching television, especially 'Westerns' and football matches. Always a meticulous letter writer, he now decided not to write any more, except when he was obliged to do so.

Although he was still capable of flashes of insight and wit, his memory and judgment were impaired. He turned to mysticism more than ever and maintained that he was in daily communication with his wife. He continued to read, though mainly mystery and detective stories, but he had no real will to live and scorned those who tried to cheer him up. When his literary executor suggested to him that he might write his autobiography, he was very taken with the idea and, with the aid of his typewriter, given him by the parishioners of Stonegate some years previously, he managed to compose about three-quarters of it before his death, also leaving behind him sufficient notes and rough drafts for it to be completed. He had already written something about himself and his early days in *The New Poly-Olbion*. But he now added further details.

On 10 December 1970, he had a serious fall in his house in the middle of the night, and was discovered next morning with a broken thigh and severe bruising of the face. He was admitted to St Richard's Hospital, Chichester, on the following day, which, in spite of the great attention it paid to him, he regarded as a prison. He made a good recovery from the fracture after a successful operation, taking into consideration his age and osteo-arthritis, but it was clear that he was in no state to return to Yapton. He entered a nursing home in Bognor Regis on 1 February 1971, and was then transferred to Moseley Hall Hospital, Birmingham, where he was visited daily by his daughter and her husband, Edward Lowbury, and often by his son and daughter-in-law from Leeds, his grandchildren and friends. While in Birmingham he began work on his anthology of religious poetry. He was transferred to another nursing home, Ravenna House, in Bognor Regis, on 16 April 1971. And it was there that he died on 25 November.

His funeral service took place in Chichester Cathedral, with several poets and other close friends present, and he was after-wards cremated at Chichester Crematorium. Mrs Young's ashes had been scattered on the Downs; his were scattered in the grounds of the Cathedral.

Andrew Young could have been mistaken for a farmer up in town for the day. He was five foot nine in height, sturdily built and large-boned, with a powerful frame which had strong powers of endurance, and legs capable of walking many miles without apparent fatigue. It can well be understood why he had been a fine runner, a storming rugby player and a good golfer in his younger days. The eyes were blue, the hair fair. The hands were particularly striking. John Arlott wrote of them, 'they can be gentle; christening a child, his touch seems a blessing of friend-liness: but his fingers rarely seem technically capable. Yet his handwriting is so delicate as to leave no imprint on the paper, merely fine, light, absolutely neat lines.'

He was a man of considerable reserve. He was not unsociable, but he was not a social person. As with his poems, he was a man of few words. Walter de la Mare once wrote to him and said, 'You watch words as a cat watches a mouse.' He had reduced speech to a minimum, but when he asked his friends questions they were shrewd and always to the point, and normally asked in order to lead to the next matter about which he had been thinking in silence for some time. Yet this man was an eloquent preacher. His sermons, though simple, were originally conceived, theologically sound, imaginative, and beautifully delivered, with the Scots accent which he never lost.

He was forthright in all he did and said. Once he had made up his mind, he was not easily shaken. His long silences and directness of speech could be devastating, and there were those who found that they could make little headway with him. Andrew Young was a man of steel but, at the same time, he was also a man of tenderness and innocence, given to sly humour and wit. He rarely laughed out loud, but his face became wreathed in smiles when something bizarre caught his fancy.

Religion and poetry meant everything to him. Although he had many friends who were distinguished poets, he had little to do with literary cliques or sophisticated social circles. John Arlott wrote of him: 'The stipend of a country parson cannot be large, yet Andrew Young has never made any attempt to "market" or "present" his work. He has sent his poetry to publishers and, on their acceptance, agreed without question to the terms offered and put the matter from his mind . . . even in recent years when his quality has been recognised, he has sent poems to editors who have asked for them, but has never submitted any unasked. His prose works were suggested and commissioned by publishers.' Arlott wrote these words in 1957.

When Andrew Young's publisher decided to issue his third *Collected Poems*, in 1960, the editor of that volume visited the poet to discuss the proposal. It transpired that Andrew Young had little idea of what he had written or what poems had been published. When pressed, he produced from his bureau the majority of the poems which later were to be included. They were in no kind of order and many were in duplicate; neither was the editor able to discover from the poet himself, with any degree of accuracy, when some of them had been written. He had to determine, on other evidence, the exact chronological order of the poems. Andrew Young entirely accepted the editor's decision as to the dates of their composition. One of his characteristics was that he had strong likes and dislikes. He remained faithful to the traditional poets, and once said, 'Before I settle down to a winter of poetry, I always read Spenser's *Faërie Queen*, because it was written with such a perfect ear.' He had a well-stocked library, largely consisting of works of theology, mysticism, poetry and topography and, in addition, a vast number of cheap thrillers in paperback. He once declared that Rex Stout was his favourite author.

Much of his reading he shared with his wife. In his eighties they embarked upon the re-reading together of *Paradise Lost,* and did not miss a day's study of it until the task had been completed. Although firm in his judgment of poetry, he read few books of criticism. Yet he had a ranging knowledge of poetry which had been written up to about the year 1930. Not that he was entirely ignorant of the work of his younger contemporaries. many of whom sent him their books, but, in general, he disliked 'modern' poetry because of its 'dearth of memorable or fine sounds.' He admired the work of de la Mare and Auden but had reservations about the poetry of T. S. Eliot, Gerard Manley Hopkins and, surprisingly, John Clare. Even for Auden, he did not display a great deal of enthusiasm. In a recorded interview towards the end of his life he said that he preferred some of the more recent writers to some of the writers of the 1930s, for example, Spender, Day Lewis and MacNeice. He had a great devotion to Hardy's short poems, enjoyed Edward Thomas and Robert Frost, but disliked the poetry of Yeats. Few men could have read more theology; he knew his Bible backwards, but would rarely enter into religious controversy. Although he was a faithful country priest, he did not involve himself in church politics and had no ambitions for promotion. Yet he was very proud of his Canonry, and greatly enjoyed the visits he paid to Chichester Cathedral for his annual sermon.

But although literature was one of his preoccupations, he also knew much about painting and china, and there were many good examples of both in his home. He had considerable knowledge of history and archaeology and few naturalists knew as much as he did about wild flowers and their habitats. Robin Tanner said of him: 'His two books, *A Prospect* and *A Retrospect of Flowers* are more closely stored with hard-earned, first-hand knowledge of plants than most botany books, and much of this knowledge is rare . . . there can be few men alive who have seen with their own eyes every member of the British flora.'

Andrew Young's poems have never been in, or out, of fashion. They are timeless in their appeal. A master of his own idiom, he did not often stray outside it and, in consequence, his work has all the marks of a distinctive character. Its roots lie deep in the pastoral traditions of English poetry. If he was a minor poet, then he was also a superb miniaturist, for he could compress vivid experience into a small space and yet not lose a drop of its essential life-blood. He was more than a painter in words for, by going into minute detail, he could produce a poem which was strongly suggestive and evocative.

It would be inaccurate to consider him to be only a 'nature' poet. He was much more than this. He saw nature in the larger setting of life itself, with that life always governed by the religious principles which he firmly believed. But even if he is only to be considered as a nature poet, then few have ranged more widely. It is doubtful if any poet, certainly in our own day, has written more good poems about so many wild flowers, birds and creatures, the changing seasons, local scenery, the weather, hills, rivers, sea-shores and archaeology. To name but a few of his subjects, there are poems about yellow-hammers, swans, daisies, oats, glow-worms, frogs, a dead mole, a brimstone butterfly, swedes, spiders, snails. The seasons are represented by poems on late autumn, winter mornings, a windy day, last snow, a thunderstorm, May frost, sudden thaw, drought in the Fens. He was always much affected by mist, snow, rain and wind.

Andrew Young was a great traveller in Britain. For the best part of sixty years he made himself familiar with most parts of England, Wales and Scotland, so it is hardly surprising that he wrote many poems about the places he visited, as well as about the flowers he found in them. There are, for instance, poems about Romsey Abbey, the Forest of Dean, the Paps of Jura, the Quantocks, the Wiltshire Downs, Sedgemoor, Glencoe, a flower farm in Cornwall, Grimes Graves and the rivers Rother, Lodden, Dove, Beaulieu, Tyne, Erme and Severn. Although there are many poems about Scotland, the vast majority of these 'traveller's poems' refer to places in southern England.

Sir John Betjeman has written of him: 'He is a nature poet whose sense of awe and wonder is in most of his poems, which often look on the surface as though they were clear pictures, either of some details in a hedge or wide prospect and which are seen on re-reading to have yet another meaning.' Andrew Young always saw the macrocosm within the microcosm and 'heaven in a grain of sand.'

Although Andrew Young's poetry is peculiar to him, it has affinities. He belongs to the field company of John Clare, Robert Frost, Thomas Hardy, Edward Thomas and Edmund Blunden. Yet it is doubtful if he was ever consciously influenced by any of these. Tennyson and Housman may have been greater influences. The fact is that there is no other poetry in English quite like it. A poem by Andrew Young is instantly recognisable. It has the same immediacy as the water-colours of Morland, Constable, Couzens, Girtin and Cotman, and the wood engravings of Bewick.

It is the highly controlled emotional intensity and the ability to communicate an exact thought and sensation that distinguishes Andrew Young's poetry. Further, the intelligence that directed all this was self-critical. He was a very fundamental poet, close to the earth, realistic, ironical, aware of the contradictions inherent in existence, as well as being a visionary. By introducing fancies and conceits into his poems, he could shock his readers into a realisation of some fact or significant thought which, until that moment, had escaped notice and consideration. He saw beyond the simple elements of this world; and through a few cracks into eternity, he peered for a while into what is infinite.

It could be claimed that Andrew Young put more of himself, and of his knowledge, into the two long poems: 'Into Hades' and 'A Traveller in Time', and that in so doing he increased his poetic span. And yet only Andrew Young could have written both the short 'nature' poems and the two long ones, for they are the products of the same imagination, and of one who was blessed with a profound awareness of life, death and resurrection.

Andrew Young's poetry will continue to give delight to future generations as it has to those who have already discovered and enjoyed it. The general reader will be refreshed and informed by it, and poets, whatever their gifts and attitudes, will learn much from its technique, and recognise its individual voice, and significance.

Leonard Clark

Part 1

The Leaf

Sometimes an autumn leaf
  That falls upon the ground,
  Gives the heart a wound
And wakes an ancient grief.

But I weep not that all
  The leaves of autumn die,
  I only weep that I
Should live to see them fall.

On the Cliff

Earth with my little pathway ends
  Abruptly, and I stand
Where in a wall of snow extends
  The breakage of the land.

White birds, like fragments of the cliff,
  Fly on the empty air,
Crying as though from hearts made stiff
  With straitening despair.

And far beneath me on the beach
  Sings the incessant sea,
And sighs like love that cannot reach
  To Love's eternity.

Lord, in the weakness of my words
  Let all these pray for me,
The broken cliff, the crying birds
  And the foam-mottled sea.

The Bee-Orchis

I saw a bee, I saw a flower;
I looked again and said, For sure
Never was flower, never was bee
Locked in such immobility.

The loud bees lurched about the hill,
But this flower-buried bee was still;
I said, O Love, has love the power
To change a bee into a flower.

Daisies

The stars are everywhere tonight,
Above, beneath me and around;
They fill the sky with powdery light
And glimmer from the night-strewn ground;
For where the folded daisies are
In every one I see a star.

And so I know that when I pass
Where no sun's shadow counts the hours
And where the sky was there is grass
And where the stars were there are flowers,
Through the long night in which I lie
Stars will be shining in my sky.

Islands

These new songs that I sing
   Were islands in the sea
That never missed a spring,
   No, nor a century.

A starry voyager,
   I to these islands come
Knowing not by what star
   I am at last come home.

A Child's Voice

On winter nights shepherd and I
   Down to the lambing-shed would go;
Rain round our swinging lamp did fly
   Like shining flakes of snow.

There on a nail our lamp we hung,
   And O it was beyond belief
To see those ewes lick with hot tongue
   The limp wet lambs to life.

A week gone and sun shining warm
   It was as good as gold to hear
Those new-born voices round the farm
   Cry shivering and clear.

Where was a prouder man than I
   Who knew the night those lambs were born,
Watching them leap two feet on high
   And stamp the ground in scorn?

Gone sheep and shed and lighted rain
   And blue March morning; yet today
A small voice crying brings again
   Those lambs leaping at play.

Waiting

We waited for the spring,
   My love and I;
The larks were in the sky,
The lambs were on the hill:
Did we not hear them sing?
Did we not hear them cry?
Yes, yes, O yes, but still
We waited for the spring
   My love and I.

We waited for the spring,
   My love and I;
Speedwell that robs the sky,
Trumpeting daffodil
And blackthorn's blossoming,
We watched them all go by;
These came and went but still
We waited for the spring
   My wife and I.

Cuckoo

   Cuckoo, cuckoo!
Is it your double note I hear
   Now far away, now near,
     Now soft, now clear,
      Cuckoo?

   Cuckoo, cuckoo!
Laughs now through the spring's misty wood
   And leaf-winged sap in flood
     Your mocking mood,
      Cuckoo?

Cuckoo, cuckoo!
So sits among sky-tangling trees
　Our Mephistopheles
　　Singing at ease,
　　　Cuckoo.

　Begone, cuckoo!
For soon your bubble-note twin born,
　Pricked by the June rose-thorn,
　　Shall burst in scorn,
　　　Cuckoo.

The Stars

The stars rushed forth tonight
Fast on the faltering light;
So thick those stars did lie
No room was left for sky;
And to my upturned stare
A snow-storm filled the air.

Stars lay like yellow pollen
That from a flower has fallen;
And single stars I saw
Crossing themselves in awe;
Some stars in sudden fear
Fell like a falling tear.

What is the eye of man,
This little star that can
See all those stars at once,
Multitudinous suns,
Making of them a wind
That blows across the mind?

34

If eye can nothing see
But what is part of me,
I ask and ask again
With a persuasive pain,
What thing, O God, am I,
This mote and mystery?

The Last Leaf

I saw how rows of white raindrops
    From bare boughs shone,
And how the storm had stript the leaves
    Forgetting none
Save one left high on a top twig
    Swinging alone;
Then that too bursting into song
    Fled and was gone.

Late Autumn

The boy called to his team
    And with blue-glancing share
Turned up the rape and turnip
    With yellow charlock to spare.

The long lean thistles stood
    Like beggars ragged and blind,
Half their white silken locks
    Blown away on the wind.

But I thought not once of winter
    Or summer that was past
Till I saw that slant-legged robin
    With autumn on his chest.

The Yellow-Hammers

All up the grassy many-tracked sheep-walk,
    Low sun on my right hand, hedge on my left
    Blotted by a late leaf, else leaf-bereft,
I drove my golden flock.

Yellow-hammers, gold-headed, russet-backed,
    They fled in jerky flight before my feet,
    Or pecked in the green ranks of winter-wheat,
While I my footsteps slacked.

Myself, the road, the hedge, these flying things,
    Who led, who followed as we climbed the hill?
    Loud as their repeated trembling trill-trill
Was the swift flirt of wings.

So tame I would have touched them with my hand,
    But they were gone, darting with rise and fall;
    I followed, till at the hedge-end they all
Dispersed over the land.

There, where the hillside scattered the sheep-walk,
    Deserted by the birds I stood to muse
    How I but now had served so sweet a use,
Driving my golden flock.

The Flood

The winter flood is out, dully glazing the weald,
The Adur, a drowned river, lies in its bed concealed;
Fishes flowing through fences explore paddock and field.

Bushes, waist-deep in water, stand sprinkled here and there;
A solitary gate, as though hung in mid-air,
Waits idly open, leading from nowhere to nowhere.

These bushes at nightfall will have strange fish for guests,
That wagtail, tit and warbler darkened with their nests;
Where flood strays now, light-headed lapwings lifted crests.

But soon comes spring again; the hazel-boughs will angle
With bait of yellow catkins that in the loose winds dangle
And starry scarlet blossoms their blind buds bespangle;

Dogs'-mercury from the earth unfold seed-clasping fists
And green-leaved honeysuckle roll in tumbling twists
And dreams of spring shake all the seeds that sleep in cists.

O blue-eyed one, too well I know you will not awake,
Who waked or lay awake so often for my sake,
Nor would I ask our last leavetaking to retake.

If lesser love of flower or bird waken my song,
It is that greater love, too full to flow along,
Falls like that Adur back, flood-like, silent and strong.

The Lane

Years and years and man's thoughtful foot,
Drip and guttering rains and mute
Shrinkage of snows, and shaggy-hoofed
Horse have sunk this lane tree-roofed
   Now patched with blossoming elder,
   Wayfaring-tree and guelder;
Lane that eases the sharp-scarped hill
Winding the slope with leisurely will.

Foot of Briton, formal Roman,
Saxon and Dane and Sussex yeoman
Have delved it deep as river-bed
Till I walk wading to my head
   In air so close and hot

And by the wind forgot,
It seems to me that in this place
The earth is breathing on my face.

Here I loiter a lost hour,
Listen to bird, look on a flower.
What will be left when I am gone?
A trodden root, a loosened stone
   And by the blackthorn caught
   Some gossamery thought
Of thankfulness to those dead bones
That knit hills closer than loose stones.

The Old Tree

The wood shakes in the breeze
   Lifting its antlered heads;
Green leaf nor brown one sees
   But the rain's glassy beads.

One tree-trunk in the wood
   No tangled head uprears,
A stump of soft touchwood
   Dead to all hopes and fears.

Even the round-faced owl
   That shakes out his long hooting
With the moon cheek-a-jowl
   Could claw there no safe footing.

Riddled by worms' small shot,
   Empty of all desire,
It smoulders in its rot,
   A pillar of damp fire.

Green Hellebore

Wind has an edge that cleaves
  Like hook of hedger, for
A blood-stain marks the leaves
  Wind-cut of hellebore.

Green with the loss of blood
  No heavy head looks up,
But in this Easter wood
  Hangs down an empty cup.

The Tumulus

Here to the leeward of this Roman mound
  The wind is quiet
As any battle-shout that shook the ground
  Long ago nigh it.

Here the dead sleep in bones through centuries
  With earth for flesh,
Their own long woven in flower-tapestries
  And turf's green mesh.

No bugle shatters sleep for them, so surely
  They keep the peace;
I in their old decease mourn prematurely
  My own at ease.

In Romsey Abbey

'Lady, the angel-heads
  That cusp your canopy
Are looking the other way;
  Why should not I
Stoop down and kiss your lips

Or even your brow?
The little hound at your feet
  Would not bark Bow-wow.'

'Stranger, from the earth
  They dug me to sleep thus
In this organ-shaken church
  Like Eutychus;
Look! Time's clumsy fingers
  Broke my neck-bone;
I think that your lips too
  Would turn to stone.'

On the Beaulieu Road

Oaks stand bearded with lichen
  Like witches that knot the birch;
But hark! the cow-bells chiming
  That call no one to church.

Oak-leaves to crown an empire
  Lie sodden as brown dulse,
While chiming bells in the distance
  Die like a fitful pulse.

Kingley Bottom

Beneath these bine-looped yew-boughs
  Gorse blossom is outspread
Like gold that lies unguarded
  By dragons that hang dead.

All but one pterodactyl
  That hid in mist and rain
High over Kingley Bottom
  Hums like an aeroplane.

The Oak-Wood

Tree behind tree they stand;
  Their slavish roots roll through the ground
And veined like the flat ivy's hand
  Their heavy boughs lean out around.

Is it not thus and thus
  The branched veins issuing from the heart
Like tentacles of an octopus
  Go up and down through every part?

How many saps have sunk?
  How many more shall yet run fresh
Till these trees too like this dead trunk
  Shall turn to touchwood, soft as flesh?

Rother in Flood

Between twin banks the Rother
  With slow contentment goes;
Bush-sprinkled lakes spread this side and
    the other
  Flowing as the wind flows.

High on the upper lands
  White-cowled oasthouses stare
And piled poles in hop gardens seem like hands
  Whose fingers point in prayer.

Gathered by stormy weather
  The rooks and sea-gulls meet
Like black angels and white mingling together
  At God's last judgment-seat.

At Oxford

Though cold December rains draw vanishing rings
   On the choked Isis that goes swirling by,
These academic gowns flap like the wings
   Of half-fledged blackbirds that attempt to fly.

The Signpost

Snowflakes dance on the night;
   A single star
Glows with a wide blue light
   On Lochnagar.

Through snow-fields trails the Dee;
   At the wind's breath
An ermine-clad spruce-tree
   Spits snow beneath.

White-armed at the roadside
   Wails a signpost,
'Tonight the world has died
   And left its ghost.'

The Pines

The eye might fancy that those pines,
With snow-struck stems in pallid lines,
Were lit by the sunlight at noon,
Or shadow-broken gleam of the moon;
But snowflakes rustle down the air,
Circling and rising here and there
As though uncertain where to fall,
Filling the wood with a deep pall,
The wood that hastens darkness to hide all.

The hurricane of snow last night
Felled one; its roots, surprised by light,
Clutch at the air in wild embrace;
Peace like an echo fills the place
Save for the quiet labour of snow,
That falling flake on flake below
The torn limbs and the red wounds stanches,
And with a sheet the dead trunk blanches,
And lays white delicate wreaths among the branches.

Loch Brandy

All day I heard the water talk
From dripping rock to rock
And water in bright snowflakes scatter
On boulders of the black Whitewater;
But louder now than these
The silent scream of the loose tumbling screes.

Grey wave on grey stone hits
And grey moth flits
Moth after moth, but oh,
What floats into that silver glow,
What golden moth
That rises with a strange majestic sloth?

O heart, why tremble with desire
As on the water shakes that bridge of fire?
The gold moth floats away, too soon
To narrow to a hard white moon
That scarce will light the path
Stumbling to where the cold mist wreathes the strath.

The Star

A white mist swathed the valley;
    Each huge uncertain tree
Came looming through the darkness
    An island in a sea;
But when I climbed to Hawkley
    The stars held all the night,
Spangles and glittering ouches
    And clouds of hollow light.

I thought they were blest spirits
    Borne upward on a wind
And the white mist the cerements
    That they had left behind;
And you, your body sleeping,
    In their bright numbers moved
And with raised face I questioned,
    Which is my well-beloved.

The Green Woodpecker

Whether that popinjay
    Screamed now at me or at his mate
I could not rightly say,
    Not knowing was it love or was it hate.

I hoped it was not love
    But hate that roused that gaudy bird;
For earth I love enough
    To crave of her at least an angry word.

The Nest

Four blue stones in this thrush's nest
I leave, content to make the best
Of turquoise, lapis lazuli
Or for that matter of the whole blue sky.

On the Pilgrims' Road

That I had hit the Road
    I partly knew
From a great Roman snail
    And sombre yew;
But that my steps went from
    And not towards
The shrine of good St Thomas,
    I thought of afterwards.

So I adored today
    No, not his ghost,
But the saints in Westwell window,
    And her the most
Who knelt there with no head
    But was so very
Adorable a saint
    In dress of crushed strawberry.

March Hares

I made myself as a tree,
No withered leaf twirling on me;
No, not a bird that stirred my boughs,
As looking out from wizard brows
I watched those lithe and lovely forms
That raised the leaves in storms.

I watched them leap and run,
Their bodies hollowed in the sun
To thin transparency,
That I could clearly see
The shallow colour of their blood
Joyous in love's full flood.

I was content enough,
Watching that serious game of love,
That happy hunting in the wood
Where the pursuer was the more pursued,
To stand in breathless hush
With no more life myself than tree or bush.

Round Barrows

The prophet's cloudy hand
Was not so small
As those grave-howes that stand
Along the skyline of the rig,
No, nor so big
Now as the shades of evening fall.

But what of their dead bones?
Not stiff and stark they lie,
But as a family,
Fathers, mothers and sons,
With indrawn knees
They lie or lean or sit at ease.

The Flint-Breaker

After the rain was gone
The wind among the trees rained on;
I listening to that scattered tread

Heard what the old flint-breaker said
(Two years or three before):
'Some flints have water at the core.'

Did I walk that sea-bank
Where flints with fluid mouths once drank
The drop they hold apart
In rusty hollow of their heart,
And lingers too in me—
One drop of that old Nummulitic Sea?

In Moonlight

We sat where boughs waved on the ground
But made no sound;
'They cannot shake me off,'
Shrieked the black dwarf,
Impudent elf,
That was the shadow of myself.

I said to him, 'We must go now';
But from his bough
He laughed, securely perched,
'Then you rise first';
It seemed to me
He spoke in wicked courtesy.

We rose and 'Take my hand,' he whined,
Though like the wind
Each waving bough he leapt;
And as we stept
Down the steep track
He seemed to grow more hunched and black.

The Spider

A single white dewdrop
That hung free on the air sang, Stop!
From twig to twig a speckled spider,
Legged like a hermit-crab, had tied her
Invisible web with WELCOME
For sign, and HOME SWEET HOME.

That spider would not stir,
Villain of her Greek theatre,
Till as I heedlessly brushed past her
She fled fast from her web's disaster
And from a twig-fork watched it swing,
Wind tangling string with string.

Now she weaves in the dark
With no light lent by a star's spark
From busy belly more than head
Geometric pattern of thin thread,
A web for wingy midge and fly,
With deadly symmetry.

The Wood

Summer's green tide rises in flood
Foaming with elder-blossom in the wood,
And insects hawk, gold-striped and blue,
On motion-hidden wings the air looks through,
And 'Buzz, buzz, buzz',
Gaily hums Sir Pandarus,
As blue ground-ivy blossom
Bends with the weight of a bee in its bosom.

Heavy with leaves the boughs lean over
The path where midges in a loose ball hover,
And daisies and slow-footed moss

And thin grass creep across,
Till scarcely on the narrow path
The sparrow finds a dusty bath,
And caterpillars from the leaves
Arch their green backs on my coat-sleeves.

Bright as a bird the small sun flits
Through shaking leaves that tear the sky in bits;
But let the leaf-lit boughs draw closer,
I in the dark will feel no loser
With myself for companion.
Grow, leafy boughs; darken, O sun,
For here two robins mate
That winter held apart in a cold hate.

The Rain

Fair mornings make false vows!
    When to that wood I came
I stood beneath fast-dripping boughs
    And watched the green leaves wink
    Spilling their heavy drink;
Some flowers to sleeping buds returned,
Some, lit by rain, with clear flames burned;
'Cuckoo' — again, again
    A cuckoo called his name
Behind the waving veil of dismal rain.

The rain bit yellow root
    And shone on the blue flints
And dangled like a silver fruit
    From blackened twigs and boughs;
    I watched those running rows
Splash on the sodden earth and wet
The empty snail-shells marked 'To Let',

And whitened worms that lay
    Like stalks of hyacinths,
The last end of a children's holiday.

I heard a dead man cough
    Not twenty yards away —
(A wool-wet sheep, likely enough,
    As I thought afterwards);
    But O those shrieking birds!
And how the flowers seemed to outstare
Some hidden sun in that dim air,
As sadly the rain soaked
    To where the dead man lay
Whose cough a sudden fall of earth had
    choked.

The Beech

Strength leaves the hand I lay on this beech-bole
    So great-girthed, old and high;
Its strawling arms like iron serpents roll
    Between me and the sky.

One elbow on the sloping earth it leans,
    That steeply falls beneath,
As though resting a century it means
    To take a moment's breath.

Its long thin buds in glistering varnish dipt
    Are swinging up and down
While one young beech that winter left unstript
    Still wears its withered crown.

At least gust of the wind the great tree heaves
    From heavy twigs to groin;
The wind sighs as it rakes among dead leaves
    For some lost key or coin.

And my blood shivers as away it sweeps
    Rustling the leaves that cling
Too late to that young withered beech that keeps
    Its autumn in the spring.

The Evening Star

I saw a star shine in bare trees
That stood in their dark effigies;
With voice so clear and close it sang
That like a bird it seemed to hang
Rising and falling with the wind,
Twigs on its rosy breast outlined.

An obvious moon high on the night
And haloed by a rainbow light
Sounded as loud as silver bell
And trees in flight before it fell,
Their shadows straggling on the road
Where glacier of soft moonlight flowed.

But moon nor star-untidy sky
Could catch my eye as that star's eye;
For still I looked on that same star,
That fitful, fiery Lucifer,
Watching with mind as quiet as moss
Its light nailed to a burning cross.

The Feather

Briar, spindle and thorn tangled together
    Made dark the narrow track,
And from some hoarse-voiced rook the fallen feather
    That lay silent and black.

Gold lees left in the pink cup of dog-roses
   Nor the red campion
That the June cuckoo when his voice he loses
   Cast his white spittle on.

Nothing could lighten that track's narrow gloom,
   Except on ground or bark
Some honied light straggling through branches from
   The sun that made it dark.

The Roman Wall

Though moss and lichen crawl
   These square-set stones still keep their serried ranks
Guarding the ancient wall,
   That whitlow-grass with lively silver pranks.

Time they could not keep back
   More than the wind that from the snow-streaked north
Taking the air for track
   Flows lightly over to the south shires forth.

Each stone might be a cist
   Where memory sleeps in dust and nothing tells
More than the silent mist
   That smokes along the heather-blackened fells.

Twitching its ears as pink
   As blushing scallops loved by Romans once
A lamb leaps to its drink
   And, as the quavering cry breaks on the stones,

Time like a leaf down-drops
   And pacing by the stars and thorn-trees' sough
A Roman sentry stops
   And hears the water lapping on Crag Lough.

Loch Luichart

Slioch and Sgurr Mor
Hang in the air in a white chastity
Of cloud and February snow
That less to earth they seem to owe
Than to the pale blue cloud-drift or
The deep blue sky.

Though high and far they stand,
Their shadows over leagues of forest come,
Here, to a purer beauty thinned
In this true mirror, now the wind,
That held it with a shaking hand,
Droops still and dumb.

As I push from the shore
And drift (beneath that buzzard) I climb now
These silver hills for miles and miles,
Breaking hard rock to gentle smiles
With the slow motion of my prow
And dripping oar.

Winter Morning

All is so still;
The hill a picture of a hill
With silver kine that glimmer
Now whiter and now dimmer
Through the fog's monochrome,
Painted by Cotman or Old Crome.

Pale in the sky
The winter sun shows a round eye,
That darkens and still brightens;

And all the landscape lightens
Till on the melting meadows
The trees are seen with hard white shadows.

Though in the balk
Ice doubles every lump of chalk
And the frost creeps across
The matted leaves in silver moss,
Here where the grass is dank
The sun weeps on this brightening bank.

Penelope

The leaves hang on the boughs
Filemot, ochreous,
Or fall and strangely greet
Green blades of winter wheat
The long buds of the beech
Point where they cannot reach.

A sad Telemachus,
I stand under the boughs;
Patient Penelope,
Her heart across the sea,
Another year unweaves
Her web of wasted leaves.

Is bud and leaf and flower
All we are waiting for?
But we shall wait again
When these are gone, and then
When they are gone and gone
Penelope alone.

Illic Jacet

This was his little house;
    Its moth-bright eye
Looks through the orchard-boughs
    At the starry sky.

I never crossed his door
    But still preferred
To hunt some orchid or
    Watch for a bird.

We went one day to church
    His friends and he;
We left him in the lurch,
    As it seemed to me.

But still from hs grave he says,
    'You know the house;
You must one of these days
    Drop in on us.'

The Dead Bird

Ah, that was but the wind
Your soft down stirred,
O bird, lying with sidelong head;
These open eyes are blind,
I cannot frighten you away;
You are so very dead
I almost say
'You are not a dead *bird*.'

The Shadow

Dark ghost
That from tree-trunk to tree-trunk tost,
Flows with me still,
When on the shoulder of the hill
The late sunrise
Tangles its rainbows on my eyes —

Although
Each time I wave to you below
I see you stand
And wave back with a distant hand,
I ask, Can you be mine,
O shade gigantic and divine?

On White Down

In a high wood,
Wind chilling my premonitory blood,
I play at death
Closing my eyes and holding back my breath.

Ah glad surprise
To wake from death, and breathe, and open eyes
To see again
This mist-capped hill that is so bright with rain.

But from a bough
A blackbird mocks, 'Blind eyes are not enough;
You act the ghost
With sight and breathing that you never lost.'

O bird, be still;
When I would walk on an immortal hill
You drag me back
As though I had not left this dim hill-track.

After the Funeral

Standing beneath the jewelled trees
That waved with slow mournful unease;
I lifted up my eyes to them —
The stars caught in the trees' dark stratagem.

But when I asked which is the wonder,
All stars above the earth and under
And in the vast hollow of space
Or the stern look on that defeated face;

I said, 'Not even the Milky Way
Shines like the golden streak of clay —
All, all of her that I could save —
My foot has gathered from her open grave.'

The Sheaf

I'd often seen before
That sheaf of corn hung from the bough —
Strange in a wood a sheaf of corn
Though by the winds half torn
And thrashed by rain to empty straw.
And then today I saw
A small pink twitching snout
And eyes like black beads sewn in fur
Peep from a hole in doubt,
And heard on dry leaves go tat-tat
The stiff tail of the other rat.
And now as the short day grows dim
And here and there farms in the dark
Turn to a spark,
I on my stumbling way think how
With indistinguishable limb
And tight tail round each other's head

They'll make tonight one ball in bed,
Those long-tailed lovers who have come
To share the pheasants' harvest-home.

The Burnt Leaves

They have been burning leaves,
Dead leaves the little shrew upheaves
Poking in winter for his trifling food.
And large black pools lie in the wood
As though the sky had rained down ink;
It all means nothing as I think
That more and more are left behind
To rise and rustle in the wind,
That paws them as a cat plays with a mouse,
And June will bring green leafy boughs;
Yet often as I watched them run
I thought of you, O blue-eyed one,
Or thought about my thoughts of you,
Fitful and feeble too:
For as these ran a little way and stopped
When the wind rose and dropped,
So I would think of you a little, yet
So soon forget.

Mist

Rain, do not fall
Nor rob this mist at all,
That is my only cell and abbey wall.

Wind, wait to blow
And let the thick mist grow,
That fills the rose-cup with a whiter glow.

Mist, deepen still
And the low valley fill;
You hide but taller trees, a higher hill.

Still, mist, draw close;
These gain by what they lose,
The taller trees and hill, the whiter rose.

All else begone,
And leave me here alone
To tread this mist where earth and sky are one.

A Man with a Horse

I wondered at the mighty horse
   So meekly since the day began
Toiling to make himself a corse,
   And then I wondered at the man.

The Men

I sat to listen to each sound
Of leaf on twig or ground
And finch that cracked a seed
Torn from a limp and tarnished weed
And rapid flirt of wings
As bluetits flew and used as swings
The bines of old man's beard,
When suddenly I heard
Those men come crashing through the wood
And voices as they stood,
And dog that yelped and whined
At each shrill scent his nose could find;
And knowing that it meant small good
To some of us who owned that wood,
Badger, stoat, rabbit, rook and jay

And smoky dove that clattered away,
Although no ill to me at least,
I too crept off like any stealthy beast.

Palmistry

I lifted from the ground my grass-pressed hand
And pondered, as its strange new lines I scanned,
What is foretold? What hope, what fear,
What strife, what passion is prefigured here?

The Rat

Strange that you let me come so near
    And send no questing senses out
From eye's dull jelly, shell-pink ear,
    Fierce-whiskered snout.

But clay has hardened in these claws
    And gypsy-like I read too late
In lines scored on your naked paws
    A starry fate.

Even that snake, your tail, hangs dead,
    And as I leave you stiff and still
A death-like quietness has spread
    Across the hill.

Killed by a Hawk

I stir them with my stick,
    These trembling feathers left behind
To show a hawk was sick,
    No more to fly except on the loose wind.

How beautiful they are
   Scattered by death yet speaking of
Quick flight and precious care
   Of those great gems, the nest-eggs, warm with love.

Feathers without a bird!
   As though the bird had flown away
From its own feathers, fired
   By strange desire for some immortal spray.

A Barrow on the Quantocks

Each night I pass the dead man's mound
I keep on turning round;
I almost stumble on the track
With looking back.

Although that mound of ling and stones
May hide his brittle bones,
I do not think that there he sleeps
Or wakes and peeps.

He is too intimately near
To see or touch or hear;
I only feel my blood is crossed
By his chill ghost.

It may be that all things are made
Of substance and of shade
And such a hill as I walk here
He walks elsewhere.

I know not which the substance is,
This hill of mine or his,
Nor which of us is the true ghost
In shadows lost.

An Old Road

None ever walks this road
That used to lie open and broad
And ran along the oakshaw edge;
The road itself is now become the hedge.

Whatever brambles say
I often try to force a way,
Wading in withered leaves that spread
Over dead lovers' tracks a sighing bed.

Is it the thought of one
That I must meet when most alone
That makes me probe a place like this,
Where gossamer now gives the only kiss?

I shall see no one there
Though I had eyes to see the air,
But at the waving of a bough
Shall think I see the way she went but now.

The Forest of Dean

'Now here you could not lose your way,
Although you lost it,' seemed to say
Each path that ran to left or right
Through narrowing distance out of sight.

'Not here, not here,' whistled a thrush
And 'Never, never,' sighed a thorn-bush;
Primroses looked me in the face,
With, 'O too lovely is this place.'

A larch-bough waved a loose green beard
And 'Never, never,' still I heard;
'Wayfarer, seek no more your track,
It lies each side and front and back.'

The Farmer's Gun

The wood is full of rooks
That by their faded looks
No more on thievery will thrive,
As when they were alive,
Nor fill the air with the hoarse noise
That most of all is England's pleasant voice.

How ugly is this work of man,
Seen in the bald brain-pan,
Voracious bill,
Torn wing, uprooted quill
And host of tiny glistening flies
That lend false lustre to these empty eyes.

More delicate is nature's way
Whereby all creatures know their day,
And hearing Death call 'Come,
Here is a bone or crumb,'
Bury themselves before they die
And leave no trace of foul mortality.

In December

I watch the dung-cart stumble by
    Leading the harvest to the fields,
That from cow-byre and stall and sty
    The farmstead in the winter yields.

Like shocks in a reaped field of rye
   The small black heaps of lively dung
Sprinkled in the grass-meadow lie
   Licking the air with smoky tongue.

This is Earth's food that man piles up
   And with his fork will thrust on her,
And Earth will lie and slowly sup
   With her moist mouth through half the year.

The Round Barrow

A lark as small as a flint arrow
Rises and falls over this ancient barrow
And seems to mock with its light tones
The silent man of bones;

Some prince that earth drew back again
From his long strife with wind and mist and rain,
Baring for him this broad round breast
In token of her rest.

But as I think how Death sat once
And with sly fingers picked those princely bones,
I feel my bones are verily
The stark and final I.

I climbed the hill housed in warm flesh,
But now as one escaped from its false mesh
Through the wan mist I journey on,
A clanking skeleton.

The Loddon

Through hoof-marked meadows that lie sodden
From winter's overflow, the Loddon
Winds by the winding pollard hedge —
Stunt willow-trunks that line the edge,
Whose roots like buried eels are sunk,
A grove of saplings on each trunk.

Its water with a white-frothed mouth
Chewing and gnawing the uncouth
Loose sticks and straws that in disorder
Lie littered on its leaping border,
As breath of wind roughens its hide,
This way or that way makes its tide.

This way or that — But O let come
May-blossom that in buds lies dumb,
This water that laps bush and tree
Shall long have drifted to the sea;
I almost feel that I too go
Caught in its secret lapsing flow.

The Cuckoo

This year the leaves were late and thin,
And my eye wandering softly in
Saw perched upon a topmost twig,
Small bird to have a voice so big,
A cuckoo with long tail behind,
Twig and bird aswing on the wind,
That rose and flew with outspread tail
Guiding his flight like steering sail.

I waited, listened; came again
Across the distance of the rain
'Cuckoo' so faint and far away

It sounded out of yesterday,
Making me start with sudden fear
Lest spring that had seemed new and near
Was gone already. A sparrow hopped
In white plum-tree and blossom dropped.

The Secret Wood

Where there is nothing more to see
Than this old earth-bound tree
That years ago dry sawdust bled
But sprouts each spring a leaf or two
As though it tried not to be dead,
Or that down-hanging broken bough
That keeps its withered leaves till now,
Like a dead man that cannot move
Or take his own clothes off,
What is it that I seek or who,
Fearing from passer-by
Intrusion of a foot or eye?
I only know
Though all men of earth's beauty speak
Beauty here I do not seek
More than I sought it on my mother's cheek.

Stay, Spring

Stay, spring, for by this ruthless haste
You turn all good to waste;
Look, how the blackthorn now
Changes to trifling dust upon the bough.

Where blossom from the wild pear shakes
Too rare a china breaks,
And though the cuckoos shout
They will forget their name ere June is out.

That thrush, too, that with beadlike eye
Watches each passer-by,
Is warming at her breast
A brood that when they fly rob their own nest.

So late begun, so early ended!
Lest I should be offended
Take warning, spring, and stay
Or I might never turn to look your way.

The Slow Race

I followed each detour
Of the slow meadow-winding Stour,
That looked on cloud, tree, hill,
And mostly flowed by standing still.

Fearing to go too quick
I stopped at times to throw a stick
Or see how in the copse
The last snow was the first snowdrops.

The river also tarried
So much of sky and earth it carried,
Or even changed its mind
To flow back with a flaw of wind.

And when we reached the weir
That combed the water's silver hair,
I knew I lost the race —
I could not keep so slow a pace.

Sea Wormwood

It grew about my feet
Like frost unmelted in the summer heat;
I plucked it and such oozes
Flowed from its broken bruises
That as I turned inland
Its loosened scent was hanging from my hand.

And so I thought the people
Stayed from pea-picking by the road to Steeple,
No, not to watch the stranger
Who landed from Goldhanger,
But breathe the odorous oil
That flowing from his hand sweetened their toil.

An Evening Walk

I never saw a lovelier sky;
The faces of the passers-by
Shine with gold light as they step west
As though by secret joy possessed,
Some rapture that is not of earth
But in that heavenly climate has its birth.

I know it is the sunlight paints
The faces of these travelling saints,
But shall I hold in cold misprision
The calm and beauty of that vision
Upturned a moment from the sorrow
That makes today today, tomorrow tomorrow.

The Fallen Tree

The shade once swept about your boughs
Quietly obsequious
To the time-keeping sun;
Now, fallen tree, you with that shade are one.

From chalky earth as white as surf
Beneath the uptorn turf
Roots hang in empty space
Like snakes about the pale Medusa's face.

And as I perch on a forked branch,
More used to squirrel's haunch,
I think how dead you are,
More dead than upright post or fence or chair.

To the River Dove

Swift under hollow shelf
Or spreading out to rest yourself
You flow between high ridge and ridge
To brim the heavy eyebrows of the bridge.

No, Dove, it is not mine
To stroke you with a fly and line,
A legless trunk wading your water;
I leave your fish to heron, pike and otter.

And him who haunts that inn
With 'Isaac Walton' for its sign,
Living there still as he lived once,
A wind-blown picture now, with creaking bones.

The Stockdoves

They rose up in a twinkling cloud
And wheeled about and bowed
To settle on the trees
Perching like small clay images.

Then with a noise of sudden rain
They clattered off again
And over Ballard Down
They circled like a flying town.

Though one could sooner blast a rock
Than scatter that dense flock
That through the winter weather
Some iron rule has held together.

Yet in another month from now
Love like a spark will blow
Those birds the country over
To drop in trees, lover by lover.

The Bird

The blackbird darted through the boughs
Trailing his whistle in a shrill dispute
'Why do you loiter near our house?'
But I was mute,
Though as he perched with sidelong head
I might have said,
'I never notice nests or lovers
In hedges or in covers;
I have enough to do
In my own way to be unnoticed too.'

Last Snow

Although the snow still lingers
Heaped on the ivy's blunt webbed fingers
And painting tree-trunks on one side,
Here in this sunlit ride
The fresh unchristened things appear,
Leaf, spathe and stem,
With crumbs of earth clinging to them
To show the way they came
But no flower yet to tell their name,
And one green spear
Stabbing a dead leaf from below
Kills winter at a blow.

The Knotted Ash

Is this a lover's vow?
Who else should tie it and for what
This olive-coloured sapling in a knot,
Till now spring's sap must stoop
And bend back in a gouty loop
Rising from root to sooty-budded bough?

They may be tired of love,
Who found it not enough
To twine the glances of their eyes
Like kissing brimstone butterflies;
But death itself can not untwist
This piteous tree-contortionist.

The Fairy Ring

Here the horse-mushrooms make a fairy ring,
 Some standing upright and some overthrown,
A small Stonehenge, where heavy black snails cling
 And bite away, like Time, the tender stone.

The Swans

How lovely are these swans,
That float like high proud galleons
Cool in the summer heat,
And waving leaf-like feet
Divide with narrow breasts of snow
In a smooth surge
This water that is mostly sky;
So lovely that I know
Death cannot kill such birds,
It could but wound them, mortally.

Eryngo

I came on that blue-headed plant
 That lovers ate to waken love,
Eryngo; but I felt no want,
 A lovesick swain, to eat thereof.

Young Oats

These oats in autumn sown,
That stood through all the winter's dearth
In so small ranks of green
That flints like pigmies' bones lay bare
And greater stones were seen
To change to hares and rise and run,

Today to such a height are grown
That drawn up by the sun,
That Indian conjuror,
The field is levitated from the earth.

The Stones

Though the thick glacier,
That filled the mountain's rocky jaws
And lifted these great rocks like straws
And dropped them here,
Has shrunk to this small ale-brown burn,
Where trout like shadows dart and turn,
The stones in awkward stance
Still wait some starry circumstance
To bring the ice once more
And bear them to a distant shore.

The Copse

Here in the Horseshoe Copse
The may in such a snow-storm drops
That every stick and stone
Becomes a tree with blossom of its own.

And though loose sun-spots sway
The night so lasts through all the day
That no bird great or small
Sings in these trees but is a nightingale.

Time might be anything,
Morning or night, winter or spring;
One who in this copse strays
Must walk through many months of night and days.

The Paps of Jura

Before I crossed the sound
  I saw how from the sea
These breasts rise soft and round,
  Not two but three;

Now, climbing, I clasp rocks
  Storm-shattered and sharp-edged,
Grey ptarmigan their flocks,
  With starved moss wedged;

And mist like hair hangs over
  One barren breast and me,
Who climb, a desperate lover,
  With hand and knee.

The Track

Trodden by man and horse
Tracks change their course
As rivers change their bed;
And this that I now tread,
Where the lean roots obtrude,
Was not the first track through the wood.

There older traces flow,
Where ghosts may go
But no one else save I;
And as in turn I try
Each faint and fainter track,
Through what long ages I fall back.

The Sunbeams

The tired road climbed the hill
Through trees with light-spots never still,
Gold mouths that drew apart and singled
And ran again and met and mingled,
Two, three or five or seven,
No other way than souls that love in heaven.

Sunny and swift and cool
They danced there like Bethesda's pool;
Ah, if in those pale kissing suns
My halting feet could bathe but once
No slender stick would crack,
My footstep falling on its brittle back.

The Dark Wood

O wood, now you are dark with summer
Your birds grow dumber
And ink-stained leaves of sycamore
Slide slowly down and hit your floor;
But there are other signs I mark,
In ivy with sunlight wet
And dried rains streaming down your bark,
A withered limb, a broken shoulder,
Signs that since first we met
Even you, O wood, have grown a little older.

The White Blackbird

Gulls that in meadows stand,
The sea their native land,
Are not so white as you
Flitting from bough to bough,
You who are white as sin
To your black kith and kin.

Wood and Hill

Nowhere is one alone
And in the closest covert least,
But to small eye of bird or beast
He will be known;
Today it was for me
A squirrel that embraced a tree
Turning a small head round;
A hare too that ran up the hill,
To his short forelegs level ground,
And with tall ears stood still.
But it was birds I could not see
And larks that tried to stand on air
That made of wood and hill a market-square.

Mole-Hills on the Downs

Here earth in her abundance spills
Hills on her hills,
Till every hill is overgrown
With small hills of its own;
Some old with moss and scorpion-grass,
Some new and bare and brown,
And one where I can watch the earth
Like a volcano at its birth
Still rise by falling down;

And as by these small hills I pass
And take them in my stride
I swell with pride,
Till the great hills to which I lift my eyes
Restore my size.

Thistledown

Silver against blue sky
These ghosts of day float by,
Fitful, irregular,
Each one a silk-haired star,
Till from the wind's aid freed
They settle on their seed.

Not by the famished light
Of a moon-ridden night
But by clear sunny hours
Gaily these ghosts of flowers
With rise and swirl and fall
Dance to their burial.

The Tree

Tree, lend me this root,
That I may sit here at your foot
And watch these hawking flies that wheel
And perch on the air's hand
And red-thighed bees
That fan the dust with their wings' breeze.
Do you not feel me on your heel,
My bone against your bone?
Or are you in such slumber sunk,
Woodpeckers knocking at your trunk
Find you are not at home?
To winds you are not dumb;

Then tell me, if you understand:
When your thick timber has been hewn,
Its boards in floors and fences sewn,
And you no more a tree,
Where will your dryad be?

Fenland

Where sky is all around
And creeps in dykes along the ground,
I see trees stand outlined
Too distant to be tossed with wind.

And farther still than these
Stand but the tops of other trees,
As on the ocean's rim
Vessels half-sunk in water swim.

Where there is so much sky
And earth so level to my eye,
Trees and trees farther hide
Far down the steep world's mountain-side.

The Dead Crab

A rosy shield upon its back,
That not the hardest storm could crack,
From whose sharp edge projected out
Black pinpoint eyes staring about;
Beneath, the well-knit cote-armure
That gave to its weak belly power;
The clustered legs with plated joints
That ended in stiletto points;
The claws like mouths it held outside:
I cannot think this creature died
By storm or fish or sea-fowl harmed

Walking the sea so heavily armed;
Or does it make for death to be
Oneself a living armoury?

In Teesdale

No, not tonight,
Not by this fading light,
Not by those high fells where the forces
Fall from the mist like the white tails of horses.

From that dark slack
Where peat-hags gape too black
I turn to where the lighted farm
Holds out through the open door a golden arm.

No, not tonight,
Tomorrow by daylight;
Tonight I fear the fabulous horses
Whose white tails flash down the steep water-courses.

A Windy Day

This wind brings all dead things to life,
Branches that lash the air like whips
And dead leaves rolling in a hurry
Or peering in a rabbits' bury
Or trying to push down a tree;
Gates that fly open to the wind
And close again behind,
And fields that are a flowing sea
And make the cattle look like ships;

Straws glistening and stiff
Lying on air as on a shelf
And pond that leaps to leave itself;

And feathers too that rise and float,
Each feather changed into a bird,
And line-hung sheets that crack and strain;
Even the sun-greened coat,
That through so many winds has served,
The scarecrow struggles to put on again.

The Ruined Chapel

From meadows with the sheep so shorn
They, not their lambs, seem newly born
Through the graveyard I pass,
Where only blue plume-thistle waves
And headstones lie so deep in grass
They follow dead men to their graves,
And as I enter by no door
This chapel where the slow moss crawls
I wonder that so small a floor
Can have the sky for roof, mountains for walls.

The Comet

Why do I idly stand
And digging with my finger-tips
Tear the tree-trunk in strips?
Because such touchwood soft and damp
I once would stuff in a clay lamp
And blow on it with fiery face
To coax a sparkling light
And through the darkness race,
That lit lamp in my hand
A comet streaming through the autumn night.

Gossip

The wind shaking the gate
Impatiently as though in haste and late
Shook and shook it making it rattle,
And all the other tittle-tattle
It rushed to tell —
Of how mahogany chestnuts fell
And how the gamekeeper
Had crackling paper here and there and there
To frighten pheasants back into the wood,
And how the flapping scarecrow stood
And guarding seeds from harm
Saluted with a broken arm,
And how the thin-voiced lamb
Still in the autumn sucked his dam,
A late and casual love-begot,
All that I heard and proudly thought
That I, a man, whom most things hate,
Shared country gossip with the wind and gate.

By the Tyne

What foolish birds were they
That build these nests exposed to day,
A score on every tree
So darkly clear between the river and me?

Not birds that haunt these woods,
But heavy, hurrying winter floods
With their foam-hissing billows
Left these wild driftwood nests on the lean willows.

Ploughing in Mist

Pulling the shoulder-sack
Closer about his neck and back,
He called out to his team
That stamped off dragging the weigh-beam;
And as he gripped the stilts and steered
They plunged in mist and disappeared,
Fading so fast away
They seemed on a long journey gone,
Not to return that day;
But while I waited on
The jingle of loose links I caught,
And suddenly on the hill-rise,
Pale phantoms of the mist at first,
Man and his horses burst
As though before my eyes
Creation had been wrought.

The Eagle

He hangs between his wings outspread
    Level and still
And bends a narrow golden head,
    Scanning the ground to kill.

Yet as he sails and smoothly swings
    Round the hillside,
He looks as though from his own wings
    He hung down crucified.

The Fear

How often I turn round
To face the beast that bound by bound
Leaps on me from behind,

Only to see a bough that heaves
With sudden gust of wind
Or blackbird raking withered leaves.

A dog may find me out
Or badger toss a white-lined snout;
And one day as I softly trod
Looking for nothing stranger than
A fox or stoat I met a man
And even that seemed not too odd.

And yet in any place I go
I watch and listen as all creatures do
For what I cannot see or hear,
For something warns me everywhere
That even in my land of birth
I trespass on the earth.

On Middleton Edge

If this life-saving rock should fail
Yielding too much to my embrace
And rock and I to death should race,
The rock would stay there in the dale
While I, breaking my fall,
Would still go on
Farther than any wandering star has gone.

A Heap of Faggots

Faggots of ash, elm, oak
That dark loose snowflakes touch and soak,
An unlit fire they lie
With cold inhospitality.

Nothing will light them now,
Sticks that with only lichen glow
And crumble to touchwood
Soft and unfit for fire's food.

And with wren, finch and tit
And all the silent birds that sit
In this snow-travelled wood
I warm myself at my own blood.

Black Rock of Kiltearn

They named it Aultgraat — Ugly Burn,
This water through the crevice hurled
Scouring the entrails of the world —
Not ugly in the rising smoke
That clothes it with a rainbowed cloak.
But slip a foot on frost-spiked stone
Above this rock-lipped Phlegethon
And you shall have
The Black Rock of Kiltearn
For tombstone, grave
And trumpet of your resurrection.

In the Fallow Field

I went down on my hands and knees
Looking for trees,
Twin leaves that, sprung from seeds,
Were now too big
For stems much thinner than a twig.
These soon with chamomile and clover
And other fallow weeds
Would be turned over;

And I was thinking how
It was a pity someone should not know
That a great forest fell before the plough.

Autumn

A new Teiresias and unreproved,
Not stricken by the goddess that I loved,
Today I looked and saw the earth undress
With intimate and godlike carelessness.

Nicodemus: A Mystery

PERSONS

> JOHN as an old man
> JOHN as a young man
> NICODEMUS
> A BLIND MAN
> SIMON PETER
> JUDAS
> CAIAPHAS, the High Priest
> ANNAS, formerly the High Priest
> Clerk and Members of the Sanhedrin
> Constables
> SAUL
> An Angel

Prelude I

In a house. Darkness; then a spot of light discloses JOHN, *as an old man, writing his Gospel: he sits at the side.*

JOHN: Now when he was in Jerusalem at the passover, in the feast day, many believed in his name, when they saw the miracles which he did. But Jesus did not commit himself unto them, because he knew all men, and needed not that any should testify of man: for he knew what was in man. There was a man of the Pharisees, named Nicodemus, a ruler of the Jews; the same came to Jesus by night and said unto him —

What did he say?
Where are the notes that Peter sent from Rome?
— He too was crucified — I see
He writes a sprawling hand like Paul — 'Rabbi,
We know thou art a teacher come from God.'
And what did Jesus say? 'Except a man

Be born again —' that puzzled Nicodemus.
'How can a man be born when he is old?'
I was not born till I was nearly thirty;
Poor Nicodemus had a lot to learn.
Then Jesus spoke about the wind. 'The wind —'
He said, 'it bloweth where it listeth —'
That was a night of wind; I thought the wind
Would blow the Paschal moon out of the sky;
Trees kept their backs to it, bending like divers.
But we were snug indoors; we felt it strange,
We fishermen, to be there in the city,
Not in the wave-lit darkness of the lake.
It was the night that Simon cooked the supper;
He raised the cover from a dish of eels;
'See, they have lost their heads like John the Baptist,'
Said Andrew; and we all looked grave at first,
Till Jesus smiled, and then we burst out laughing.
Fishers of men!
We little thought of the rich lustrous fish
That even then was nosing at the net.
Supper was ended and we sang our hymn;
The hymn we often sang;
We were a happy band of brothers then;
          'Behold how good a thing it is,
               and how becoming well' —
No sooner had we sung it than a knock
Came at the door. 'Go, John,' the Master said,
'We have a visitor; see who he is.'

Scene I

*Outside the door of a house. It is a windy night with a full
moon. A hymn is being sung in the house.*

(NICODEMUS *enters during the singing*)

Behold how good a thing it is,
   and how becoming well,
Together such as brethren are
   in unity to dwell!

Like precious ointment on the head,
   that down the beard did flow,
Ev'n Aaron's beard, and to the skirts
   did of his garments go.

As Hermon's dew, the dew that doth
   on Sion's hills descend;
For there the blessing God commands,
   life that shall never end.

(NICODEMUS *enters hesitatingly, knocks at the door, and* JOHN, *as a young man, opens it*)

NICODEMUS: Is this where Jesus lodges?
JOHN: Nicodemus!
NICODEMUS: Hush, do not shout my name. I see you know
                                                  me.
JOHN: Know you? Surely I know you; only —
NICODEMUS: You are surprised to see me. Have I not
Seen you with Jesus? You are His disciple?
What is your name?
JOHN: John
NICODEMUS: A relative of John the Baptist?
JOHN: A distant cousin.
NICODEMUS: Indeed? John was a most outspoken man,
And he is dead. It does not always do
To say too much. Is Jesus in the house?
JOHN: You think He says too much?
NICODEMUS: He might say less; and yet I do not know.
JOHN: Is He in danger? Is that why you come?
NICODEMUS: No, not immediately; but who can tell?
JOHN: You come to warn Him?
NICODEMUS: Listen! what is that sound?

JOHN: Only the wind.

NICODEMUS: No, no; that other sound; that tap-tap-tapping.

JOHN: I hear it; somewhere down the street.

NICODEMUS: Now it has stopped; no, it begins again.

JOHN: It sounds like someone knocking.

NICODEMUS: There, someone has passed that lighted window.

JOHN: It is his stick that taps.

NICODEMUS: He stops; he peers about him like a bird.
Stand in the shadow till he passes

JOHN: No need; the man is blind.

(*The* BLIND MAN *enters*)

BLIND MAN: Who says that I am blind? If I am blind,
I see you well enough, you standing there.
I raise my stick; ah, does that frighten you?
You will not speak lest I should beg for money;
I do not beg at night when I am rich.
Listen; these coins chink sweeter than house-sparrows,
They sing like nightingales.
Will you not speak?
God curse this world; I say God curse this world
Where blind men make the others deaf and dumb.
I see you there; you think that I am blind;
I am not blind except I cannot see.
God gave me eyes; I feel them with my finger;
They died the day that I was born. Alas,
That you should stand and feel me with your eyes
And my eyes should be dumb and cannot answer.
I know the dogs better than I know men;
We share the street and have our meals together;
They do not even know that I am blind.
I know you stand there, for you stand so still.
A curse upon you, you that I heard speak
And you that have been silent like a spirit.
But I know someone who will speak to me,
And one day I shall meet him — Jesus the Prophet
Have you not heard He gives sight to the blind?

He is not such as you who grudge us sight.
You mock at me because you think me blind;
My eyes are only blind until I see Him.

(*The* BLIND MAN *goes out*)

JOHN: What shall I do? Shall I go after him?
NICODEMUS: No, let him go; I know the fellow well;
He sits all day at the Gate Beautiful;
His blindness is a profitable business.
Your Master has more sense than heal him — yet,
Why not, why not? Quick, call him back.
JOHN: You want him back?
NICODEMUS: I want to see a miracle.
JOHN: Blind man, blind man! — I cannot hear his stick.
Blind man, blind man! — can he have gone so far?
NICODEMUS: The man is sly; he listens like a mouse.
JOHN: Blind man, blind man, if you would have your sight —
It is the wind that blows my voice away.
Blind man! Hello! Jesus is here.
NICODEMUS: Hush, you will wake the street. The man is gone;
Perhaps he will come back. In any case —

(SIMON PETER *comes out from the house*)

SIMON PETER: Who calls on Jesus?
JOHN: Simon!
SIMON PETER: John, was it you? I thought it was your voice.
JOHN: I called to a blind man who passed just now.
SIMON PETER: What did he want?
JOHN: Simon, go in; I will explain.
SIMON PETER: Who have you there? Someone stands in the
shadow.
JOHN: Go in just now; we have a wonderful guest.
SIMON PETER: What guest? Who is he?
JOHN: Someone whose name you know: it is — —
NICODEMUS: Tell him to close the door.
SIMON PETER: The wonderful guest tells me to close the door.

But hurry, John; your supper will get cold.

(SIMON PETER *goes into the house, closing the door*)

NICODEMUS: Who is that man?
JOHN: His name is Simon; Jesus calls him Peter.
NICODEMUS: Peter; that means a rock.
JOHN: I know; He says that on this rock —
NICODEMUS: What rock? You mean that man?
JOHN: I know that it sounds strange; He said —
But no; you would not understand. Come in.
Jesus would like to speak to you.
NICODEMUS: He is at supper; I will come again.
JOHN: Will you not join us?
NICODEMUS: I have already supped.
JOHN: Not even in a cheerful cup? I know
That Jesus will be disappointed.
NICODEMUS: Tell me one thing; why do you follow Jesus?
JOHN: It was because of John the Baptist first.
NICODEMUS: But why because of him?
JOHN: One day, when we were standing by the Jordan,
John and my cousin Andrew and myself,
We saw a man pass by, tall as a spirit;
He did not see us though he passed quite near;
Indeed we thought it strange;
His eyes were open but he looked on nothing;
And as he passed, John, pointing with his finger,
Cried — I can hear him cry it now —
'Behold, The Lamb of God!'
NICODEMUS: And He, what did He say? What did He do?
JOHN: Nothing; we watched Him slowly climb the hill;
His shadow fell before Him; it was evening.
Sometimes He stopped
To raise His head to the home-flying rooks
Or greet a countryman with plough on shoulder.
NICODEMUS: John said, 'Behold, the Lamb of God'?
JOHN: He said so.
NICODEMUS: And from that day you followed Him?

JOHN: No, that was afterwards in Galilee.

NICODEMUS: But tell me why; why did you follow Him?

JOHN: I think it was our feet that followed Him;
It was our feet; our hearts were too afraid.
Perhaps indeed it was not in our choice;
He tells us that we have not chosen Him,
But He has chosen us.   I only know
That as we followed Him that day He called us
We were not walking on the earth at all;
It was another world,
Where everything was new and strange and shining;
We pitied men and women at their business,
For they knew nothing of what we knew —

NICODEMUS: Perhaps it was some miracle He did.

JOHN: It was indeed; more miracles than one;
I was not blind and yet He gave me sight;
I was not deaf and yet He gave me hearing;
Nor was I dead, yet me He raised to life.

(JUDAS *enters from the house and looks about suspiciously,
opening and closing the door carefully.   He looks about him
and goes out*)

NICODEMUS: Who is that man?

JOHN: Judas Iscariot.

NICODEMUS: Is he one of your company?

JOHN: He is.

NICODEMUS: Why did he look like that? Where is he going?

JOHN: I do not know. He often walks at night.

NICODEMUS: If he has left the house, supper is ended.

JOHN: Listen; they sing the hymn.

(*A hymn is sung from the house*)

The Lord's my shepherd, I'll not want,
   He makes me down to lie
In pastures green; he leadeth me
   the quiet waters by.

My soul he doth restore again;
 and me to walk doth make
Within the paths of righteousness,
 ev'n for his own name's sake.

Yea, though I walk in death's dark vale,
 yet will I fear none ill;
For thou art with me; and thy rod
 and staff me comfort still.

My table thou has furnished
 in presence of my foes;
My head thou dost with oil anoint,
 and my cup overflows.

Goodness and mercy all my life
 shall surely follow me:
And in God's house for evermore
 my dwelling-place shall be.

JOHN: Nicodemus!
NICODEMUS: Nothing, nothing; the music wrought on me.
I shiver too in the night wind;
And that man who went out, he bodes some evil.
The night is growing late; it is too late;
Tomorrow I will come —
JOHN: Tomorrow He returns to Galilee.
NICODEMUS: But He will come again.
JOHN: But not this hour. O Nicodemus, look!
A miracle; you asked a miracle;
Look, look, the wind has blown the door wide open.
NICODEMUS: A miracle?
JOHN: He used the wind to work a miracle;
Even the wind obeys Him.
NICODEMUS: I scarcely think it is a miracle.
JOHN: It is, it is.

(SIMON PETER *appears at the open door*)

SIMON PETER: John, John, will you stop railing in the street?
There is no miracle about the door.
I opened it myself. The wind's hand too
Plucked at it; we both opened it at once.
I told the Master of our visitor;
Why do you keep him standing at the door?
What is that sound?
JOHN: The blind man coming back; you hear his stick
Tap-tapping; he is coming down the street;
Now it has stopped.
I will stay here and speak to him. You, Peter,
Take Nicodemus in, if he will go.
SIMON PETER: Nicodemus!
NICODEMUS: I — I will go in.

(PETER *and* NICODEMUS *go into the house;* JOHN *waits till the*
BLIND MAN *enters*)

JOHN: Blind man.
BLIND MAN: Ah, voice, we meet again. Still standing there?
Have you no feet to walk about?
Good voice, take care of your invisible throat;
Voices can catch a cold and cough and spit.
Voice, be a voice and speak. Where are you?
I cannot see to hit you with my stick.
JOHN: Keep your stick quiet.
BLIND MAN: A stick? a serpent; this is Moses' serpent;
Jump quick or he will bite your heels.
JOHN: Listen. I heard you ask —
BLIND MAN: And why did you not answer? Tell me that.
And where is your voice's friend, the other voice,
The dumb voice that cannot speak? Is he about?
Hiss at him, serpent.
JOHN: Keep your stick quiet and listen.
BLIND MAN: Listen? What does a blind man do but listen?
I listen like an echo in a cave;
I am a drum that listens to be struck.
And when did you, you paste-faced hypocrite,

Listen to me? Have you not seen me sit
Outside the Temple, mewing like a cat,
'An alms, an alms, for God's sake give an alms;
Pity a poor blind beggar.' And did you listen?
JOHN: I might say something for your good.
BLIND MAN: All day I sit there with my sleeping eyes
And look up at the sun.   God thinks I pray.
But when night comes
And I can rattle money in my purse,
Ah, then I am a king, night is my kingdom.
O I can see to spy a tavern door,
And there I meet my friends; I know their voices;
Some blind like me, some deaf or dumb or halt;
One has a palsy, he trembles like an earthquake;
And there is one that often drops down dead;
And there we sing our — well, not our psalms.
JOHN: I do not doubt it, friend.
BLIND MAN: You cannot see by night, but I can see;
O that my eyes could see that Man called Jesus.
JOHN: Perhaps they will; I think they will;
But not tonight.
BLIND MAN: No, not tonight; I will be healed by day;
I should be only half-healed in the dark.
My eyes must look up at the blessed sun.
They say it is no bigger than an apple
And made of fire.   How can a fire be round?
I do not understand about the moon;
How can men see the moon when it is night?
No, it must be by day my eyes are born.
How they will sit on either side my head,
Those new-born twins, and look up at the sun!
But with two eyes will I not see two suns?
JOHN: You will see all the sun.
BLIND MAN: For I have heard men say that they saw only
Half of the moon.
JOHN: No, with one eye you would see all the sun.
BLIND MAN: Well, God is wise, giving the blind two eyes.
I must see Jesus.

JOHN: If you see Jesus, you will see indeed.
Goodnight, my friend.

(*The* BLIND MAN *goes out;* NICODEMUS *comes from the house*)

JOHN: Nicodemus!
NICODEMUS: My name! Who speaks the name I had forgotten?
My eyes are stupid coming from the light.
John, is it you? Have you been waiting here:
Still waiting? O how long ago it is
Since you and I stood talking at this door.
It was another life. I did not know
Your Master then; O John, I know Him now.
I had a mother once and she is dead;
I think she did not bear me till this hour.
Or 'born again' was what the Master said;
Have I been born again? O God, I pray
I be not cast out like a stillborn child.
He is to blame to let me go — But no;
I cannot now go back: never again.
It was a stillborn child my mother bore,
But I am come alive tonight. O John,
Not only I am born again tonight,
The world is born again. Look at the stars;
Though small they jostle in the sky for room,
Shining so bright, they drop down through the air;
Are they not born again? Look at the street;
The stones are nestling down to their hard sleep,
Stone nudging neighbour stone, whispering 'Friend,
Are we not born tonight?' Look at the door,
An open sepulchre; I went in dead,
Now I come out again and walk in heaven.
Who could have thought that our poor earth was heaven?
I kiss you, John, my brother.

(JUDAS *enters, looks at* NICODEMUS *and slowly passes into
the house*)

NICODEMUS: Who was that man?

JOHN: Judas;

I told you that he often walks by night.

NICODEMUS: Can corpses walk in heaven?

JOHN: What do you mean?

It was the moonlight on his face.

NICODEMUS: I fear that man.

JOHN: Why do you fear him? He is one of us.

NICODEMUS: Of us? he too? Has he been born again?

JOHN: Why do you ask of him?

NICODEMUS: I do not know;

I cannot tell you more than that I ask;

Or is it that I ask about myself?

No, no; go, brother John, back to the Master

And tell Him that I walk tonight in heaven.

(NICODEMUS *goes out;* JOHN, *looking after him, enters the house, and closes the door*)

Prelude II

As in Prelude I

JOHN *(writing):*   Then they sought to take him: but no man laid hands on him, because his hour was not yet come. And many of the people believed on him, and said, When Christ cometh, will he do more miracles than these which this man hath done? The Pharisees heard that the people murmured such things concerning him: and the Pharisees and chief priests sent officers to take him.

How clearly I remember; I was there
Outside the door, where Nicodemus told me;
He said that he might call me as a witness;
He did not call me;
I saw the constables go out to take Him;
'Make way, make way,' they cried, pushing a path,
Until the people closing in like water

Hid them from sight; I saw them come again;
They shuffled in with slow uncertain steps,
But Jesus was not with them. —
How costly is this parchment that I write on;
I must write nothing but the words He spoke,
Lest men living in far-off lands and ages
Should read this Gospel I am writing now
And blame my wasted words. —
I think it was the third day of the Feast;
I never saw so great a throng before.
I heard the Levites blow the silver trumpets,
And all the people waving myrtle branches,
That stirred the sleepy dust about their feet,
Flowed on toward the golden Candelabra
Singing the harvest hymn. When that was ended,
Nicodemus came and gripped me by the arm;
We looked more than we spoke.
And then the Council entered; Caiaphas,
As High Priest for that year; then Annas followed,
His white beard streaming like a waterfall,
Then Summas, Alexander, Datan
And others that I could not name.
They took their seats. Then Caiaphas arose,
Lifting his hand, and all stood up to pray.

Scene II

The Hall of Hewn Stones

(JOHN *stands at the door, which opens to the Temple court.*
Outside people pass, waving branches and singing a hymn)

Thou crownest the year with thy goodness: and thy clouds
drop fatness.
They shall drop upon the dwellings of the wilderness: and

the little hills shall rejoice on every side.

The folds shall be full of sheep: the valleys also shall stand so thick with corn, that they shall laugh and sing.

(NICODEMUS *enters*)

NICODEMUS: John.
JOHN: Nicodemus.
NICODEMUS: What does the Master say?
JOHN: His hour is not yet come.
NICODEMUS: You are prepared to be a witness?
JOHN: I am. But, Nicodemus —
NICODEMUS: But what?
JOHN: Remember when you came to Him that night.
NICODEMUS: Remember! How can I forget that night?
I live there yet;
No sun for me has risen on that night;
It is still night; that night.
JOHN: Then be yourself the witness; why not now
Come out into the light as His disciple?
NICODEMUS: I will, but — is the time now ripe?
He says His hour is not yet come.
Here in the Council I am a listening ear;
I can report. And meantime I can work
In other ways. Joseph of Arimathea,
Last night I sounded him — but see, they come,
Caiaphas, Annas and the rest.

(CAIAPHAS, ANNAS, *the* CLERK *and other members of the Sanhedrin enter*)

CAIAPHAS: Why, here is Nicodemus.
NICODEMUS: The High Priest's servant; and, Annas, yours.
ANNAS: Mine too? As Master of the Waterworks
Take care there is no poison in the water.

(*All take their seats.* CONSTABLES *stand near the door*)

CAIAPHAS: Rise, let us pray.

True is it that Thou art the Lord our God and the God of our Fathers: our King and the King of our fathers: our Redeemer and the Redeemer of our fathers: our Maker and the Rock of our salvation. A new song did they that were redeemed sing to Thy name by the sea shore. For the sake of our fathers who trusted in Thee, and Thou taughtest them the statutes of life, Have mercy upon us and enlighten our darkness. Blessed be the Lord, who in love chose His people Israel. Amen.

ALL: Amen.

CAIAPHAS: Apologies for absence.

CLERK: Gamaliel writes to say he has a cold,
And Joseph of Arimathea writes to say
He has a chill; both beg to be excused.

NICODEMUS: Why are these brethren absent from our Council?

CAIAPHAS: One has a cold, the other has a chill.

NICODEMUS: I fear they do not favour these proceedings.

ANNAS: No more do you; yet you are here.

CAIAPHAS: The Clerk will read the minutes of the last meeting.

CLERK: On the eleventh day of Tishri, in the Hall of Hewn Stones; at which time and place the Sanhedrin met and was duly constituted by prayer; the High Priest presided, and there were also present Annas, Nicodemus, Summas, Alexander, Datan, Gamaliel, Joseph of Arimathea, Nepthalim, Cyris and other members. The High Priest reported that on the Day of Atonement He had entered the Holy of Holies. Estimates for repairing the pipes that drain the High Altar were submitted; these were referred to the Finance Committee. Following a report sent from the Sanhedrin of Capernaum and the hearing of witnesses a discussion arose about a man called Jesus, said to be an agitator of the people. Nicodemus moved that the report be left on the table; this was not seconded. Annas then moved that as Jesus might be present at the forthcoming Feast of Tabernacles the matter be brought up at the next meeting. This was seconded and carried. There being no other business the Sanhedrin adjourned to meet on the eighteenth of Tishri in the Hall of Hewn Stones at the hour of Evening Sacrifice. The meeting closed with prayer.

CAIAPHAS: Is it your pleasure that I sign these minutes?
ALL: Agreed, agreed.
CAIAPHAS: The only business rising from these minutes
Is the report concerning this man, Jesus.
Since the last meeting of the Sanhedrin
I took it on myself,
Seeing the charges made in the report
Were of so serious a character,
To have it copied out and circulated
Among the members; it is in your hands.
NICODEMUS: Has this Man come up to the Feast?
CAIAPHAS: I hear He came two days ago.
NICODEMUS: And yet I see the charge against Him here,
That He observes no Sabbath-days or Feasts;
How can that be if He comes to the Feast?
ANNAS: He is a most notorious Sabbath-breaker.
CAIAPHAS: That matter was discussed at the last meeting.
Fathers and brethren,
I take it you have studied the report;
Are you prepared to come to a decision?
ALL: Agreed, agreed.
ANNAS: Then, Caiaphas, I rise to make a motion.
I need not now take up the Council's time
Traversing what I said at our last meeting;
My views were clearly voiced on that occasion;
So at this juncture I will merely move
This Jesus be sent for and brought before us.
NICODEMUS: I, Caiaphas, would second that. But first,
Before you put the motion to the meeting,
I have a witness.
CAIAPHAS: Another witness? We have heard enough.
NICODEMUS: Those witnesses were on one side.
ANNAS: The right side.
NICODEMUS: That does not yet appear.
ANNAS: It shall.
CAIAPHAS: Order! I call you both to order. Fathers,
Is it your will to hear a further witness?
NICODEMUS: I claim the right; can you deny my right?

ANNAS: Or mine?

CAIAPHAS: You too? You too would call a witness?

ANNAS: Why not, if Nicodemus claims the right?

CAIAPHAS: We will hear both. You, Annas, call your witness.

ANNAS: Fathers, at the last meeting of our Council
We heard such evidence of this blasphemer
It burnt our ears; it might have singed our beards;
Who would have thought we needed to hear more?
But Nicodemus says 'All on one side,'
As though white were not white and black not black.
That he would call — mark the effrontery! —
One of this Man's disciples as a witness,
A lying tongue in our holy convocation,
An angel whispered in my ear.

NICODEMUS: An angel? A spy, a snake;
Behold a High Priest changed to a snake-charmer!
He keeps a garden full of snakes.

ANNAS: You, Nicodemus, hide behind your wealth,
But God will call you one day to account.

CAIAPHAS: Order! Proceed.

ANNAS: And so I am prepared.
I have a witness; fathers, take note of him,
A young man with a future, Saul of Tarsus.

(SAUL *enters*)

CAIAPHAS: Your name is Saul? you come from Tarsus?

SAUL: Saul is my name; I come from Tarsus.

NICODEMUS: Why is he blinking like an owl?

ANNAS: He is half-blind with studying our Law.

CAIAPHAS: What is your occupation?

SAUL: A student.

CAIAPHAS: Who is your professor?

SAUL: Gamaliel.

CAIAPHAS: Gamaliel is not here to vouch for you.

ANNAS: He has a cold, a most convenient cold;
But I can vouch for him.

CAIAPHAS: You know the Man called Jesus.

SAUL: I know Him; I am His disciple.

CAIAPHAS: What!

SAUL: None follows Him more faithfully than I.

CAIAPHAS: What are you saying? Are you mad?
Here, Annas, is a change of wind.

SAUL: No, Caiaphas, I am not mad.
I follow Him about like His own shadow;
I drink His words as a dog drinks water;
They change to gall and wormwood in my belly.

CAIAPHAS: Another change of wind — what do you mean?
Are you this Man's disciple, Yes or No?

SAUL: Is it not written in our holy Law
That the Lord said to Moses, Send out men,
One man of every tribe, to spy the land?

CAIAPHAS: Well, what of that?

SAUL: And God, who leads men by a way they know not,
Sent me from Tarsus to spy out this Man.

NICODEMUS: A spy and self-confessed!

SAUL: Those spies came bringing from the brook of Eshcol
Clusters of mighty grapes, pomegranates, figs;
I bring you Dead Sea fruit, apples of Sodom.

CAIAPHAS: I cannot make out what you say.

NICODEMUS: The man is fortified in lunacy.

CAIAPHAS: I ask again, are you this Man's disciple?

SAUL: The hunter on the mountain stalks the hind,
The hawk pursues —

ANNAS: Come down from your high mountain and talk sense.
Fathers, this man is no disciple.
He means — the thing is plainer than a post —
That he has watched the heretic; set himself
To watch Him closely and catch up His words;
This man can tell you the whole lying truth.

CAIAPHAS: Then let him tell us; let the man speak plainly.
Come, witness, speak.

SAUL: Caiaphas, Annas, Fathers of the Council,
I have your leave to speak and I will speak.
Though born in Tarsus, which is no mean city,
I am a man that am a Jew; for, know,

After the strictest sect of our religion
I was brought up a Pharisee —
CAIAPHAS: You must not make a speech.
ANNAS: Say what you said to me last night.
What does this Jesus say of us?
That is the point. Fathers, listen.
SAUL: His word is in mine heart,
As a burning fire shut up within my bones,
And I am weary with forbearing.
ANNAS: Stop quoting scripture and speak sense.
NICODEMUS: Why must we listen to this ranting fellow?
ANNAS: Come, tell us what He says of us.
SAUL: Hypocrites!
ANNAS: Ha, now we get the truth.
SAUL: Blind leaders of the blind!
ANNAS: We are blind leaders of the blind!
SAUL: Whited sepulchres!
ANNAS: You hear it? We are whited sepulchres.
You hear this truthful witness, what he says.
I knew that we would get the truth.
CAIAPHAS: So we are whited sepulchres, hypocrites,
Blind leaders of the blind; is this the truth?
SAUL: It is the truth.
CAIAPHAS: He says these things of us?
SAUL: These words with which I have defiled my mouth
Tickle the people's ears and make them laugh.
CAIAPHAS: This is hot blasphemy.
ANNAS: It is indeed;
Blaspheming us he blasphemes God.
CAIAPHAS: What does the Council say?
ALL: Blasphemy, blasphemy!
Let Him be sent for; we have heard enough.
NICODEMUS: Caiaphas.
CAIAPHAS: Silence! Let Nicodemus speak.
NICODEMUS: Fathers, I wonder an old man like Annas
Should mock us in our holy Convocation
With this play-acting fellow. You heard him say
'I have defiled my mouth to speak these words';

But with what relish did he speak them! A witness?
Behind the false face of his evidence
The fellow leered at us; in shrewd pretence
Of holy zeal he plucked us by the beard.
Annas, if old in years, is young in wisdom
To be deceived by such a mocker. Why,
He owns himself a spy; you heard him own it;
And being so great a student of our Scripture
He quotes it to approve his vile profession.
You saw the serpent flick his double tongue,
'I am and I am not this Man's disciple';
You saw too how the serpent turned and twisted,
No one could catch his meaning. Look at him,
This man called Saul, whom God has sent from Tarsus,
This young man with a future —
No, do not blink at me and work your hands;
I know that they would clutch my throat. Listen!
Have you no fear of God to play this part,
To spy on this most righteous Man?
ANNAS: Most righteous man! Listen to Nicodemus.
If Jesus is most righteous, what are we
But hypocrites, blind leaders of the blind?
CAIAPHAS: Order, order!
I rule that we are finished with this witness.
You, Saul of Tarsus, leave the Council.
ANNAS: But wait outside the door.

(SAUL OF TARSUS *goes out*)

CAIAPHAS: You have a witness, Nicodemus.
ANNAS: Why need he call another witness in?
Let Nicodemus call himself as witness.
CAIAPHAS: Himself?
ANNAS: Why not?
Am I in order if I ask a question?
CAIAPHAS: What is your question?
ANNAS: I ask of Nicodemus —
CAIAPHAS: What?

ANNAS: Is he too a disciple of the Man?

CAIAPHAS: Let Nicodemus answer if he will.

NICODEMUS: The question — does not seem — in order.

ANNAS: No, it is not; it is far out of order
That I should need to ask it. Caiaphas,
I, who am old in years and young in wisdom,
Think I can gauge the feeling of the Council.
If Nicodemus will not speak himself,
We will not hear his mouthpiece.

CAIAPHAS: Are you agreed?

ALL: Agreed, agreed.

ANNAS: I made a motion — it was seconded —
That Jesus be sent for and brought before us.
Is it not time you put it to the meeting?

CAIAPHAS: I put that motion to the meeting —

NICODEMUS: Wait!

CAIAPHAS: Well, we are waiting.

NICODEMUS: No; put the motion.

CAIAPHAS: All those in favour?

ALL: Agreed, agreed.

CAIAPHAS: Go, constables, and bring the Man before us,
The Man called Jesus; if He will not come,
Bring Him by force.

A CONSTABLE: Here is a crowd and with them a mad fellow
Who dances as he walks; they all are crying,
'A miracle, a miracle.'

ANNAS: Why, this may be the mystagogue Himself.

CAIAPHAS: Hold back the people.

CONSTABLES: Back, back; stand back, stand back.

CAIAPHAS: What do they want? Let one man speak.

CONSTABLES: What do you want? Let one man speak.

CAIAPHAS: What do they say?

A CONSTABLE: They say they bring a miracle to show you.

CAIAPHAS: A miracle? What kind of miracle?

A CONSTABLE: A man; the dancing fellow.

CAIAPHAS: Then bring this dancing fellow in before us;
But keep the others back.

(The BLIND MAN *enters)*

CAIAPHAS: Who are you?
BLIND MAN: Truly the light is sweet and a pleasant thing
It is for a blind man to see the sun.
Where is the sun? I cannot see the sun.
O friends, I hope I have not lost the sun.
ANNAS: This man is drunk.
NICODEMUS: No, no, he is not drunk. Look, Caiaphas,
I call you all to look; this man was blind
And now you see his eyes are open.
ANNAS: A trick, a trick! The man was never blind.
NICODEMUS: But I have seen him begging.
ANNAS: Why, any man can shut his eyes and cry,
'An alms, an alms, pity the blind.' A kick
Is all the miracle such fellows need
To give them sight enough to skip.
CAIAPHAS: Go, constables, and bring the Man called Jesus;
As for this fellow, leave him here with us.
BLIND MAN: Good constables, go bring the Man called Jesus;
That Jesus is the Man that I would see.
CAIAPHAS: That you would see, you, fellow?
BLIND MAN: And why should I not see? Have I not sight?
My eyes were dead, but they are living now.
O I can see so much I scarcely know
If I am here or there or where I am.
I see so many things that I would need
A hundred hands to tell me what they are.
I see you there; I see you seeing me;
You are the Sanhedrin, High Priest and all;
The holy men. God tells me you are men,
Or else I should not know it.
CAIAPHAS: Constables, stop staring at this man and go.

(The CONSTABLES *go out)*

BLIND MAN: Go, constables; no, stay and take me with you.
Where are you, constables? God curse these eyes;

Why do I stumble when I try to walk?
I must be blind again to see my way.

ANNAS: I say the man is drunk.

BLIND MAN: Ho, ho; a voice says I am drunk. Who spoke?
I have been often drunk; God pity me,
But what else would He have a blind man be?
But not today; no, I am worse than drunk;
Today I have my sight and see.

ANNAS: You have been drinking at the Feast.

BLIND MAN: O you are speaking; you with the long beard;
A holy man. Where are the prayers that drip
Like gravy from your beard? You look like God —
But where is God? I had not thought of that.
Now I have eyes, I must see God as well.
Where is the Temple where they say He lives?
I used to know but now I have my sight
I lose my way.

CAIAPHAS: Stay where you are.

BLIND MAN: What, would you have a blind man not see God?
Why have I eyes then? Why should I not see Him?
Ha, ha, perhaps you have not seen God either.
Perhaps you frighten Him; I should not wonder;
Perhaps when you, the priests, go in the Temple
God scampers like a little careful mouse
And runs and hides Himself behind the curtains.
I must go to the Temple and see God.
Besides, now I remember, Jesus said
I must go to the priest and show myself.
He said it; I must go.

ANNAS: Here is the priest, the High Priest.

BLIND MAN: And here am I. Look well at me, High Priest;
The people praise me as a miracle,
And so I am. Lift up your voice in prayer;
Offer a prayer of gladness and thanksgiving.
I know that you can pray;
I know by your long beard and scowling face.
How could a poor blind beggar pray himself?

CAIAPHAS: Be quiet, fellow.

BLIND MAN: I will be quiet; I do not want to speak;
When I have sight, why should I want to speak?
CAIAPHAS: Now listen to the question of the Council;
Do you say this Man, Jesus, gave you sight?
BLIND MAN: I say He made the clay, as God made Adam,
And laid it on my eyes and gave me sight.
CAIAPHAS: You say that to the Council?
BLIND MAN: No, no; I do not say it; I am dumb;
A poor dumb beggar who can only see.
Where is the door? The light must be the door.
My eyes are tired; my eyes are tired with seeing;
O I must close them and be blind again.
Where are you, friends? Here is your miracle.
Jesus and God, I have a lot to see.

(The BLIND MAN *goes out, and the people cry, '*A miracle,
a miracle!*')*

CAIAPHAS: Bring back that man. Where are the constables?

(The CONSTABLES *enter)*

A CONSTABLE: Here, here; shall we bring back the miracle?
ANNAS: Be careful, Caiaphas;
The people count him as a miracle.
CAIAPHAS: No, let him go. Bring in the Man called Jesus.
Where is He? Why, fools, are you dumb?
Have you not brought Him?
Why do you stand there shuffling on your feet?
Is this another miracle?
A CONSTABLE: We went to take Him —
CAIAPHAS: Well, did you not take Him?
A CONSTABLE: But no man ever spoke as that Man speaks.
His words were living things, part of Himself;
They were an arm stretched out to hold us back.
NICODEMUS: O Caiaphas, let me fill up the silence.
I see you staring at these men; they say
That no man ever spoke as that Man speaks.

You think that they are foolish ignorant men;
But what if I, a member of the Council,
As having spoken with the Man myself,
Should say the same, that no man ever spoke
As that Man speaks, what would you say?
ANNAS: Nothing; there is no need to say. From now
We know you, Nicodemus; this Man too;
The thing is plain as a whitewashed sepulchre;
I say this Jesus must be put to death.
NICODEMUS: Our Law can judge no man before it hear him.
ANNAS: He has resisted our authority;
I at the proper time will vote for death.
He is as good as dead. You, Nicodemus,
Are you too His disciple? Why then, go
And buy some unguent to anoint His body;
The Man is dead already.
NICODEMUS: Caiaphas, I protest.
ANNAS: I know my words have the cold sound of death
In Nicodemus' ears; and why is that?
Have I not said, he too is a disciple?
If he is not, he needs only to say it.
We know this Man's disciples who they are,
A pack of fishermen from Galilee;
Can any good come out of Galilee?
Tax-gatherers and other publicans,
And wicked women too. Come, Nicodemus,
You are this Man's disciple, are you not? —
Fathers, you hear his silence?
NICODEMUS: I say again
Our Law can judge no man before it hear him.
ANNAS: He shouts so loud that you can hear his silence;
Jesus is dead and buried in that silence.
Fathers, let us be joyful. Hark, the music!
Here is a happy ending to our Council.
The flutes are playing in the Temple court.
The night grows brighter as the day grows darker,
Young priests have climbed and lit the Candelabra.
The people sing and join the holy dance;

You hear their voices lifted in the psalm,
And God can hear the shuffling of their feet.
See how the gold light treads across the chamber;
Come, let us join the dance. But wait;
Let Caiaphas first close the meeting.

CAIAPHAS: Is it your will I close the meeting?

ALL: Agreed, agreed.

CAIAPHAS: Then let us pray.

Praised be Thou, Lord, who bestowest abundant grace and rememberest the promises to the fathers, and bringest a redeemer to their children's children, for Thy name's sake, out of love. O God, who bringest help and salvation, and art a shield, praised be Thou, O shield of Abraham. Amen.

ALL: Amen.

ANNAS: Fathers, step out; I too will shake my beard,
Joining the people in the holy dance;
Come, Nicodemus,
And dance as David danced before the Ark,
No Michal looks out through her lattice window.
The Spirit of the Lord lifts up our steps.
You, foolish constables, can dance as well;
But close the door behind.

(The Members of the Council dance out with slow swinging movement, singing the hymn. NICODEMUS *remains behind)*

He will not suffer thy foot to be moved: and he that keepeth thee will not sleep.

Behold, he that keepeth Israel: shall neither slumber nor sleep.

The Lord himself is thy keeper: the Lord is thy defence upon thy right hand.

So that the sun shall not burn thee by day: neither the moon by night.

The Lord shall preserve thee from all evil: yea, it is even he that shall keep thy soul.

The Lord shall preserve thy going out, and thy coming in: from this time forth for evermore.

(The CONSTABLES *close the door behind them)*

Prelude III

JOHN *sitting as before writing his Gospel.*

JOHN *(writing):* For these things were done, that the scripture should be fulfilled. A bone of him shall not be broken. And again another scripture saith, They shall look on him whom they pierced. And after this Joseph of Arimathea, being a disciple of Jesus, but secretly for fear of the Jews, besought Pilate that he might take away the body of Jesus: and Pilate gave him leave. He came therefore, and took the body of Jesus. And there came also Nicodemus, which at the first came to Jesus by night, and brought a mixture of myrrh and aloes, about an hundred pound weight.

About an hundred pound! Why, Mary's gift
Was but a pound, and Judas thought it costly,
And that was to anoint His living feet;
And this, an hundred pound of myrrh and aloes
Was to embalm His body for a night,
One night, for Jesus was no sleeping Pharaoh.
My lamp burns down;
The flame lies on the oil and soon will die;
And this old body that grows cold with time
Has no more life left than that floating flame.
How different was it on that Easter morning,
That first of Easters;
We raced together to the sepulchre,
Peter and I, and I outran my friend.
But Peter has outrun me in the end;
His course is finished, he has gained the crown.
James too and brother Paul and all of them
Have left me far behind. I am the last.
Yet not so far behind; no, not far now;
I run a race where old age outruns youth;

My weakness is my strength, my slowness speed,
And I am hastening on towards the mark.
How strange I am the last,
The only one now living on the earth
Who saw and talked with Jesus as a friend.
If I should die, would He not die again?
No, He will live still in His living Church —
I must be writing. But I cannot see
By this small dying flame.
Caius may be awake still; I will ring —
So Nicodemus, the same who came by night,
Came with his hundred pound of myrrh and aloes;
Alas, he came too late.

(An ANGEL *enters)*

ANGEL: You struck the bell.
JOHN: But who are you?
ANGEL: I am the one who rolled away the stone.
JOHN: The stone?
ANGEL: I rolled it from the sepulchre; God said,
'Go, take an earthquake, roll away the stone.'
JOHN: Are you a servant of the house?
ANGEL: I am the angel of the sepulchre.
JOHN: An angel!
ANGEL: Body and clothes are one material;
I put them on just now outside the door.
Give me your hand, for you must come with me.
JOHN: You come to take me? I must die tonight?
ANGEL: Tonight: some other night; it is the same.
JOHN: I think you are God's angel; it would not matter
Though you were not; you could not take me far.
I see that I must die.
Well, I will go with you; here is my hand.
But this is not like dying; though I am old.
How can I die when I am still alive?
ANGEL: No, you mistake me; this is not your hour.
It was another died tonight.

JOHN: Another of us martyred?

ANGEL: Nicodemus.

JOHN: Nicodemus!

ANGEL: Killed by the Jews; his spirit fled to heaven;
I met him on the way.

JOHN: O God be praised! You came to tell me that?

ANGEL: I came to tell you that; I also came
To lead you back through fifty years and more
To that dark morning at the sepulchre
And show you something Nicodemus saw;
Though Mary and the women went there early
He was the first.

JOHN: He told us nothing.

ANGEL: It was forbidden him to speak;
For once when he might have spoken he was silent.
Hold fast my hand and we are there.

Scene III

Outside the Sepulchre.

(Two CONSTABLES *stand at the door. Two other* CONSTABLES
enter)

1ST CONSTABLE: Halt! Who goes there?

3RD CONSTABLE: The Temple Guard.

1ST CONSTABLE: Then pass the word.

3RD CONSTABLE: May angels guard the constables.

1ST CONSTABLE: Why are you so late in relieving us?

3RD CONSTABLE: We came the moment that the captain sent

us.

Is this the sepulchre?

1ST CONSTABLE: Did you hear music on the way?

3RD CONSTABLE: We heard the soldiers singing in the castle.

1ST CONSTABLE: But afterwards; here in the garden?

3RD CONSTABLE: We heard the nightingales.

1ST CONSTABLE: That is not music. No, music in the air,

High in the air; sounds without instruments,
Voices without people, as though the air
Were playing of itself and singing too.
3RD CONSTABLE: No, we heard no such music.
1ST CONSTABLE: We are well quit of it;
It sounded too like heaven for my taste.
Good night and a safe watch.
3RD CONSTABLE: Good night and a sound sleep.

(The first two CONSTABLES *go out)*

4TH CONSTABLE: What is this music in the air?
3RD CONSTABLE: They must have dreamt it.
4TH CONSTABLE: They would not sleep on guard.
3RD CONSTABLE: They would not sleep — do you think that,
young friend?
Why does the captain set us two and two,
Except that one should sleep and one should wake?
We will take turns; and I will sleep first.
But pass the cider.
4TH CONSTABLE: The bottle is three-quarters empty.
3RD CONSTABLE: That is their music in the air.
I will hear music too, music for nothing.
Good health, a long life, and fat purse.
4TH CONSTABLE: I am too cold to sleep; it is the dew.
They say dew falls; I never felt it fall;
I think it rises from the ground.
3RD CONSTABLE: It is the heat that makes the dew.
4TH CONSTABLE: How can heat make the dew? The dew is
cold.
3RD CONSTABLE: I do not know. I wish I were a dog,
That wakes and listens while he's still asleep.
4TH CONSTABLE: It will be morning in an hour.
Do you remember —
3RD CONSTABLE: Remember what?
4TH CONSTABLE: The day they sent us to arrest Him?
3RD CONSTABLE: The Council? I remember.
4TH CONSTABLE: And we came back without Him;

And we could only stand and tell the Council
That no one ever spoke as that Man spoke.
3RD CONSTABLE: Death was a better constable.
4TH CONSTABLE: I did not think He would be crucified.
3RD CONSTABLE: He went about it the right way.
4TH CONSTABLE: Perhaps He lies there on the shelf and listens.
3RD CONSTABLE: But He is dead.
4TH CONSTABLE: A dead man lies so still he seems to listen.
The dead are far more cunning than the living;
I think too that they have the sharper hearing,
Although they never will let on they hear.
3RD CONSTABLE: He could not hear us from behind the stone.
4TH CONSTABLE: Perhaps a spirit can pass through a stone.
3RD CONSTABLE: A stone would be an open door to spirits,
If there were spirits.
4TH CONSTABLE: You think there are no spirits?
3RD CONSTABLE: No, there are none.
4TH CONSTABLE: But if there are no spirits, why do you say
A stone would be an open door to spirits?
3RD CONSTABLE: Because I speak of nothing.
4TH CONSTABLE: But if there were no spirits, how could you
                                                          say
There are no spirits?
3RD CONSTABLE: In the same way that I can speak of nothing.
4TH CONSTABLE: To speak of nothing would be not to speak;
If you can speak of spirits, there are spirits.
Listen, Listen!
3RD CONSTABLE: I hear it.
4TH CONSTABLE: The music in the air.

(A hymn is heard in the distance)

I bless the Lord because he doth
    by counsel me conduct:
And in the seasons of the night
    my reins do me instruct.

Because of this my heart is glad,
   and joy shall be exprest,
Ev'n by my glory; and my flesh
   in confidence shall rest.

Because my soul in grave to dwell
   shall not be left by thee;
Nor wilt thou give thine Holy One
   corruption to see.

Thou wilt show me the path of life;
   of joys there is full store
Before thy face; at thy right hand
   are pleasures evermore.

4TH CONSTABLE: Angels, angels!
Were these not angels singing?
3RD CONSTABLE: They were not jackals or hyenas.
4TH CONSTABLE: Perhaps they sing because of Jesus.
3RD CONSTABLE: They do not sing because of us.
4TH CONSTABLE: What shall we do?
3RD CONSTABLE: We cannot cheer them as we cheer a circus
And ask for it again, no, certainly.
4TH CONSTABLE: We must do something; they were angels.
3RD CONSTABLE: Go and arrest them then.
4TH CONSTABLE: Shall we report it to the captain?
3RD CONSTABLE: Why not report it to the priest?
Come, take a drink of cider; you will feel better;
Let me drink first. Health to the angels,
Though no need to wish immortals a long life.

(The BLIND MAN *enters with a sack)*

BLIND MAN: I come in time; leave some for me, good friend.
3RD CONSTABLE: Halt, who goes there?
BLIND MAN: I halt; and why should I not halt?
I have come fast enough. You, sack, lie there;
O how the earth smells sweet, struck by the sack;

It smells of flowers and roses.

3RD CONSTABLE: The dancing fellow!

BLIND MAN: The singing constables! I heard you sing.
Who would have thought you had such pleasant voices?
Or did you bring the Temple choir? Where are they?

3RD CONSTABLE: What have you in the sack?

BLIND MAN: It might afflict your noses. Myrrh and aloes;
Surely it stinks enough. It makes the place
Smell like the holy Temple. Bees will wake
And come and sting us. A hundred pound;
Lift it; a hundred pound of precious smell.
Samson could not have carried it. O I
Shall stink of it for ever. I am a garden;
A sweet herb-border like the Shulamite.
I shall not need to die; I am embalmed
Like an Egyptian mummy. But tell me, friends,
Is this the sepulchre of Jesus?

3RD CONSTABLE: What is His sepulchre to you?

BLIND MAN: Why, surely, you are the wise constables
To ask what is His sepulchre to me.
Did you not know this Jesus gave me sight?
For how could I have known that I was blind
Unless He gave me sight?
Perhaps it was His own sight that He gave me;
He lies so blind there in the sepulchre.

3RD CONSTABLE: Why have you come here?

BLIND MAN: To see you, constables; was that not right?
Now I have eyes I must see all I can.
My eyes are blest to see such men as you.

3RD CONSTABLE: We know you; you are one of His disciples;
We saw you at the Council; the dancing fellow.

BLIND MAN: And I saw you; they sent you to arrest Him;
Why was it that you did not bring Him back?

3RD CONSTABLE: Are you not His disciple?

BLIND MAN: Why should you think it?

3RD CONSTABLE: He gave you sight.

BLIND MAN: Why did He give me sight? Come, tell me that.
Why did He take away my livelihood?

When I was blind, could I not eat and drink?
I did not need to close my eyes to sleep.
I had no sins; a blind man cannot sin.
Earth was a heaven that I could not see
And men who had their sight were walking angels
Or devils when they cursed me.

3RD CONSTABLE: Why have you brought this sack?

BLIND MAN: That sack, too, is a problem; I must work;
I must do this and that for Nicodemus;
You see I have to work both day and night;
I am a servant.

3RD CONSTABLE: Servant to Nicodemus?

BLIND MAN: Why not? He is a good man, Nicodemus,
Although he makes a blind man work for money.
And he is kind; I think he pities me,
Now I have lost my blindness.

3RD CONSTABLE: Why have you come?

BLIND MAN: It is this dead Man in the sepulchre
That I would speak to, if He is alive.
Jesus, Jesus, wake up and answer me,
Why did you take away a poor man's blindness?
Was I not a great blessing to the city,
Stirring the spirit of alms-giving?
Misers have wept to see me. Now, alas,
For want of a blind beggar to give alms to
The rich must die and go to hell.

4TH CONSTABLE: He mocks the dead.

3RD CONSTABLE: Or he is mocking us.

4TH CONSTABLE: I think he plays for time.

3RD CONSTABLE: It is some trick, we must arrest him.

BLIND MAN: Wake up, and save me from the constables;
Make them as blind as the vile men of Sodom
Who wandered round the door.

3RD CONSTABLE: Come, we arrest you, fellow.

BLIND MAN: Leave go, leave go!

3RD CONSTABLE: Come, come.

BLIND MAN: Well, have you got me fast; what will you do?

3RD CONSTABLE: How can we tie him up?

4TH CONSTABLE: We passed a vineyard; I could smell the
blossoms;
The young vine-shoots would tie him safe enough;
It is close by.
3RD CONSTABLE: Then go and pull them.
4TH CONSTABLE: This eel will wriggle from your hands.
3RD CONSTABLE: Then let us take him with us.
4TH CONSTABLE: We cannot leave the sepulchre.
3RD CONSTABLE: We shall not be long gone.
BLIND MAN: Hold, I must wait for Nicodemus here.
3RD CONSTABLE: When you are tied up you will wait the
better.

(The two CONSTABLES *go out with the* BLIND MAN.
NICODEMUS *enters)*

NICODEMUS: O Jesus, if your spirit haunts this place —
I feel that you are here, here in this garden,
Where they have brought and planted your poor body,
But not to rise again — forgive, forgive me!
You see me kneeling here, my sin as dark
As the black shadows of this moon-washed garden.
I tried and yet I did not try to save you;
Something I said and yet I did not speak.
O had I spoken boldly, or even said,
'I am this man's disciple,' I do not think
They would have dared to do what they have done.
My silence was the witness that condemned you.
I was afraid; afraid of nothing, for me
They could not crucify as they did you.
I was afraid of nothing but to speak,
Afraid to tell them what they knew. That silence
Became a weight upon my lips, a chain
That bound me, a dumb devil that afflicted me;
And now it is become a wilderness
Where I must ever wander and be lost.
I thought that you would save yourself at last;
I thought — O God, I even thought — that day —

Only two days ago — when I went out
And looked towards the crowd at Calvary
And saw you stand above the people's heads
That you had saved yourself — and then I knew
It was the cross that held you in its arms.
I come again by night; but now too late,
For I can only come to your dead body.
This is a vain work that I come about,
Bringing this useless load of myrrh and aloes;
For to embalm your body with these unguents
Is to perpetuate the wounds and blood.
It is your death that I would keep alive;
And it was I who crucified you, I
Who might have spoken and did not speak.
Forgive me, Lord. Why do I call you Lord?
Is it that in some majesty of death
Your spirit has grown greater than a man's?
Or was it always so, and now in death
I know you, what you are?
Lord, Lord, forgive me, Lord!

(The two CONSTABLES *enter with the* BLIND MAN *bound)*

3RD CONSTABLE: Here is another at the sepulchre.
BLIND MAN: Nicodemus!
NICODEMUS: What, is that you?
BLIND MAN: The constables have taken me.
NICODEMUS: Leave go my servant. Who are you?
3RD CONSTABLE: The Temple Guard.
NICODEMUS: Why are you here?
3RD CONSTABLE: We watch the sepulchre.
NICODEMUS: Well, I commend your watching; but this man,
He came here at my bidding. Set him free.
BLIND MAN: I told you, fools.

(The CONSTABLES *unbind the* BLIND MAN*)*

NICODEMUS: You constables, come here and lend a hand;
I want the stone rolled from the sepulchre.
3RD CONSTABLE: We have no orders from the captain.
NICODEMUS: Take them from me, then.
3RD CONSTABLE: We were sent here to guard the body.
NICODEMUS: I do not come to steal but to embalm.
Come, help my servant to roll back the stone.
4TH CONSTABLE: The music in the air!
NICODEMUS: What is that music?
4TH CONSTABLE: It is created music, made from nothing.

(A hymn is heard from the air)

Ye gates, lift up your heads on high;
   ye doors that last for aye,
Be lifted up, that so the King
   of glory enter may.

But who of glory is the King?
   the mighty Lord is this;
Ev'n that same Lord, that great in might
   and strong in battle is.

Ye gates, lift up your heads; ye doors,
   doors that do last for aye,
Be lifted up, that so the King
   of glory enter may.

But who is he that is the King
   of glory? who is this?
The Lord of hosts, and none but he
   the King of glory is.

(An earthquake, with thunder and lightning)

BLIND MAN: O master, master, look! the earth is drunk;
It is not I this time.
The earth is turned to sea; we rock like boats;

It gives me a cold rising stomach.

NICODEMUS: This is an earthquake.

BLIND MAN: The constables are shipwrecked; they have fallen.

NICODEMUS: Kneel down, kneel down.

BLIND MAN: O master, I am frightened.
The ground is rising up to swallow me.

NICODEMUS: Look at the stone, the stone!

BLIND MAN: What stone?

NICODEMUS; There at the sepulchre; it moves.

BLIND MAN: O God, the stone is frightened too.

NICODEMUS: It trembles like a curtain.

BLIND MAN: It will fall back and crush us.

NICODEMUS: Look! it is rolling like a wheel.
The light, the light!

(A lighted Altar is disclosed)

BLIND MAN: O master, is this heaven? am I dead?

NICODEMUS: The tomb is full of light.

BLIND MAN: Or am I blind again to see this sight?
Only the blind could see it.

NICODEMUS: Light, light; nothing but light;
The tomb is empty; He is gone.

BLIND MAN: Where is He gone? Go in the tomb and look;
He may be there.

NICODEMUS: The Lord is risen.

BLIND MAN: But He was dead; could the earthquake wake
Him?

NICODEMUS: Waken these sleeping men; they too must see it.

BLIND MAN: Waken, waken! They will not waken;
They seem alive and dead at the same time.

NICODEMUS: Then let them lie; this sight is not for them.

BLIND MAN: But where is Jesus? Call on Him;
If He is gone, He cannot have gone far.

NICODEMUS: Go, leave me here.

BLIND MAN: Go where?

NICODEMUS: Back to Jerusalem.

BLIND MAN: He may be going there.

NICODEMUS: Go quickly; I will follow soon.

BLIND MAN: I am afraid to meet Him, a dead man;
He may come walking to me through the trees;
I wish I never had received my sight.

(The BLIND MAN *goes out)*

NICODEMUS: O risen Lord,
I do not ask you to forgive me now;
There is no need.
I came tonight to speak to your dead body,
To touch it with my hands and say 'Forgive',
For though I knew it could not speak to me
Or even hear, yet it was once yourself;
It is dissolved and risen like a dew,
And now I know,
As dawn forgives the night, as spring the winter,
You have forgiven me. It is enough.
Why do I kneel before your empty tomb?
You are not here, for you are everywhere;
The grass, the trees, the air, the wind, the sky,
Nothing can now refuse to be your home;
Nor I. Lord, live in me and I shall live.
This is the word you spoke,
The whole earth hears it, for the whole earth cries,
I AM THE RESURRECTION, AND THE LIFE: HE THAT BELIEVETH IN ME
THOUGH HE WERE DEAD, YET SHALL HE LIVE: AND WHOSOEVER LIVETH
AND BELIEVETH IN ME SHALL NEVER DIE.

The Chalk-Cliff

Blasted and bored and undermined
  By quarrying seas
Reared the erect chalk-cliff with black flints lined.
  (Flints drop like nuts from trees
When the frost bites
The chalk on winter nights.)

Save for frail shade of jackdaw's flight
  No night was there,
But blue-skyed summer and a cliff so white
  It stood like frozen air;
Foot slipped on damp
Chalk where the limpets camp.

With only purple of sea-stock
  And jackdaw's shade
To mitigate that blazing height of chalk
  I stood like a soul strayed
In paradise
Hiding my blinded eyes.

The Ventriloquists

The birds sang in the rain
  That rhythmically waving its grey veil
From smoking hilltop flowed to misty plain,
  Where one white house shone sharply as a sail;

But not so bright as these,
  The anemones that held the wood snow-bound,
The water-drops waiting to fall from trees,
  The rusty catkins crawling on the ground.

March buds give little shelter;
   Better seek shelter in the open rain
Than where tree-gathered showers fall helter-skelter,
   I meditated; but 'Turn, turn again,'

The birds shrieked through their song;
   So rooted to the leaf-soft earth I stood,
Letting my restless eye wander among
   The thick sky-scrawling branches of the wood.

But no bird could I see
   In criss-cross of thin twigs or sudden twists
Where branching tree interrupted branching tree;
   Yet everywhere those hidden ventriloquists

Were singing in the wood,
   Flinging their cheating voices here and there;
But seeing nothing though I walked or stood
   I thought the singing grew out of the air.

August

The cows stood in a thundercloud of flies,
   As lagging through the field with trailing feet
I kicked up scores of skipper butterflies
   That hopped a little way, lazy with heat.

The wood I found was in deep shelter sunk,
   Though bryony leaves shone with a glossy sweat
And creeping over ground and up tree-trunk
   The ivy in the sun gleamed bright and wet.

Songs brief as Chinese poems the birds sung
   And insects of all sheens, blue, brown and yellow,
Darted and twisted in their flight and hung
   On air that groaned like hoarse sweet violoncello.

No leaf stirred in the wood-discouraged wind,
　　But foliage hung on trees, like heavy wigs;
The sun, come from the sky, was close behind
　　The fire-fringed leaves and in among the twigs.

Autumn Seeds

Although a thoughtful bee still travels
And midge-ball ravels and unravels,
Yet strewn along the pathway lie
Like small open sarcophagi
The hazel-nuts broken in two
And cobwebs catch the seed-pearl dew.

Now summer's flowers are winter's weeds,
I think of all the sleeping seeds;
Winds were their robins and by night
Frosts glue their leafy cover tight;
Snow may shake down its dizzy feathers,
They will sleep safely through all weathers.

Snow

Ridged thickly on black bough
　　And foaming on twig-fork in swollen lumps
At flirt of bird-wing or wind's sough
　　Plump snow tumbled on snow softly with sudden dumps.

Where early steps had made
　　A wavering track through the white-blotted road
Breaking its brightness with blue shade,
　　Snow creaked beneath my feet with snow heavily shod.

I reached a snow-thatched rick
  Where men sawed bedding off for horse and cow;
There varnished straws were lying thick
  Paving with streaky gold the trodden silver snow.

Such light filled me with awe
  And nothing marred my paradisal thought,
That robin least of all I saw
  Lying too fast asleep, his song choked in his throat.

The Missel-Thrush

That missel-thrush
Scorns to alight on a low bush,
And as he flies
And tree-top after tree-top tries,
His shadow flits
And harmlessly on tree-trunk hits.

Shutting his wings
He sways and sings and sways and sings,
And from his bough
As in deep water he looks through
He sees me there
Crawl at the bottom of the air.

The Chalk-Quarry

A solitary yew,
  Fern-haired and ruddy-thewed,
That light with no sharp needle can prick through,
  Itself makes a small forest in the wood.

The strong sun darkening still
   That yew's *memento mori*
Fills with a fiercer light out on the hill
   The open sepulchre of the old chalk-quarry.

South Downs

No water cries among these hills,
   The mist hides and enlarges,
Though rain in every road-rut spills
   Where leaves have sunk their barges.

No freshet in a hollow brake
   Utters its shy cold fears,
Only the chiming sheep-bells make
   One Sabbath of the years.

Cuckoo in May

Cuckoo that like a cuckoo-clock
Calls out the hours so fast,
Days, months and years go slipping past,
O for a while be dumb
Lest in a moment I become
Old as that man I stopped to watch
And chat with in my morning walk,
His back as rounded as a hoop,
Who did not need to stoop
To pull out weeds in his potato-patch.

The Elm Beetle

So long I sat and conned
That naked bole
With the strange hieroglyphics scored

That those small priests,
The beetle-grubs, had bored,
Telling of gods and kings and beasts
And the long journey of the soul
Through magic-opened gates
To where the throned Osiris waits,
That when at last I woke
I stepped from an Egyptian tomb
To see the wood's sun-spotted gloom,
And rising cottage smoke
That leaned upon the wind and broke,
Roller-striped fields, and smooth cow-shadowed pond.

Walking in Beech Leaves

I tread on many autumns here
    But with no pride,
For at the leaf-fall of each year
    I also died.

This is last autumn, crisp and brown,
    That my knees feel;
But through how many years sinks down
    My sullen heel.

February

So thick a mist darkened the day
Not two trees distant flew my friend, the jay,
    To keep love's angry tryst
    Somewhere in the damp mist,
    And as I brushed each bush
    Rain-buds fell in a rush,
One might have said it rained,
While green buds on the barer boughs remained.

But where with looped and twisted twine
Wild clematis, bryony and woodbine
  And such reptilian growth
  Hung in decaying sloth,
  I stood still thinking how
  Two months or three from now
The green buds would not tarry
More than those flashing drops of February.

The Echoing Cliff

White gulls that sit and float
Each on his shadow like a boat,
Sandpipers, oystercatchers
And herons, those grey stilted watchers,
From loch and corran rise,
And as they scream and squawk abuse
Echo from wooded cliff replies
So clearly that the dark pine boughs,
Where goldcrests flit
And owls in drowsy wisdom sit,
Are filled with sea-birds and their cries.

The Scarecrow

He strides across the grassy corn
That has not grown since it was born,
A piece of sacking on a pole,
A ghost, but nothing like a soul.

Why must this dead man haunt the spring
With arms anxiously beckoning?
Is spring not hard enough to bear
For one at autumn of his year?

The Mountain

The burn ran blacker for the snow
And ice-floe on ice-floe
Jangled in heavy lurches
Beneath the claret-coloured birches.

Dark grouse rose becking from the ground
And deer turned sharp heads round,
The antlers on their brows
Like stunted trees with withered boughs.

I climbed to where the mountain sloped
And long wan bubbles groped
Under the ice's cover,
A bridge that groaned as I crossed over.

I reached the mist, brighter than day,
That showed a specious way
By narrow crumbling shelves,
Where rocks grew larger than themselves.

But when I saw the mountain's spire
Looming through that damp fire,
I left it still unwon
And climbed down to the setting sun.

Man and Cows

I stood aside to let the cows
Swing past me with their wrinkled brows,
Bowing their heads as they went by
As to a woodland deity
To whom they turned mute eyes
To save them from the plaguing god of flies.

And I too cursed Beelzebub,
Watching them stop to rub
A bulging side or bony haunch
Against a trunk or pointing branch
And lift a tufted tail
To thresh the air with its soft flail.

They stumbled heavily down the slope,
As Hethor led them or the hope
Of the lush meadow-grass,
While I remained, thinking it was
Strange that we both were held divine,
In Egypt these, man once in Palestine.

The Swallows

All day — when early morning shone
With every dewdrop its own dawn
And when cockchafers were abroad
Hurtling like missiles that had lost their road —

The swallows twisting here and there
Round unseen corners of the air
Upstream and down so quickly passed
I wondered that their shadows flew as fast.

They steeplechased over the bridge
And dropped down to a drowning midge
Sharing the river with the fish,
Although the air itself was their chief dish.

Blue-winged snowballs! until they turned
And then with ruddy breasts they burned;
All in one instant everywhere,
Jugglers with their own bodies in the air.

The Thunderstorm

When Coniston Old Man was younger
And his deep-quarried sides· were stronger,
Goats may have leapt about Goat's Water;
But why the tarn that looks like its young daughter
Though lying high under the fell
Should be called Blind Tarn, who can tell?

For from Dow Crag, passing it by,
I saw it as a dark presageful eye;
And soon I knew that I was not mistaken
Hearing the thunder the loose echoes waken
About Scafell and Scafell Pike
And feeling the slant raindrops strike.

And when I came to Walna Pass
Hailstones hissing and hopping among the grass,
Beneath a rock I found a hole;
But with sharp crack and rumbling roll on roll
So quick the lightning came and went
The solid rock was like a lighted tent.

A Wet Day

Breasting the thick brushwood that hid my track
Diffuse wetness of rain had stained me black;
My clinging coat I hung on a bough-knop
And sodden shapeless hat I laid on top.

With heavy hat and coat left on the bough
I felt a snake that had cast off his slough
And joined the slow black slugs that strolled abroad
Making soft shameless love on the open road.

But, turning on my steps, startled I stood
To see a dead man hanging in the wood;
By two clear feet of air he swung afloat,
One who had hanged himself in hat and coat.

Wiltshire Downs

The cuckoo's double note
Loosened like bubbles from a drowning throat
Floats through the air
In mockery of pipit, lark and stare.

The stable-boys thud by
Their horses slinging divots at the sky
And with bright hooves
Printing the sodden turf with lucky grooves.

As still as a windhover
A shepherd in his flapping coat leans over
His tall sheep-crook
And shearlings, tegs and yoes cons like a book.

And one tree-crowned long barrow
Stretched like a sow that has brought forth her farrow
Hides a king's bones
Lying like broken sticks among the stones.

Christmas Day

Last night in the open shippen
    The Infant Jesus lay,
While cows stood at the hay-crib
    Twitching the sweet hay.

As I trudged through the snow-fields
  That lay in their own light,
A thorn-bush with its shadow
  Stood doubled on the night.

And I stayed on my journey
  To listen to the cheep
Of a small bird in the thorn-bush
  I woke from its puffed sleep.

The bright stars were my angels
  And with the heavenly host
I sang praise to the Father,
  The Son and Holy Ghost.

The Gramophone

We listened to your birds tonight
By the firelight,
The nightingales that trilled to us
From moonlit boughs.

Though golden snowflakes from the gloom
Looked in the room,
Those birds' clear voices lingered on
Your gramophone.

'Goodnight' we said and as I go
High-heeled with snow
I almost hope to hear one now
From a bare bough.

The Archaeologist

Although men may dig up
A broken Bacchus with a vine-wreathed cup
Or helmeted chryselephantine goddess;
Though Aphrodite divine and godless,
Helped by a rope, rise from the sea,
None is immortal but Persephone.

See, by an English lane
Cold Hades lets her rise again.
In celandines that in a blaze
Spread like gold starfish their flat rays
Revisiting our earth and sky
Death's wife reveals her immortality.

She glitters with a light
That sharpens, as is said, the swallow's sight;
I am not like that twittering bird;
Too clear a memory my eyes has blurred;
Not this side heaven I'll see again
As once I saw it a gold English lane.

The Falls of Glomach

Rain drifts forever in this place
Tossed from the long white lace
The Falls trail on black rocks below,
And golden-road and rose-root shake
In wind that they forever make;
So though they wear their own rainbow
It's not in hope, but just for show,
For rain and wind together
Here through the summer make a chill wet weather.

Glow-Worms

As though the dark had called
To chrysolite and emerald,
Earth brings out jewel by jewel,
Love stoking their bright fires, itself the fuel.

To flying beetles, 'Come,
Find here your children and your home,'
They sing with a green light,
Each glow-worm her own Venus in the night.

Beaulieu River

Largest of Forest snakes, by heath and scrog
It stretches in its blue sky-borrowed coat,
For while its tail trails in a cotton bog
It grips with foaming mouth the Solent's throat.

The Frogs

Each night that I come down the strath
Frogs turn heels-over-head,
And their white bellies on the path
Tell where to tread.

Of fox with brush above the brake
And kestrel pinned to air
And thin dark river of a snake
Let them beware!

Fat acrobats, I watch them turn
Kicking the evening dew,
Till in white waves that ride the burn
I see frogs too.

The Dunes

These heavy hills of sand,
That marram-grasses bind
Lest they should fly off on the wind,
Hold back the sea from Sea-kings' Land.

Such a waste holds me too
From fields where shadows fly,
Wolds, woods and streams that quote the sky,
All the sweet country that is you.

Long Meg and her Daughters

When from the Druid's Head I came
The low sun doubled tussock-tump
And half in shadow, half in flame
Stood the Stone Circle. Lump by lump
Viewing her daughters Long Meg said,
'Come, stranger, make your choice of one;
All are my children, stone of stone,
And none of them yet wed;
They wait to play at kiss-in-the-ring
With only now the wind to sing.'
But I, 'No, mother, all are fat
And some too old have fallen down flat.'
Meg frowned, 'You should be dead
To take instead a young tombstone to bed.'

Hibernating Snails

Here where the castle faces south
The ivy spreading its flat tree
Hides snails in heaps thick and uncouth,
All fast asleep with open mouth,
Although they breathe no air,
Each china throat sealed up with glair;

Yet some will never wake at all,
For two years old or even three
They crawled alive to their own funeral.

Nightfall on Sedgemoor

The darkness like a guillotine
   Descends on the flat earth;
The flocks look white across the rhine
   All but one lamb, a negro from its birth.

The pollards hold up in the gloom
   Knobbed heads with long stiff hair
That the wind tries to make a broom
   To sweep the moon's faint feather from the air.

What makes the darkness fall so soon
   Is not the short March day
Nor the white sheep nor brightening moon,
   But long June evenings when I came this way.

A Prehistoric Camp

It was the time of year
   Pale lambs leap with thick leggings on
Over small hills that are not there,
   That I climbed Eggardon.

The hedgerows still were bare,
   None ever knew so late a year;
Birds built their nests in the open air,
   Love conquering their fear.

But there on the hill-crest,
  Where only larks or stars look down,
Earthworks exposed a vaster nest,
  Its race of men long flown.

The Flesh-Scraper

If I had sight enough
Might I not find a fingerprint
Left on this flint
By Neolithic man or Kelt?
So knapped to scrape a wild beast's pelt,
The thumb below, fingers above,
See, my hand fits it like a glove.

Essex Salt-Marsh

Now the tide's task is done,
Marsh runnels turn and chuckling run
Or come to a standstill,
The level ground for them a breathless hill.

And as they run or faint
Through mud that takes the sunset's paint,
The gullies they have worn
Shine as with purple grapes and golden corn.

Drought in the Fens

How often from the shade of trees
I thought of that rich man, Dives,
And how no diamond drop was given
To his or earth's cracked lips from heaven.

Green apples fell and lay around
As though they grew upon the ground,
And ditches, shrunk to muddy roads,
Starved limbless fish and man-legged toads.

So when the sand-walled flats I crossed
Hardened by heat as by a frost,
How strange it was that there could be
Still so much water in the sea.

Morning in the Combe

The low sun halves the combe,
One side in sunlight, one in gloom,
And where they meet together
I walk from winter into summer weather.

There hard mud kept the cast
Of hoof and claw and foot that passed,
While here I stumble over
Moist earth that draws me backward like a lover.

The Cuillin Hills

Each step a cataract of stones
So that I rise and sink at once,
Slowly up to the ridge I creep;
And as through drifting smoke
Of mist grey-black as a hoodie-crow
The ghostly boulders come and go
And two hoarse ravens croak
That hopped with flapping wings by a dead sheep,
All is so hideous that I know
It would not kill me though I fell
A thousand feet below;
On you, Black Cuillin, I am now in hell.

Cuckoos

When coltsfoot withers and begins to wear
Long silver locks instead of golden hair,
And fat red catkins from black poplars fall
And on the ground like caterpillars crawl,
And bracken lifts up slender arms and wrists
And stretches them, unfolding sleepy fists,
The cuckoos in a few well-chosen words
Tell they give Easter eggs to the small birds.

Climbing in Glencoe

The sun became a small round moon
And the scared rocks grew pale and weak
As mist surged up the col, and soon
So thickly everywhere it tossed
That though I reached the peak
With height and depth both lost
It might as well have been a plain;
Yet when, groping my way again,
On to the scree I stept
It went with me, and as I swept
Down its loose rumbling course
Balanced I rode it like a circus horse.

Suilven

It rose dark as a stack of peat
With mountains at its feet,
Till a bright flush of evening swept
And on to its high shoulder leapt
And Suilven, a great ruby, shone;
And though that evening light is dead,

The mountain in my mind burns on,
As though I were the foul toad, said
To bear a precious jewel in his head.

Mountain View

Can those small hills lying below
Be mountains that some hours ago
I gazed at from beneath?
Can such intense blue be the sea's
Or that long cloud the Hebrides?
Perhaps I prayed enough
By crawling up on hands and knees
The sharp loose screes,
Sweat dripping on the lichen's scurf,
And now in answer to my prayer
A vision is laid bare;
Or on that ledge, holding my breath,
I may have even slipped past Death.

The Shepherd's Hut

Now when I could not find the road
Unless beside it also flowed
This cobbled beck that through the night,
Breaking on stones, makes its own light,

Where blackness in the starlit sky
Is all I know a mountain by,
A shepherd little thinks how far
His lamp is shining like a star.

144

Children Gathering Violets

Children, small Herods, slay these Innocents
With blue untidy faces and sweet scents;
But violets gone or even autumn here
Spring in the children lasts through all the year.

Walking in Mist

At first the river Noe
Like a snake's belly gleamed below,
And then in mist was lost;
The hill too vanished like a ghost
And all the day was gone
Except the damp grey light that round me shone.

From Lose Hill to Mam Tor,
Darkness behind me and before,
I gave the track its head;
But as I followed where it led,
That light went all the way
As though I made and carried my own day.

Reflections on the River

Rose-petals fall without a touch
As though it were too much
I should be standing by,
And poplars in no wind at all
Keep swaying left and right
With the slow motion of their height
Beneath a small white cloud that soon
Will pluck light from the dark and be the moon.

But where roach rise and bite the Ouse
Round ripples spread out like the first
Drops of a storm about to burst
And in the water toss the boughs
And crack the garden wall;
And as I gaze down in the sky
I see the whole vault shake
As though the heavens were seized with an earthquake.

A Dead Mole

Strong-shouldered mole,
That so much lived below the ground,
Dug, fought and loved, hunted and fed,
For you to raise a mound
Was as for us to make a hole;
What wonder now that being dead
Your body lies here stout and square
Buried within the blue vault of the air?

Fields of Asparagus

From their long narrow beds
Asparagus raise reptilian heads
(Even the sand in May awakes)
And men who think that they are snakes
With shining knives
Walk to and fro, taking their scaly lives.

My path goes to the sea
But turning round comes back to me
In clouds of wind-blown sand
Making a desert of the land,
Where men must fight
With purple snakes that grow up in a night.

Overtaken by Mist

Like lightning on the mountain-slope
The stalker's path zigzagged,
And climbing it with steps that lagged
I often raised my eyes in hope
To where Scour Ouran's head was bare;
But mist that gathered from nowhere
With a bright darkness filled the air,
Until, both earth and heaven gone,
Never was man or angel so alone.

Walking on the Cliff

But for a sleepy gull that yawned
    And spread its wings and dropping disappeared
This evening would have dawned
    To the eternity my flesh has feared.

For too intent on a blackcap
    Perched like a miser on the yellow furze
High over Birling Gap,
    That sang 'Gold is a blessing not a curse,'

How near I was to stepping over
    The brink where the gull dropped to soar beneath,
While now safe as a lover
    I walk the cliff-edge arm in arm with Death.

Idleness

God, you've so much to do,
To think of, watch and listen to,
That I will let all else go by
And lending ear and eye
Help you to watch how in the combe

Winds sweep dead leaves without a broom;
And rooks in the spring-reddened trees
Restore their villages,
Nest by dark nest
Swaying at rest on the trees' frail unrest;
Or on this limestone wall,
Leaning at ease, with you recall
How once these heavy stones
Swam in the sea as shells and bones;
And hear that owl snore in a tree
Till it grows dark enough for him to see;
In fact, will learn to shirk
No idleness that I may share your work.

Autumn Mist

So thick a mist hung over all,
Rain had no room to fall;
It seemed a sea without a shore;
The cobwebs drooped heavy and hoar
As though with wool they had been knit;
Too obvious mark for fly to hit!

And though the sun was somewhere else
The gloom had brightness of its own
That shone on bracken, grass and stone
And mole-mound with its broken shells
That told where squirrel lately sat,
Cracked hazel-nuts and ate the fat.

And sullen haws in the hedgerows
Burned in the damp with clearer fire;
And brighter still than those
The scarlet hips hung on the briar
Like coffins of the dead dog-rose;
All were as bright as though for earth
Death were a gayer thing than birth.

The Nightingale and Owl

How often had I tried to see
A nightingale, and only seen the tree;
Tonight I went with new belief
That I should see one, looking leaf by leaf.

And I was glad too that I went,
For as I listened, drinking the may's scent,
Another came, drawn by the tale
Of that Greek girl changed to a nightingale.

O Philomela, but for me
Who frightened that dark shadow from the tree,
A further change you had gone through,
Your 'Tereu-tereu' now 'Too-whit too-whoo!'

A Brimstone Butterfly

The autumn sun that rose at seven
Has risen again at noon,
Where the hill makes a later heaven,
And fringing with bright rainbow hair
The boughs that lace the sky
Has wakened half a year too soon
This brimstone butterfly,
That fluttering every way at once
Searches in vain the moss and stones, —
Itself the only primrose there.

Ba Cottage

There at the watershed I turned
And looked back at the house I burned —
Burnt, too, by many another tramp
Who sought its shelter, dry or damp.

For coming from the mist-thick moor
I made the window-sill my door
And, wet incendiary, tore up wood
And fed the grate's wide mouth with food.

Then leaning on the mantelshelf
As though a mountain now myself
I smoked with mist and dripped with rain
That slowly made me dry again.

Culbin Sands

Here lay a fair fat land;
   But now its townships, kirks, graveyards
Beneath bald hills of sand
   Lie buried deep as Babylonian shards.

But gales may blow again;
   And like a sand-glass turned about
The hills in a dry rain
   Will flow away and the old land look out;

And where now hedgehog delves
   And conies hollow their long caves
Houses will build themselves
   And tombstones rewrite names on dead men's graves.

After the Gale

I pity trees that all their life
Have ivy for a wife
Or with dark mistletoe they bear
Keep Christmas through the year.

So seeing oak-twigs grow on thorn
Where they were never born,
And sprays of ash-keys and pine-cones
Grow on a briar at once.

I blamed the gale that through the night
Had with perverse delight
Quartered rich children on the poor
Like foundlings at their door.

A Prospect of Death

If it should come to this
You cannot wake me with a kiss,
Think I but sleep too late
Or once again keep a cold angry state.

So now you have been told —
I or my breakfast may grow cold,
But you must only say
'Why does he miss the best part of the day?'

Even then you may be wrong;
Through woods torn by a blackbird's song
My thoughts may often roam
While graver business makes me stay at home.

There will be time enough
To go back to the earth I love
Some other day that week,
Perhaps to find what all my life I seek.

So do not dream of danger;
Forgive my lateness or my anger;
You have so much forgiven,
Forgive me this or that, or Hell or Heaven.

The Stone Eagles

Purple and gold and wet
  To Toller Fratrum, Wynyard Eagle,
Both roads in the sunset
  Shone with a light so rich and regal.
Which choose without regret?

Chance led me by the one
  Where two lean-headed eagles perched
Rain-pitted to the bone
  And the last dregs of daylight searched
With their blind eyes of stone.

What were they watching for?
  Wild eagles that again would fly
Over a waste land or
  Scything wide circles in the sky
Mechanic birds of war?

Snow Harvest

The moon that now and then last night
Glanced between clouds in flight
Saw the white harvest that spread over
The stubble fields and even roots and clover.

It climbed the hedges, overflowed
And trespassed on the road,
Weighed down fruit-trees and when winds woke
From white-thatched roofs rose in a silver smoke.

How busy is the world today!
Sun reaps, rills bear away
The lovely harvest of the snow
While bushes weep loud tears to see it go.

Passing the Graveyard

I see you did not try to save
The bouquet of white flowers I gave;
So fast they wither on your grave.

Why does it hurt the heart to think
Of that most bitter abrupt brink
Where the low-shouldered coffins sink?

These living bodies that we wear
So change by every seventh year
That in a new dress we appear.

Limbs, spongy brain and slogging heart,
No part remains the selfsame part;
Like streams they stay and still depart.

You slipped slow bodies in the past;
Then why should we be so aghast
You flung off the whole flesh at last?

Let him who loves you think instead
That like a woman who has wed
You undressed first and went to bed.

In Moonlight

Rain pattered in the poplar trees,
    And yet there was no rain;
It was clear moon; the trees' unease
    Made me hear water plain.

It seemed that lover walked by lover
    So sharp my shadow showed;
We never needed to step over
    The tree-trunks on the road.

The moon too on the other side
  From tree to tree flew on,
As though she had forsook the tide
  For her Endymion.

The truest lovers I could have —
  So to myself I said —
The shadow marking out my grave
  And moon lending a spade.

The Blind Children

Where caterpillars ate their fill
On hazels' mealy leaves until
The boughs were stript half-bare
And leaves hung riddled with clear holes of air,

I met with children who upturned
Faces to where the blue sky burned,
Some blinking in the glare,
Some looking up with a white open stare.

I did not need to question which
Should leave the road and take the ditch;
I felt it was small kindness
To children walking arm in arm in blindness.

From their blind eyes I borrowed sight
To see the leaves against the light
Rich and not ruinous,
Set with bright diamonds on the fire-fringed boughs.

154

On the Hillside

What causes the surprise
That greets me here under the piecemeal skies
Of this thick-wooded scar?
Is it the look that the familiar
Keeps as of something strange
When so much else is constant but to change?
No, it's the thought that this white sun that cleaves
A silvery passage through the leaves
Is the same sun that cleft them
A week ago, as though I never left them
And never went in the sad interval
To my friend's funeral,
Though crossing the churchyard today I shivered
To see how fast on a fresh grave the flowers had withered.

The Day Ends

The day ends and its heat
Lies in chill dews about our feet;
But though its twelve hours seemed as soon
Gone as the twelve strokes struck at noon,
So much those hours have freed
To blow away for memory's seed,
Will they not still be ours,
Fixed like the church-tower's gilt and holy hours?

The Shower

The cherry-pickers left their picking
And ladders through the branches sticking
And cherries hung like gouts of blood
Down the long aisles of white-washed wood.

But now the sun is breaking through
Dark clouds that dry to pools of blue
And the smooth Medway lies uncreased
Except for drops the boughs released.

What is it makes the sun so proud
He will not suck a passing cloud
But needs raindrops to quench his thirst?
Well, let him do his picking first.

In Avebury Circle

I see the white clouds blow
From cottages thick-thatched with snow
More clearly than I read
This great stone monster without feet, wings, head:

A huge night-blackening shadow
Set up by kings in this holy meadow,
Where of his fellows most
With those antique Cimmerians are lost.

I wonder if King Sil
Will rise and ride from Silbury Hill
Where buried with his horse
He sits, a strange invulnerable corse,

And grey wethers that keep
On Clatford Down their lichened sleep
Drive to this ancient fold
And bring again an age of stone and gold.

In Burnham Beeches

Walking among these smooth beech-boles
   With cracks and galls
And beetle-holes
   And ivy trickling in green waterfalls,

I noted carvings on their barks,
   Faint and diffuse
As china-marks
   On Worcester or Old Bow: I wondered whose.

I feared that time had played its part
   With those whose token
Was a twin heart,
   So many hearts the swelling bark had broken.

Prospect of a Mountain

Though cuckoos call across the kyle
And larks are dancing everywhere
To their thin bagpipe's air,
My thoughts are of the autumn day
I climbed that Quinaig, monstrous pile,
And striding up its slaggy brow
Stood outside time and space;
It looks so empty of me now,
More years than miles away,
The mountain-cairn might mark my burial-place.

Cornish Flower-Farm

Here where the cliff rises so high
The sea below fills half the sky
And ships hang in mid-air,
Set on the cliff-face, square by square,

Walls of veronica enclose
White gladioli in their neat rows
And blue and golden irises;
But though the walls grow tall as trees,
Some flowers from their quiet quillets pass
To mix with wayside weeds and grass,
Like nuns that from their strict retreats
Go visiting the poor in their plain streets.

The Revenant

O foolish birds, be dumb,
   And you, jay, stop your mocking laughter;
A revenant I come
   Today as I might come fifty years after.

Why, birds, I am no stranger,
   For as I cross the copse and back,
I feel a double-ganger,
   Who meets himself at each turn of the track.

A better welcome give
   To one who may have bent and blessed
Your fathers four or five
   Laid in the smooth round hollow of a nest.

Come less than fifty years,
   Owls may have cause to mock at one
Who stalks this wood and wears
   A frosty coat that will not stand the sun.

Spring Flowers

Now we enjoy the rain,
When at each neighbour's door we hear
'How big primroses are this year' —
Tale we may live to hear again —

And dandelions flood
The orchards as though apple-trees
Dropped in the grass ripe oranges,
Boughs still in pink impatient bud,

When too we cannot choose,
But one foot and the other set
In celandine and violet,
Walking in gold and purple shoes,

Rain that through winter weeks
Splashed on our face and window pane,
And rising in these flowers again
Brightens their eyes and fats their cheeks.

The Blind Man

Speak of the birds, he lifts a listening finger
And 'chiff-chaff' 'willow-warbler' names each singer,
'Hedge-sparrow' 'robin' 'wren'; he knows their cries,
Though all are nightingales to his blind eyes.

A Mountain Graveyard

Sheep-fold, I thought — till by the dyke
    I saw it lying deep in dock
And knew he never whistled tyke,
    The herd who folded that quiet flock.

May Frost

It was the night May robbed September
Killing with frost the apple-bloom,
The sunset sunk to its last ember,
I climbed the dew-webbed combe;
There floating from the earth's round rim
I saw the red sun rise.
At first I only thought 'How soon,'
And then 'Surely I must be dying;
These are death's cobwebs on my eyes
That make the dawn so dim;'
And yet my sight was lying:
The frost had set on fire the full-faced moon.

The Shepherd's Hut

The smear of blue peat smoke
That staggered on the wind and broke,
The only sign of life,
Where was the shepherd's wife,
Who left those flapping clothes to dry,
Taking no thought for her family?
For, as they bellied out
And limbs took shape and waved about,
I thought, She little knows
That ghosts are trying on her children's clothes.

A Sussex Ghyll

Primroses thick on its steep floor,
This ghyll deserves a better door
Than an old doubled sack
Flung over the barbed fence's narrow back.

The stream has its own way to come;
And though leaves try to keep it dumb
And even choke it dead,
Like a sick man it lies and sings in bed.

The trees are old; some ivy climbs;
Others like lepers drop their limbs;
But this stream delved the ghyll
Till each bank 'Good-bye' said — a distant hill.

Sudden Thaw

When day dawned with unusual light,
Hedges in snow stood half their height
And in the white-paved village street
Children were walking without feet.

But now by their own breath kept warm
Muck-heaps are naked at the farm
And even through the shrinking snow
Dead bents and thistles start to grow.

Lady's Slipper Orchid

Though I know well enough
To hunt the Lady's-Slipper now
Is playing blindman's-buff,
For it was June She put it on
And grey with mist the spiders' lace
Swings in the autumn wind,
Yet through this hill-wood, high and low,
I peer in every place;
Seeking for what I cannot find
I do as I have often done
And shall do while I stay beneath the sun.

In Breckland

Why is it when I cross the warren,
That last year's thistles make more barren,
Rabbits standing upright like men
Dive in their holes again,
And turtle that to turtle purrs
Rises and swerves from the blue belt of firs,
And even the mole that works beneath
Like a small earthquake holds its breath?
Hated by all for other's sins
I bless this rat that only grins,
Stayed by the stiff indifference of death.

The Haystack

Too dense to have a door,
Window or fireplace or a floor,
They saw this cottage up,
Huge bricks of grass, clover and buttercup
Carting to byre and stable,
Where cow and horse will eat wall, roof and gable.

The Mud

This glistening mud that loves a gate
Was mashed by cows of late,
But now its puddles lie so still
They hold the clouds and trees and hill;
But when the painted cows come out
From milking-shed to grass
And churn the mud up as they pass,
How cloud and tree and hill will dart about!

Field-Glasses

Though buds still speak in hints
And frozen ground has set the flints
As fast as precious stones
And birds perch on the boughs, silent as cones,

Suddenly waked from sloth
Young trees put on a ten year's growth
And stones double their size,
Drawn nearer through field-glasses' greater eyes.

Why I borrow their sight
Is not to give small birds a fright
Creeping up close by inches;
I make the trees come, bringing tits and finches.

I lift a field itself
As lightly as I might a shelf,
And the rooks do not rage
Caught for a moment in my crystal cage.

And while I stand and look,
Their private lives an open book,
I feel so privileged
My shoulders prick, as though they were half-fledged.

A Dead Bird

Finding the feathers of a bird
Killed by a sparrow-hawk,
I thought, What need is there to walk?
And bound them on my feet;
And as I flew off through the air,
I saw men stare up from a street
And women clasp their hands in prayer.
'To Hades' was no sooner said

Than a winged Hermes I was there;
And though I peered round for the dead,
Nothing I saw and nothing heard
But a low moaning from a bough,
'Ah, who is wearing my poor feathers now?'

Twilight

As daylight drains away
And darkness creeps out of the wood
And flowers become too faint to tell,
My eyesight failing me as well
And chill dew watering my blood,
I might imagine night was my last day.

But why need I rehearse
What I must play with my whole heart?
Spectators may be moved to tears
To see me act these now-feigned fears;
While others summing up the part
May with approval say, His lines were terse.

On the Common

The chaffy seeds by the wind blown
Are here so strangely sown,
That one night almost say
The spider's-webs the bushes wear
Have been put down to hay,
And though no crop they bear
Ploughed and cross-ploughed on empty air,
So thick these hay-fields swarm,
That every gorse-bush is become a farm.

Dundonnel Mountains

Through mist that sets the hills on fire
And rising, never rises higher
Looms a stone figure, gross and squat,
An idol carved out by the weather,
Face, limbs and body lumped together;
And while for none but mountain fox
Eagle or buzzard or wild cat
Its worship may be orthodox,
Death fawning on me from these rocks,
A false step would suffice
To make me both its priest and sacrifice.

The Beech-Wood

When the long, varnished buds of beech
Point out beyond their reach,
And tanned by summer suns
Leaves of black bryony turn bronze,
And gossamer floats bright and wet
From trees that are their own sunset,
Spring, summer, autumn I come here,
And what is there to fear?
And yet I never lose the feeling
That someone close behind is stealing
Or else in front has disappeared;
Though nothing I have seen or heard,
The fear of what I might have met
Makes me still walk beneath these boughs
With cautious step as in a haunted house.

The Dead Sheep

There was a blacksmith in my breast,
That worked the bellows of my chest
   And hammer of my heart,
As up the heavy scree I pressed,
   Making the loose stones scream, crag-echoes start.

Rocks, rising, showed that they were sheep,
But one remained as though asleep,
   And how it was I saw,
When loath to leave the huddled heap
   A hoodie crow rose up with angry craw.

Though stiller than a stone it lay,
The face with skin half-flayed away
   And precious jewels gone,
The eye-pits darted a dark ray
   That searched me to my shadowy skeleton.

Hard Frost

Frost called to water 'Halt!'
And crusted the moist snow with sparkling salt;
Brooks, their own bridges, stop,
And icicles in long stalactites drop,
And tench in water-holes
Lurk under gluey glass like fish in bowls.

In the hard-rutted lane
At every footstep breaks a brittle pane,
And tinkling trees ice-bound,
Changed into weeping willows, sweep the ground;
Dead boughs take root in ponds
And ferns on windows shoot their ghostly fronds.

But vainly the fierce frost
Interns poor fish, ranks trees in an armed host,
Hangs daggers from house-eaves
And on the windows ferny ambush weaves;
In the long war grown warmer
The sun will strike him dead and strip his armour.

The Swedes

Three that are one since time began,
Horse, cart and man,
Lurch down the lane patched with loose stones;
Swedes in the cart heaped smooth and round
Like skulls that from the ground
The man has dug without the bones
Leave me in doubt
Whether the swedes with gold shoots sprout
Or with fresh fancies bursts each old bald sconce.

By the Erme

No trace of absent years
Water or bank or boulder wears;
All is the same as when I went away.

Even my floating face
Seems looking up from the same place,
More steadfast than the stream that cannot stay.

I might have left it there,
Although I notice that my hair
Now stirs a little foam in the smooth bay.

View from Mountain

When through the parting mist,
That the sun's warm gold mouth had kissed,
The hills beneath me came to view
With lochans gleaming here and there,
It was not like the earth I knew;
Another world was shining through,
As though that earth had worn so thin
I saw the living spirit within,
Its beauty almost pain to bear
Waking in me the thought,
If heaven by act of death were brought
Nearer than now, might I not die
Slain by my immortality?

The Salmon-Leap

Leaves, and not birds, now flit,
Brighter than yellow wagtail and cole-tit,
Or on the water lie
Making a sunset of the fishes' sky.

Autumn for salmon-trout
Is spring, and Io Hymen boulders shout,
Spate drawing them to spawn
Where on high hills the river keeps its dawn.

From rock-lipt lynn to lynn,
Shaking the ferns and grasses with their din,
The cascades overflow
And pour in pools to rise as boiling snow;

Tossing their bodies bare
The salmon-trout are seen tasting our air,
For stronger is the flood
That rages in their few small drops of blood.

The Rockland Broad

Water too clear to show,
Unless a frown ruffle its brow,
I scarcely feel afloat —
I am suspended in a flying-boat!

Sure, with the land so low
This broad will burst and overflow,
Rush on and never stop,
Till the whole world becomes one water-drop.

Though willow-carrs and reeds
And alders, too, change to seaweeds,
Let Heaven again take note,
Save this new Noah in his flying-boat.

In the Dingle

As the spring darkened into summer
This dingle rill grew dumber,
Till only sand and gravel
Showed sullen pools the way to travel;
And now no water flows
But what by root and tree-trunk goes,
Sinking and rising up
To bathe a leaf or fill an acorn's cup.

At Amberley Wild Brooks

Watching the horses stand
And bend their long heads Roman-nosed
With thick cheek veins exposed,
So close to where the brook's bank shelves
They almost meet themselves
In the smooth water sliding by,

I think it strange creatures so great
Can be shut in by wooden gate
And brook no deeper than my hand,
And not like Pegasus shoot wings and fly.

A Shot Magpie

Though on your long-tailed flight
You wore half-mourning of staid black and white,
So little did the thought of death
Enter your thievish head,
You never knew what choked your breath
When in a day turned night
You fell with feathers heavier than lead.

By a British Barrow in Wartime

Let me lie down beside you, prince,
And share — no, do not wince —
Your grave for a short hour at noon
Shaped, with molehills for stars, like the full moon.

Man in this moon of turf and chalk,
If you can hear me talk
And understand a Saxon stranger,
Listen! today our country is in danger.

Does that not stir you, man of bones?
Your country it was once,
Yours when you strode across these downs
Where walls still wave about your hilltop towns.

Or is the news stale in your world
Where hosts are hourly hurled?
Perhaps you learnt from one of these
Who by his death gained a victorious peace.

You do not hear, man in this moon;
The skylarks might as soon
Hear me as you who are not there;
I waste breath that were precious now in prayer.

At Grime's Graves

These flints that on the warren lie
And glint in moonlight like a snake's eye,
Though chipped by knappers for flint arrows
That flew away like sparrows,
Are still so fresh that one might say
Those dead men were on holiday;
'Few poems keep as fresh as flints,'
The green-eyed moonlight hints;
'Yours will not last as long;
They will not even go for an old song.'

July

Darker the track today
Than any cloudy March or April day
    When nesting birds sang louder,
For hazels hazels, elders elders meet,
Tangle and trip the sun's pale dancing feet
    That beat it to white powder.

That day in January,
I climbed the hill to this wood's sanctuary,
    The track was plain enough;
Now bryony crowds its stars yellow as honey
And close against my face hemp-agrimony
    Pushes its purple faces.

But I may find again
When autumn's fires sink under winter's rain
　　A clearer way to pass,
As when that sun with a wan ray of hope
Striking a hollow on the frost furred slope
　　Wet one green patch of grass.

Hymn

Lord, by whose breath all souls and seeds are living
　　With life that is and life that is to be,
First-fruits of earth we offer with thanksgiving
　　For fields in flood with summer's golden sea.

Lord of the earth, accept these gifts in token
　　Thou in thy works are to be all-adored,
For whom the light as daily bread is broken,
　　Sunset and dawn as wine and milk are poured.

Poor is our praise, but these shall be our psalter;
　　Lo, like thyself they rose up from the dead;
Lord, give them back when at thy holy altar
　　We feed on thee, who are the living bread.

At Formby

From that wide empty shore,
No foot had ever trod before
(Or since the sea drew back the tide),
I climbed the dune's soft slide
To where no higher than my hand
Wind-bitten pines grew in the clogging sand.

But farther from the beach
The trees rose up beyond my reach,
And as I walked, they still grew taller
And I myself smaller and smaller,
Till gazing up at a high wood
I felt that I had found my lost childhood.

At Arley

The Severn sweeping smooth and broad
A motion to the hillside gives
Till it too liquifies and lives,
For glancing from that rushing road
I see the solid hill
Flow backward for a moment and stand still.

Into Hades

1 The Funeral
One midnight in the Paris Underground
Walking along the tunnel to a train,
I saw a man leaning against the wall,
Eyes shut, head sunk on chest; selling newspapers
He had fallen asleep, but still stood on his feet.
Just so I must have stood,
When drowsily I heard, as from a distance,
Forasmuch—Almighty God—unto himself
The soul of our dear brother here departed,
We therefore commit his body to the ground;
Earth to earth, ashes to ashes—Half-asleep,
My mind took time to gather in the meaning;
Then I began to wonder, and awoke.

By an open grave
Lined with the undertaker's verdant grass,
Their backs toward me, priest and people stood.
The verger, who dropped the clods, dusting his hands,
Why, it was Fred! And this was Stonegate Church!
These were my friends, the priest the Rural Dean;
Did they think I lay ill in the vicarage,
Too ill to bury a parishioner?
Could they not see me standing in the road?
But when I saw the Three,
Who after the priest's *'I heard a voice from heaven'*
Drew closer to the grave's brink and gazed down,
I gasped and cried, 'Stop! there is some mistake;
You cannot bury me; I am not dead.'
But no one turned, for no one heard my cry.
Terrified by the silence of my own voice,
I sank down with a shudder by the lych-gate.

2 **The Prison**
        It was like waking
In a strange room; I almost hoped to hear
The opening of a door, a slippered step.
The funeral came slowly back as though
A scene from last night's play. I lay and listened
For night's stealthy noises, swaying curtain,
Sigh of spent cinders in a fire-place; but all
Was silent as myself. No wind outside
Drew its loose fingers through a bush; farm-cock
Still slept like weather-cock.
But I could wait. Soon a window would grow pale;
Already I could see my hand, my body.
I had no fear, thinking of nothing more
Than the strange novelty of being dead.

        Often I had waked
Thankful to be alive after an air-raid;
I was as thankful now to wake and to be dead.
I even grew light-headed; I had made
The long night journey in a sleeping carriage;
I had not changed at Crewe. Where was my watch?
What was the time now in Eternity?
The funeral was a hoax; how false that coffin
They slowly lowered with its puppet. Why,
It was my conjurer's box, with which I showed
The Vanishing Parson; played the trick so well
I had deceived myself. Scared the audience,
Affected by the flowers, unconscious bouquets,
I had been seized by stage-fright and cried out,
'You cannot bury me; I am not dead.'

        Would someone come?
The place must have its routine, a new arrival
Causing no sensation. I should hear voices soon,
Friends at the door. Which should we be in heaven,
Our parents' children or our children's parents?
We might be both. Time could be a clock,

No foolish face, only a pendulum,
Swinging us to and fro, backward and forward,
From age to youth, from youth again to age,
The psychological clock, our minds had lived by
In the interchange of memory and hope.

This dusk was ambiguous;
Would it thin to dawn or thicken to darkness? I waited,
Longing to hear a bird's first doubtful chirp
And then another and the whole kindled chorus.
But no birds sang that morning—if it was morning.
Birds had no time to sing, for while my eyes
Were fumbling with informal cloudy shapes,
Light entered with a step, and it was day,
Wide-open, unabashed. I stared in wonder
At what had the appearance of a prison
With thick-ribbed vault and iron-studded door.
Yet it seemed hardly real;
More like a dungeon in an opera,
Fidelio or Faust. What made it stranger,
I saw no window for the light to enter.

Frightened, yet half mocking,
I sat and viewed it. Was this one of those fits
That often seized me? Objects of themselves
Melted away to their own images,
An insubstantial world; or it only needed
That I should say, 'I see what I am seeing,'
To feel that what I looked on was unreal,
Nothing was changed, but all was visionary,
And I was in a waking dream. But this time
My sight was in reverse and what looked real
Was visionary. Reaching out my hand
To put it to the proof, I touched a stone;
It was as soft as mist; my hand went through it,
Boring a hole. This was mere make-believe,
Stuff of myself; like a silkworm I had spun
My own cocoon. I understood this prison;

A symbol of the womb, it was the presage
Of my new birth. No midwife would be needed
For this confinement; precocious embryo,
I should prick the pregnant bubble. These stones would
                                                   vanish,
The prisoner escaping with the prison.

          From this side death
Ghost tales seemed credible; could I not go back
To the vicarage? show myself to the Three,
Who thought they left me in the lowered box?
Would they be psychic? A determined ghost,
I should be palpable, besiege the house,
Lay ambushes in the garden, look through a window—
But at the thought I stiffened!
A picture came to my mind—was it from something
I had seen or read? or was it not imagined?—
Of a dead man, live ghost, who came and stood
Outside a lighted window of his house,
Face crushed against the glass, white as a mushroom,
Eyes burning like a moth's, and gazed within
On wife and children, who were so unconscious
A daughter rose and looked out on the darkness
And, seeing nothing, drew the blind. I was frightened
By that picture so intolerant of hope;
It even woke new fear.

   3 The Body
          I had seen a tree-trunk,
That hurt the ground with its dead weight, sprout leaves
Not knowing it was dead; I had caught fish,
Flounders that flapped, eels tying and untying
Slippery knots, slow to drown in our air;
Was I too living out my life's last remnant,
Not living, only lasting? Was Death a monster,
A cat that toyed with a mouse, caught but not killed?
The thought seized my brain, a fear so tumultuous

That, afraid of itself, it died in fascination,
A crouching, a yielding to the softened paw,
The sense I was safe—not to escape.

Or was I not yet myself,
Not recovered from my illness, cured by death,
Still convalescent? How had I died?
Had death come as a storm, tornado, razing
A tract of memory? There was a gap,
Days, weeks and months torn from the almanac.
I remembered my father's death;
How I had watched the hard, humiliating struggle,
That made me half ashamed that I, his son,
Spied on his weakness. I remembered her,
Who held her son's last letter in her hand
Like a passport to heaven. I remembered too
Thinking that some time I should go their way;
But had I then believed it?

Why, even now
The sight and touch of my accustomed body
Compromised the truth. Here it was out of place,
An obvious mistake. Raising my hand
I recognized a white scar on my wrist;
I felt my heart; shut in its cage of bones,
That songless lark kept time. But the funeral!
The coffin with its cargo! I was confused;
Were there two bodies, two scars, two birdcages?
Paudricia in *Palmerin of England*
In place of her lover, still alive in prison,
Buried his effigy. Trust the undertaker
Not a bury a guy

As I looked at my body,
It stared back with a strange impertinence,
Familiar, hostile, superfluous proof I was dead.
It, too, was make-believe, stuff of myself,
Old use and wont expected, therefore seen.

I was my own Pygmalion!
A fungoid outgrowth, it was not like that other
I left in the churchyard, that stiff, straight soldier
Who kept good guard in his fallen sentry-box.

       I must not sleep again;
Nothing to hold it, my body would be gone,
And, body gone, should I not also go?
The thought alarmed me; it was high time to answer
The long-unanswered knocking at my mind's
Back-door. I had heard it since I first awoke,
Steady as a clocklike dripping in a crypt.
Now I bustled about and with shamefaced 'Welcome, stranger,
You should have come up by the garden path',
I greeted my terrific visitor,
The thought of God.

   4 The Prisoner
       The thought was surgical,
But could I not disarm it of the knife?
Had I no grievance I had been kept waiting
So long in an ante-room? *O bona Patria,*
Num tua gaudia teque videbo?
How often had I sung. Not patriotic
Like Bernard de Morlaix, I yet had tasted
The honey of the land in his sweet *Rhythm.*
Where was that land? where was the mystic city?
What had I seen? A ghost with a white scar,
An opera prison.

       But nothing happened,
Time lazy, stale, dammed up by a long moment.
Was I here forever, or till the Judgment Day?
Which was this cell, convict's or anchorite's?
The prison irked me; though it looked determined,
It was stage property. What I had conjured up
Could I not conjure down? Calling to myself,
'These are the prophet's stones of emptiness',

I tried to wave it away. It answered back,
Stones shooting out on elongated necks
Fantastic gargoyles. It was like a church
Turned outside in. Waving their serpent heads,
They reached towards me, tugging at the walls;
I was seized by my oldest fear, to be buried alive,
And gave a nightmare cry.

      I outstared them in the end;
Grinning acknowledgment, they relapsed to stone.
I was their Gorgon's head!
Yet I was afraid; it was dangerous to be dead.

5 The Lover
      Why had I waked?
There was no future in this future life,
Nothing to do, no prayer, no repentance.
Dante set out to walk from hell to heaven
For his soul's health, but mine had caught a cold.
And Dante came back! Why was I singled out?
What was peculiar? What the truth, the value?
Was it in that young lover,
Who pitched his tent in heaven and read Plato?

      I had the strange feeling
Someone that moment, in looking through my relics,
Had found a ring, a ring of twisted silver
Carved with a letter, and had paused to wonder
Whose name it stood for, what the cheap treasure meant.
How little did he guess
She had been nothing I could see or touch
And had no other name than that I gave her
Unless among the angels. Unlike Psyche
Lighting her penny dip, I asked no sight
Of the flying Eros. Hermits and virgins,
Who in the love and proof of chastity
Slept side by side in the Egyptian desert,
Had not so pure a passion. Joseph and Mary

Might have been the witnesses, when at our wedding
I placed the ring, for our marriage was by proxy,
On the third finger—of my own left hand.

      Her speech a responsive silence,
(Though in undertones of streams I caught her voice),
She was the charm of woods, my Adam's rib,
My Muse, my shadow on the sunny side.
She mocked me on mountains; where hands and knees
                                               clasped rocks,
She glided as a ghost; yet in a mist's
Rich loneliness she was singularly present.
I found her most in Paris;
In the twilight, in the evening, when, behold,
A woman at the corner, she cooled my blood
More than the corpses set up in the Morgue
Like fashion dummies in a milliner's window.
I starved my body that the loosened spirit
Might break out to the prospect, the fulfilment;
Indulged in the thought of death, feeding on Plato;
For though he argued of the life to come
With only half his head, he was himself
The better argument.

      With no gross brain
Steadying it, my mind clutched at a hope;
Though I had broken my noviciate's vows,
Fallen from that envied self, now my despair,
Might she not trespass on a timid star
And, euphrasy on her eyes, see how her lover
Struggled in this strait-jacket? That Platonic love
Was withered seaweed, crawled over by bleached dead crabs,
Busy with sand-hoppers; yet it had floated once,
Waved with the water, lustrous, stranger than earthplant.
Believe what you see not and you shall see
What you will not believe: If in the words
There was heavenly logic, might she not come?
I outbid hope; she would come laughing, mocking

My artificial body, 'not one true limb,
Poor Dresden china shepherd'.   But what came instead
Was sleep, an irresistible sleep—

6 The Ghost
        Morning was late that day,
Delayed by thick fog. Trees, their tops out of sight,
Scattered irregular rain: dew-hoary cobwebs
Drooped with false geometry. Over the hedge
The mist drew round the coats of coughing sheep
A halo of silver light: they might have been
Hyperion's. How I came in the garden
Was denser fog. A moorhen on the pond,
Jetting its head with red phylactery,
Pushed forward in widening angles. Seeing a man,
It would have croaked and run with dripping legs
To shelter in the reeds: but it swam closer.
I was a ghost; I could go up to birds
And pick them like a barn-owl from a bough.
That it was my own garden I was haunting
Filled it with stinging nettles. The old boat,
Upturned with gaping wounds, was not so dead;
It came to life in summer, growing warm
And raising tarry blisters.

          The sun itself was a ghost,
A pallid ball that came and went in the haze
It helped to thin. I saw the vicarage
Across the pond; but where was my ambition
To haunt it? Achilles' horses could shed tears,
But mine were raindrops on a winter bough,
That freeze and forget to fall. For something told me
I was warned away, a trespasser in my own garden.
I had come home to learn
With how true an instinct I had dedicated
The ring of twisted silver in the end.

The bell rang for the Celebration.
It had an absent sound, but I would be present;
All mornings for a ghost were All Saints' Night.
Why, when they brought St Germain's body to church,
Choir tapers lit themselves. And I wore my cassock!
Had they buried me like a Carthusian monk
In his usual habit? And the feast was ghostly;
I should feel at home, see with St Chrysostom
The Word born on the altar; I should kneel
And worship like the Magi at the manger.

The bell stopped ringing,
As I took the road. The boy with Sunday papers
Came cycling down; I would have said 'Good morning',
But he rode past, eyes fixed ahead. I turned
And saw him jump off at the garden gate
And, feeling for a paper, disappear.
He had looked through my body! The hedge was thorny;
I clawed it, eager for the sight of blood
As the thronging ghosts Odysseus drove with his sword
From the red pool. But I was an empty ghost
And no blood came. I had seen Death at last;
He had ridden past me, not on his pale horse,
But on a cycle with the *Sunday Times*.

It mattered little
The service was begun. The Ten Commandments
I could take as read—what were they to me now?—
Omit the Offertory—silver and gold,
Could I not say, with Peter, I had none?
Reaching the lych-gate, where at first I fainted,
I almost fainted again. As I stole a glance
At the white chrysanthemums that buried my grave,
The sun made rainbows on my wet eye-lashes.
Lift up your hearts, I heard; but my heart sank;
My ghostly hands had not strength enough to turn
The door's iron handle. I darted to a window;
But the priest was not in view. I outdid Zacchaeus;

Overflying the roof, I perched on an Irish yew,
That grew on the farther side against the chancel.
The priest was kneeling: like God or an eavesdropper
I knew the words he spoke. At the Consecration,
When he stood with hovering hands over the Birth,
I watched him like a young communicant,
Who through his fingers spies on the priest's action.
But when he raised the Host,
The Bread that feeds us as we feed the Bread,
He straightened upwards in a fearful elongation,
Tall as a seraph. I gazed at him aghast
As at the sight of something that could not happen.
My trembling shook the tree. Then all grew dim,
Cloudy, tumultuous, a swirling smoke.
'Fire! your church is on fire!' I almost cried
To the sleeping villagers, but I remembered
The prophet's words, *The house was filled with smoke.*
As the candle flames, indignant eyes, burned through it,
I slid down from the tree; not church, but churchyard,
Fitted a ghost. I was excommunicated.

7 Mattins

            The fog had left the sun
A heavy dew to lift; Thomson, the farmer,
Trailed a dark track in the cow-pasture. But I,
A ghost, a little fog myself, trailed none
Through the churchyard grass. Shunning chrysanthemums,
I sat on a flat stone, alive with lichen.
It might have been a moonbeam the sun cast,
For I felt no warmth.

        Locked out by St Peter's key!
And from the church that he and I had shared
As patron saint and priest! I was the more
Aggrieved, for churches were my love and study,
Not theology. I sat and wrapt myself
In their warm memory, from Norman naves,
Huge monsters standing on elephantine legs,

Tame at the altar, to the little churches
With scarcely room for God. Stone foliage
Showed me the spring in winter at West Walton,
Angels smiled down as they spread their wooden wings
To fly off with Knapton's roof. I thought of Gloucester,
Where under the swirling fan-vault of the cloister
I walked like a river-god; of Beverley's
Dense forest of choir stalls, where I unearthed
Strange creatures, salamanders, unicorns,
Peacocks and men whose faces were their bellies.
Lincoln's rose-window so hurt me with its beauty,
It was like broken glass; sun shining through,
Apollo was a Christian.

    Was the church a well,
That filled from within? I had seen no people enter,
Yet voices sang to the organ. They sang *Venite,*
But I did not come; I sat, too, through the Psalms
Like an invalid. Gazing about the churchyard,
I saw it was autumn; berries on the hedge
Hung in bright bracelets; bryony, nightshade, how vain
To remember the names. A silence grew more than silence,
A vacuum, that drew me to a window.
One of my friends stood at the lectern eagle;
Jove's messenger, the brazen bird looked bored,
It had so often listened to the Lessons.
As I peered at the priest, the stranger in my stall,
The congregation rose, filling the church,
For the *Te Deum.* So they must have risen,
When I was shouldered out, smothered with flowers
To make my death the surer. The thought was bitter;
It turned the *Te Deum* to the *Nunc Dimittis.*
Two women stood at the other side of the window;
I could have touched the nearer but for the glass
And a lost world between. Turning her head,
She stared at me in wonder. Would she start the story

She had seen her late vicar's ghost? Though I told myself
I was only another window she looked through,
I stole from the church's shadow.

> The white chrysanthemums
Seduced my feet. I stood over my grave
At the priest's end. It was my mother Eve,
Apple still in her mouth, who tempted me
To take the plunge into that foaming gulf.
I saw a wonder: the coffin-lid mere glass,
I gazed down at the gaunt philosopher.
I hardly knew myself; here was a change
From Epicurean to the Stoic school.
But the coffin was a trap; springing to life
He rose, a towering wave of lust, and gripped me;
I choked in his close embrace, cold awful kiss.

8 World's End
> It was touch and go,
That I escaped the shaking of the sheet,
The breathless suction, being buried in my grave.
Corpses so amorous, earth was not safe
For wandering ghosts. The prison would be safer,
No fear of being murdered by a dead man.
But was I back in prison?
I gazed on nothing; even the floor had fled;
The prison, not the prisoner, had escaped!
All was so absent, I had the baffled sense
That in looking I did not look. It was like a sea
Without the water. Hung on a spacious point,
I feared to stretch a hand; I might overbalance,
Fall without end; it was dangerous as a dream.
I viewed myself with distaste. Emphatic Ego,
A speck of horrible conspicuousness,
I felt exposed. Shaming the one-eyed Cyclops,
I borrowed the whole universe for eye,
A gazing-stock to myself.

           Flowing ectoplasm,
This body would not last, not even as long
As that other body lying in its sunk boat,
Shipwrecked on land. This was a replica,
That the original. I felt for its defeat
A self-pity: face that had hoisted the white flag
To the invaders; veins, once fruitful rivers,
Stagnant canals; the heart, that had kept good time,
Stopped; inner works that had gone of their own accord,
While I, the engineer, had walked on deck,
Run down; the precious idol that all my life
I had fed with hecatombs of sheep and oxen,
Given rich libations, fallen. Though the Creed
Spoke of an exhumation and Coroner's inquest,
It lay in a world that itself had fallen to nothing.
I was further from that world than the nebulae,
Not space enough between us to drop a pin.
Trout in time's stream, nosing its solid wind,
Helped by a heavenly hook, I had leapt out
And landed on the bank.

  9 **The Rainbow**
           Was I near the Magnetic Mountain,
Climbed by those saints who, wounded by love's arrow,
Had sought for healing at their Hunter's wounds?
Rapt from themselves to a murmuring solitude,
A silent music, they were abroad in bliss,
A merry heat, and tasting marvellous honey,
They loved and burned and shone and in a tempest
Were overthrown. By comprehending not,
They comprehended and in a fathomless staring
Became the light they saw. Through an abyss
That in the Godhead's mountain-range disported,
Beyond activity, wayless and idle,
They passed to a wild estrangement, the Dark Silence
Where all lovers lose themselves.

Saints were the world's adventure.
I had explored their poor cells of self-knowledge,
Tasted their fasts; my faith leaned hard on theirs,
As substance of things hoped for, evidence
Of things not seen. Now, answering my faith,
The sudden rainbow!

       At first it puzzled my eyes;
Red, orange, green, blue, violet, the names
Did not apply; I could not read the colours
I knew for colours only by their contrast.
It was a rainbow in a foreign language,
If rainbow it was, that overflowed with flowers,
Amorous, dangling in a gay rebellion
From their strict arch. I gazed in frightened joy;
What was to follow, the Book of Revelation
Having opened at this marker? I lay still,
Awed, crouching, tightly clutched by its wide arms,
Eyes drawn up to the supernatural magnet.
Time was not long or short enough to measure
My gazing. Then the strange fires melted.

       My makeshift body, too,
Melted away. My substance was a thought,
That fell back on itself like a wave rising
White on a stream's current. Buoyant, open,
I expatiated in freedom. But not for long;
Too near to nothing, exposed, I craved for objects,
The body's mutual touch, the rough and hard,
A rock's resistance, the boundary of a thorn,
A limit to my false infinitude.

       My thought dropped to the churchyard.
It gaped with an easy earthquake, the coffin-lid
Flying open of itself and the dead man—
Did I catch his action?—pulling back the sheet.
He had drawn his skin-coat tight against the cold
And, pale ascetic, crossed his hands in prayer.

'Brother,' I said, 'I need your blind statue eyes
To see the rainbow's overflowing flowers;
Your deaf ears, so intent, to hear what gospels
Hum round its whispering gallery; a thin hand
To shade me shyly from the Deity.'

Like the soul of Hermotimus,
Returned from the air to find his body burnt,
I was at a loss. I could have hailed a stone,
Made it an idol; squeezed into a rabbit's burrow
To crush myself to shape. All was so empty,
I was not even defined by what I was not;
I might have flown for ever and not found
A desert. If others like myself were here,
Each had arrived with his own universe.
Whatever it might be after the Judgment,
Our universes now could no more mingle
Than the imaginations of a man and woman
Lying in the same bed.

Where was my ground,
Support? Trembling, naked, I was an O,
A nothing and a cry of astonishment.
Where there is nothing there is God: the word
Came to my mind; it might have been a flower
Dropt from the rainbow. My sole support was God.
The thought was electric; at the toleration,
God as my unseen, contemplated ground,
My mind began to sparkle.

10   The New Body
It was a phantom,
Not the true Helen, who was rapt to Egypt,
Paris took to Troy. Phantasmal, too, the body
I lived in, loved on earth; for now the body
I saw, knew as my own, though not yet adopted,
Was real in excess.

      Fantastic coffin,
The boat that bore it slowly sailed in sight,
Lit by St Elmo's fire; it might have come
From anchoring off the rainbow. Solomon's cargo,
The gold and silver, ivory, apes and peacocks,
Was not so precious as that solemn barge's.
Its cargo was its captain, but not dead;
In sleep surmounting sleep he lay in state
Distant, superior, unrecognising,
My new authentic body!
Holy, immortal, my eyes saw it so clearly
They stung me like jelly-fish, as I remembered
How I had profaned its earthly prototype,
Though only a phantom.

      I saw it put to shame
The miracle of loaves and fishes. It stirred,
Sprouted with life, rose spreading, multiplying,
Changed to a Jesse-tree. The sleeping Adam
Had more ribs than a wreck: warm, fertile, breathing,
They stretched as boughs, laden with all the bodies
I had worn on earth, child, lover and man.

      Gazing at the child,
In whom I saw myself, *O Hesperus,*
That bringest all things back the bright dawn scattered,
I sang with Sappho. Narcissus-like I eyed
The lover who aspired to climb love's ladder;
Petrarch had climbed it, led by Laura's eyes,
But he, who aimed at an eloping angel,
Climbed two or three steps, when beneath his weight
The ladder gave way. The man was multiple,
The one in many, the same, yet different.
I hailed the token! At the Resurrection
It was a changing Proteus who would rise,
Choosing, repeating variable ages,
His life a newel-stair, ascending, descending.

11   The New Earth
                Caught up to heaven,
Or charmed away by an Orphean lyre,
The tree vanished; it did not even leave
The progenitor. Yet I was not alone;
I knew by the different silence there was an Other,
Invisible, hiding behind himself.
I waited, listened. There was no need to listen:
Silence interpreting itself, the words
Were reflected on my mind like flowers on water,
'Come, see the Bride'. They were as plain as speech,
But whose they were, I had no time to wonder;
As tiny as a thought at first, but growing
To hazel-nut, to apple, to balloon,
A world swam up, losing its shape in size.
If worlds could speak like maps, it would have said,
'The New Earth'.

                Her beauty sparkled;
Though I knew her for the old earth, now renewed,
Reborn, she was so transfigured, so unearthly,
I felt I tarnished her even with looking.
All things were conscious, trees talking together,
Streams their own Sirens; mountains might have moved
Slow shoulders. Miraculously as in a dream
She drew close to my side. Distance so near,
Thin as a window-pane, I could have leapt
And landed on her lap, in a laughing ditch
Or cow-gate smiling with subliminal mud.
But I was stuck in space. Not for one lover,
A paralytic too, had this Venus risen.

                If the Jesse-tree,
Laden with bodies, a Christmas-tree at Easter,
Had shamed the miracle of loaves and fishes,
What I now saw excelled. It came in glimpses,
As the Earth, a changing Proteus too, repeated
Her variable ages. It flung out

Wild liberty to move both ways in time,
Backward, forward. The moment in reverse,
Past following future, as future followed past,
Clio, playing Penelope's part, would unweave
Her historic web. What sights would be disclosed,
Time ebbing: cities would unbuild themselves,
Temples fly back to their quarries; fossils unfreezing
Would show toothed birds and five-toed horses; coal,
Mining itself, would rise as ferny forests,
Air feel again the weight of flying lizards.
One glimpse I had: it was a dead volcano,
That remembering its old anger, furiously
Stoked its cold fires; perhaps I saw it clearly,
I was so blinded by the frightening flames.

       Time's two-way traffic
Would let the apelike man, a sinless satyr,
Loping into the future, view the Parthenon,
While Aristotle, hieing back to the past,
Watched fish that, coming to land, grew legs and lungs.
And myself? I should wander to and fro in time,
Historian of all—its present ages.
I should taste Eternity. Why had I said,
There was no future in this future life?
The New Earth opened out so bright a prospect,
I forgot about its sky!
I looked too late, that strange earth floating away;
But womanlike she tossed me a last word,
'Sun, moon and stars lay in that tomb with Christ.'

12   **The New Heaven**
       Vanished to permanence,
She left a hollow in the emptiness,
That waited to be filled. Should I now hear,
'Come, see the Bridegroom'?
My Monitor—for so I named the Other—
Alarmed me by his stillness. Was he waiting
Prelude, star-signal? The silence grew peculiar,

Then self-assertive, till, swelling immense,
It rocked me as it rose to bursting-point,
To the explosion! I was lifted up,
Dead and alive at once, stunned by a rock,
Assaulted by the sight—

Plato died in his dream,
But I woke muttering 'The Terrible Crystal'.
What did my lips remember? For my mind
Held nothing real; it was an empty net
Drawn up at night from a phosphorescent sea.
I even felt the distant rainbow frowned
On the effort to remember. I clutched at symbols:
The sky a mirror, feet moving to and fro,
An albatross, a fountain rising in prayer,
One who bent over me, tall as a pillar,
Reflected faces, swaying like flowers, astonished.
Had I scared the angels by my conspicuousness?
Shattered the Crystal?

I knew with a blind man's feeling
My Monitor was there: I could have kissed
His faithful, invisible feet. He even read
My dumb question, 'Why the earthquake, heavenquake,
The evocation of those foolish symbols?'
The answer came as though written on my mind,
'You flew too high: come, see the saints in flight.'
He proved a Mercury. First his soft rod
Charmed my sick memory asleep; and then!
Argus had fewer eyes shut by that rod
Than I had opened, though in a steadfast sleep.

13   The Three Hierarchies
He rose in flamelike flight,
Singing to music dumb as a music-score
A song inaudible as a bursting rosebud's,
I following in straight ascent. We halted
Where a waterfall, cascade after cascade,

Made an endless thunder. Pools swirled with wondering
                                                    bubbles
And overflowed in wide columns of water,
That in crashing down stood still. Salmon darkened
Its white tumbling extravagance, leaping out
To fall back, curved like bows, or straight as arrows
Shot through the current. I heard, close as a kiss,
'Look back; see her who sends to heaven these saints,
Missiles, love-letters.' Earth in an empty nadir
Shone like a star reflected in a pool.

        The waterfall stopped,
Salmon hooked in mid-air, the spray a frozen silence;
All was a picture waiting to come alive.
My Monitor called from above, 'Look higher.'
To look was to ascend; I was on a peak,
Exhausted pinnacle. The air was filled
With flying gannets that—Was space upturned?
Why, when they plunged, they rose and fell into the sky,
Not down into a sea. It brought to my mind
How waterdrops fall *up* to a lake's surface
Reflecting drips from an oar. Sharing my thought,
He said, 'Some birds come back; they are not lucky
Like the false water-drops that falling up
Meet their true selves to perish in a kiss.'

        'The Holy Trinity
Is celebrated in three hierarchies;
Come, see the third.' As though at my Monitor's word,
I flew up like a bubble from a stream,
Exploding, lost in air. Yet I gathered myself,
Grew sufficient, and to his mocking 'Look beyond',
I looked. My strained sight took so long to travel,
It might have been climbing an invisible mountain.
But I saw them, even to their gold and purple feathers,
The phoenixes. They struck at the Godhead,
One moment birds and the next moment ashes.
Though they flocked in thousands to their immortal deaths,

Each was God's only phoenix. My Monitor said,
'Yet an archangel's wing, darkening the sky,
Would frighten those small larks.'

     The height relaxing,
I fell away so fast the waterfall
Passed in a flash; I could have overtaken
A stone or shooting star. But I was halted;
The New Earth swam in sight. Rapidly rising,
She burned with an intolerable beauty
That would have scorched my feet, yet seemed each moment
A new creation. She carried her own morning,
A sunny light, to which her heart kept humming.
'Bridegroom waits Bride; the saints will hail the Union,
Inherit both, descending or ascending,
As they see God in creatures or creatures in God,'
My Monitor said, and put my dream to sleep.

14 The Last Look
     If he was not myself,
The primal self who never had left heaven,
My Monitor was gone. A ghostly light
Hovered over an open door; it led to a stair,
That invited my downward steps. Though I had played
Ghost in the misty garden, through the window
Watched like a thief the Celebration, stared hard
At the amorous body in his wooden bed,
All had been timeless. The funeral was not finished;
Priest and people would stand by the open grave,
Till I descended the stair.

     The light advanced as a torch,
Paving a pale way through my mind's recesses.
It illuminated notions, a knowledge lost
As I stumbled down the faulty, circular stair.
It paused at a window, where sparkling frost-ferns waved,
Commemorating summer. Touched by the torch,
A sudden repentance, they melted in tears. Outside

Floated a misty world I knew by instinct
Was the old earth. It was still in its ancient youth,
Volcanoes bending over it in level smoke,
Foundations settling. In a waste of waters
I discerned the Symbol, shadowy as a shark,
Foreseen, foreseeing, patient without pain,
Jealous and wrathful without perturbation.
The monster would rise, spreading ambitious arms,
Embracing the world, yet empty, Adam's tree,
Leafless, forlorn, clothed with a naked Man,
The Prodigal Son, who came to save the world.

A Traveller in Time

1 I Set Out
                The light was on my face,
But my thoughts were cast behind into the Shadow
I had emerged from. Was the Last Judgment passed?
With nothing seen or heard but a sounding flash
Like the soft explosion when a photograph
Is taken in the dark, it had been enough;
The illumination had been interior,
And to all self-portraits I had said Good-bye,
Meeting that stranger, myself.
Timidly as a plant stretches pale leaves
From a dim cave to the sunlight, I had stolen
Out of the Shadow. I stood on the living world's
Momentous threshold. Was I free again to play
My garden part, the ghost?

                So abrupt the border,
It was like the edge—of a flat precipice.
The way was open, but my heels still stuck.
The sun peeped over a hill, a half-closed eye
That made me restless. I moved a few slow steps.
I was in the world; it was the familiar earth,
But more familiar! Hill, meadow, trees and grass,
So like themselves, had an essential look.
Escaping ghost, dead man on holiday,
Where was I? What was I about to see?
Solvitur ambulando.

                A path offered its company.
It led me up a hill; the ascent was sharp,
But I lost no breath; ghosts borrow from Vulcan's stithy
A pair of bellows for lungs! Looking back I saw
The Shadow had vanished. Or had it not turned to trees?
A group of witchlike birches was so weird,
Demoniac, for a moment I was startled.
But I smiled at myself; for a ghost who should frighten others

I was too nervous. But it was not long before
Again I was startled. Though the air hung breathless,
No breeze to alarm a leaf, I suddenly staggered
In a strong gust of wind. Lasting a moment,
It gave me the feeling of an invisible man
Walking through my body. For a long time I stood
Still as a stone; but I was not as patient
And thoughtfully I persisted up the path.
Yet not without bravado; the invisible man
Had scared me with the sense of solitude;
No other traffic on the empty path—
It was wider than a desert—shepherd, gamekeeper,
Would pass so lightly through my ghostly body;
I should stop it with my heart.

        From a shoulder of the hill
The path fell to a wooded dale. But I hung back,
A third time startled. For, looking round for comfort,
The conscious smoke that rises from a chimney
Or dull intelligence of a ploughed field,
My eyes opened to a world I recognised
No longer in a mode of separation,
But intimate, reciprocal. Its substance
A thin device to retain the inner spirit,
It disclaimed the name of earth. It was transfigured,
Caught up beyond itself, remote from time,
Even outside space, hung in a holy trance.
I was daunted, frightened by the incarnate beauty,
The ecstatic landscape. Earth in love with heaven!
As I turned away, flowers followed me with eyes
Surprised, reproachful.

        A stream ran down the dale
With stepping-stones. The earth so visionary,
Was the water real? Or did it appear to flow
As in a picture? Descending to the dale
I dipped my hand; the stream rose round my wrist
Resenting the question. On the stepping-stones

I scared a shoal of minnows; all of one mind
They darted off in one body. How thin the love
That bound that brotherhood in their watery convent;
Yet it was love, appropriate to the place.
Though I knew my shadow shivering on the current
Kept them from coming back, I almost fancied
It was love's shyness.

       Still musing on the minnows
I was about to step from the last stone,
When I was halted. A man had crossed my path
Walking downstream. But was he a man and walking?
All I saw was a head and shoulders!

2   The Dale
       Herod was not so startled
By the Baptist's head on a charger. He ordered that dish,
But the floating head and shoulders were unannounced.
They had the timeless air of a marble bust,
Yet eyes were alive and looking straight ahead,
Intent on the future. Near, but as though from a distance,
He slowly faded from sight. If I saw nothing,
It was too real a nothing not to follow.

       Leaving the hill-path,
I took a grassy track along the bank.
At first I outpaced the stream, too lazy to flow,
Carried along by its weight. Then for no reason
My pace, too, grew slow; I laboured in my walk,
As though wading through water. Stranger still,
When the stream with gathering speed raced down a decline,
Showing white heels on the cobbles, the descent
Perplexed me like a hill. No wind was stirring;
Autumn leaves, brown as bronze, hung down as heavy;
Yet I laboured as in a gale. Foot followed foot,
Not marking time; I passed a tree, a rock,
More trees, more rocks, yet felt at every step
I was blown back a mile. Should I be carried

Out of the world? I caught hold of a branch,
But quickly let it go; it was in bud!
Autumn had changed to spring; loose hazel catkins
Dripped in a yellow rain, palm-willow wands
Stretched out gold paws. Time had moved with a jerk
Backward or forward; had I moved with time,
Not knowing I moved, the sense of motion felt
As an imaginary gale?

   3   **The Tiltyard**
       Head and shoulders again!
I saw him through the trees. Gone soon as seen,
I read the inviting sign. The air now calm,
I walked with ease. Like Amadis of Gaul
Forcing his way through the Firm Island enchantment
I had fought with the strange gale, but now my feet
Carried me smoothly, as though borne on a rhythm.
But was I not myself in an enchantment?
Nothing looked real; trees, bushes, rocks, the stream,
The small black swine routing up leaves, all seemed
A dream's decoration. Was I in the half-man's world?
And what was this new feeling? Leaving the track,
I stepped down to the stream, where water waited
In a patient pool, and gazed at my floating face.
No wonder what I saw had a startled look;
It was a young man's face. My mind went blank
As though struck by a black lightning.

      Months blown away like clouds,
It was high summer, briars with Tudor roses,
The sedge with yellow fleur-de-lis, when, waking,
I took the track again and looked around.
It passed a heath-thatched hovel; a bent figure,
Hair dangling over what he read or wrote,
Sat by the door. Had it been the Middle Ages,
I might have wondered which, hermit or wizard,

The strange man was. He did not raise his head,
And I passed on, my eyes like the half-man's
Intent on the future.

The dale soon opened out
To a broad meadow with a line of willows
Hiding and showing the stream. On level ground
Before a castle people held a pageant,
Dressed to their parts. Had I visited the earth
To view a pageant? Travelled through time to see
Time's imitation? What I saw was phantasma;
People, if not the castle, would dissolve
At my approach. But castle stayed as stone;
And the people! Amazed I saw it was no pageant;
Those were real knights, plumes tossing in the air
Like birds-of-paradise. It was a passage of arms
In a tiltyard.

It was late evening;
A swollen sun hung over the purple hills,
Its gold changing to blood. It pushed out shadows
From tree and castle, but where it struck on armour
Steel turned to shining water, shields were wounds,
White, azure, vert. A long beflagged pavilion
Was gay with people; it was as though a rainbow
Had fallen and broken. Two knights with their squires
Waited on chamfered horses in the lists,
Their fork-tailed pennons fluttering like swallows
Caught on their lances. What was the argument?
By a flying Cupid hung in the pavilion
Shooting an arrow, each upheld his love
Against the other. Was it to the utterance?
Did he with the three gold lilies on a field
Vermilion, say to his squire, 'If I am killed,
Dig out my heart and carry it to my lady;
I would not have to give account to God
For keeping what is not mine'? Did he with the swan

On a field purple pray, 'As I have held
God on my right hand, my lady on my left,
So, Jesu, sweet knight, help me'?

Cannon fired roses,
And bending peak-nosed helms, setting at rest
Long staves like pens with which they meant to write,
Those clerkly knights flew on a trumpet's flourish
To fall in a confused tumble. Both rose dazed,
Avoiding their stallions. Taking to their swords,
They traced and traversed in a shower of sparks
As though the danger were less wounds than fire.

How strange to see these knights,
Who died too long ago to be called dead,
Now fighting for life. For the ancient castle was new,
The spectacle extant. In love with love
Were they not a counterpart to the lovesick earth,
Even the shoal of minnows? The fight stopping itself,
They froze to figures in a stained glass window.
Colours fluttered away; once again I was struck
By the black lightning.

4   The Abbey
Even in the dark I knew
It was a church. And soon a tall arched window,
Twin lancets balancing a quatrefoil,
Began to kindle. Dawn stoking its rich coals,
Rubies, emeralds, opals, two saints appeared,
Their dresses bright as the vestments that St Gear
Hung on a sunbeam. Between Lauds and Prime
I guessed the hour, the monks back in their dorter
Or walking the cloister.

How unlike this church
To that cathedral, grey ghost of itself,
Where I held my Canon's stall. Here clustered columns,
Sprouting gilt foliage from the capitals,

Blossomed like Aaron's rod, and in the choir-screen
Dead timber, coming alive, renewed rich summer
With leaf, flower, berry. On the painted walls
Abraham drove the birds from the sacrifice,
And ravens fed Elijah; Yebel and Salome,
The midwives, watched an ox feed from the manger,
Its mouth close to the Child. It was strange to think
In the great Doom over the chancel arch
That Child was the seated Judge; on either side
Were naked souls, some stepping up to heaven,
Glad hands pointed in prayer, others in chains
Slowly creeping to hell, a whale's gaping mouth,
No Jonahs to return. But the congregation!
Patriarchs, prophets, kings, apostles, martyrs,
Not waiting the resurrection, had put on
Spare flesh of glass and worshipped at the windows.
St Margaret and St George had brought their dragons,
St Lawrence his iron bed; St Sebastian
Bristled with arrows like a startled hedgehog.
But all were martyrs in those burning windows,
God's salamanders. Built more of flame than stone,
But most of spirit, reared on argument
Of thrust and counterthrust, Thomistic logic,
This adoring church wooed God.

       The light of four candles,
Praying on prickets, drew me to the chancel,
Where gold stars glittering on an azure roof
Made a strange night. In front of the high altar,
Two candles at his head, two at his feet,
Sword, shield and armour peaceful by his side,
One of the knights, his three gold lilies cropt,
Lay under a white pall. Fantastic lover,
He, too, had been a religious, armour his habit,
A casque his cowl, and in the end love's martyr.

I was stooping down
To draw aside the cover from his face,
When something hurled me back. At the same moment
The abbey vanished. I saw only a man
Hastening away; he was hidden by a hedge,
All but the head and shoulders.

5   I Travel Farther
Had he grown arms and legs,
Like tadpole turned to frog? Body or not,
The determined shoulders carried off the head
As though a trophy. But what was the haste, the fear?
Should I recognise a face, a family likeness?
At the stepping-stones the face had floated past
As alien as a statue's. Had he dropped a mask?
Might I not know the man? His shoulders' shape,
Back of the head, woke in me a strange feeling
Instinctive, warm.

Gliding away so fast
Half-hidden by the hedge, he was like a centaur
Galloping on himself. I was no Achilles
To overtake that Cheiron. But the abbey?
It had slipped a hundred years behind my mind,
Was slipping still. I was travelling in time!
A strange wind had risen as in the dale,
But a softer wind, making my passage easy.
Backward or forward, which way was my journey?
Was I passing, too, through space? But I saw nothing,
All lost in a mist.

6   The Nymph's Well
So suddenly I saw
The mist was gone, it was as though I had waked,
And yet not slept. A low sun, swollen with sleep,
Lit up a land that rocks and rocklike plants
Seemed less to fill than empty. Slow black shadows
Moved on the hillsides, showing they werc goats;

All else was still; no note dropped from bird's bill,
Grasshopper's wing. I was seated by a well;
Shaped like a shrine, it was sacred to a Nymph.
I felt her presence, and bending over the pool
I saw myself in her arms. But I was warned
The fancy was profane; a wild fig-tree
Leaned over the well as though a holy Watcher,
And on a ledge, a pious offering,
Lay three small loaves. The sand stirred with her breath,
And quicksilver bubbles rose like uttered words,
But soundless, empty.

       My travelling in time
Had made me look no older. The young man's face,
That had so startled me in the windy dale,
This sacred well repeated. For its strange truth
I had the Nymph's own word! Yet I had lived
As long as Aeson. What Medea's herbs
Renewed my years? Was I in the Age of Gold
With Kronos ruling as in Plato's fable,
All in reverse, sun rising in the west,
Spring following summer, old men born in graves
And growing younger?

       But I heard voices;
Two girls were slowly climbing up the slope,
Each with a basket. Raising a festive dress,
They picked a delicate way among the stones,
Great earrings jangling. Painted to the neck,
Eyes like blue mussel-shells, they approached the shrine.
Bowing with hand on knee, each added a loaf
From her straw basket; then, breaking into laughter,
They ran down to a road. They had not glanced my way!
I was wearing Perseus' cap, invisible.
I turned to where I lay drowned in the pool;
My floating face and I, exchanging looks,
Saw more than the laughing girls.

What on the road seemed people
Were gods and goddesses, olives and poplars,
Lining a Sacred Way. It left a city
I knew for Athens; in the pure Attic air
The Acropolis was plain, even, though minute,
The Parthenon, perched like a silver beetle
Newly alighted. Ground strewn with gossamer,
I guessed it was late autumn; but what year,
What century? Was Socrates alive?
Wrestling that morning in the Gymnasium
With argument or lover? Or setting out
To sit with Phaedrus in the plane-tree's shade,
Grasshoppers his holy Muses? Going to Athens,
What should I find? I was about to rise,
When behind a tree, laden with images,
Owls and small pigs, I caught sight of the half-man!
So I wildly thought for a moment; then I knew
That head and shoulders rested on a plinth,
A roadside Hermes. Would the god's stone eyes
Be sharper than the girls'? He drove off ghosts!
What else was I?

      The fear was heathenish;
Ghost or no ghost, if there were comings and goings
Between the two worlds, why, what should I not see?
I should come in spring when red anemones
Burn up dead thistles, and in the river-beds
The oleanders make pink waterfalls.
Indifferent to space, ranging around,
I should see Dodona's oak, that talking tree,
Hear nightingales at Daulis. Choosing my moment,
I should fly in time like Merops, the Bee-eater,
Backward or forward; watch in the theatre
Theodorus play Antigone, or even,
Intruding on the Banquet, Socrates
Soaring in high discourse, while the other drinkers
Flapped feeble wings. I should witness famous battles
And truer than the Delphic pythoness

Foretell the issue. At Thermopylae
I should see the Spartans on the green sea-rocks
Combing their oily hair; young Sophocles,
A naked choir-boy, dancing with ivory lyre
After Salamis. I should go farther back,
To the Trojan war; if ghost could spare a penny
For a blind rhapsodist reciting verses,
Homer should have it. Greece for a beginning,
I should not find eternity itself
Hang heavy on my hands.

7 **The Procession**
On the eve of Salamis
Two men had seen on the Eleusis road
A cloud of dust, heard, too, a holy music
With Bacchic cries, but all had proved a phantom;
The procession I now saw approach was real,
Myself the ghost. The god in the farm-wagon,
Drawn by white oxen, was more alive than I;
He sprouted vine-leaves. By his spotted fawn-skin
Dionysos I should have named him, but the cries,
Iacche, Iacche, gave him another name,
Iacchos. ' Unlike that slant-eyed mystagogue,
Bearded, effeminate, this was a frightening god,
His mask with gaping mouth. Did a pine-cone hide
A spear-point on his staff? A throng of people,
As though goaded by his horns, waved fennel-stalks
And danced so wildly that the bearded goats
Looked philosophers. Men to the beat of drums
Stamping the ground, women to Phrygian flutes
Arching their bodies back like scorpions,
They danced the Holy Marriage. Let Heaven's rain
Impregnate Earth; then the long summer drought
Breaking, Korè will rise in her green veil,
The autumn grass and corn. It was to Eleusis,
The Mysteries, they bore the god. Iacchos,
Born of a bull's heart, would outface Hades

And bring back to her mother, virginity
Renewed like Aphrodite's, the tender Korè,
Whose spring is in the autumn.

           Had Athens emptied itself
That morning? Purple-bordered sindon dresses
Mingling with woollen peplums, parasols
With crutches, the long procession slowly passed,
Dragging a tedious tail. Then all at once
It took to wings, was flying along the road
Like a frightened goose!

           Another trick of time,
Not keeping time, I thought; time went so fast,
The slow procession was flying before my eyes.
And sure enough, already in the west
The sun, growing hot with haste, slid down the sky.
If it should strike the earth! But it slipped safely
Behind a mountain. First the air grew crimson,
Then violet; hill-slopes ran with purple,
Dionysos treading grapes; earth fell asleep
In a dream of her own beauty. A full moon rose,
And the empty road gleamed like a serpent's ghost,
A small owl moaning.

  8 **At Eleusis**
           If the flying goose was gone,
I had followed it, exchanging the Nymph's Well
For lights, cries, music. I was in Eleusis,
My journey's end the Mysteries. As I stood
Beside the wall of a tall enclosure, voices
Made me look up to two men in a tower
Leaning over the parapet in Corinthian helmets.
Were they watchers of a precinct, eyeing me,
Suspecting a temple thief? I moved away,
But came to a standstill. The moonlight showed

A yard strewn with black rocks; but the rocks breathed,
Heaps of small sleeping pigs that soon would redden
A priest's gold knife.

        I shuddered as I turned
To heads outlined against a smoky glow.
A crowd was gathered round the god's ox-wagon,
That stood on a dancing-floor. The god was gone,
But wearing mask, fawn-skin and horns, a priest
Sat in his place. Their faces smeared with gypsum,
Kobalds ran in a ring, flame-flattened torches
Trailing a roof of smoke. Within the circle
A din of drums and flutes worked wild-haired women
To a dancing frenzy; they might have been the Maenads,
Who milked the lionesses on the mountains
And made great cheeses. But where was the god gone?
To the Hall of Mysteries, the tall enclosure?
My feet almost as fast as the thought they followed,
I reached the entrance. It was guarded by two soldiers,
Leaning on spears. For a moment I hung back;
Then remembering I wore my Perseus' cap,
I cut across the barrier of their talk
And was through an open gate.

        A paved path in a garden,
Rows of white statues and dark cypresses,
The hall itself carved out of frozen moonlight,
These I remember, though vaguely as a dream,
But nothing else, not even how I entered,
Till I saw Demeter's eyes. The great jewels glowed
Through an incense-cloud, and, as it thinned and thickened,
Their flashes came and went. Was the goddess angry
My profane eyes saw her giving birth to children?
For from a fold of her black marble robe
Appeared a figure, like a dead man rising,
Naked but for a sheet. Were two old people,
Who, standing side by side, wept as they watched,
Seeing their new-born son? From the same birthplace

A woman rose; her eyes meeting a man's,
They shared one smile. So figure followed figure
From that strange womb, the goddess giving birth
To her adopted children.

        Did Iacchos lead them out,
Twice-born himself, from lightning-stricken mother
And father's thigh? What was the Hierophant
Showing the mystics? Was it the little Korè,
A barley-corn? Was he placing in their hands
The sacred cup from which Demeter drank
Water and meal? And what did they repeat?
I could not pluck the heart of the mystery,
And tortured by half-truths I ranged around,
Defied by Demeter's eyes. But as I heard
The awed audience here and there break into sobs,
I grew ashamed. Retreating to a corner,
I stood by one, an old initiate,
Who viewed the scene with disillusioned eyes.
I felt he would have said, if he had spoken:
All is the effort to accomplish death,
The returning to the safety of the womb,
First and last love.

  9 I Travel Still Farther
        The Sphinx, her riddle read,
Died of heart-failure; did the hall collapse
Because I read its secret? For all went,
Demeter, Hierophant, the new-born mystics,
Wiped from a mirror, not even the mirror left.
But had I read it? There was no time to ask;
I was in motion, travelling again.
But where and when? I could not even guess
The continent, nor by a thousand years
The hour of my arrival.

The imaginary wind,
I faced in the dale, had veered round to my back,
Was taking me with itself. What of the half-man,
Was I leaving him behind? But how had I fancied
That wandering bust was real like the knights,
The girls, the mystics? If I smiled at the thought,
The smile faded from my face when I turned my head;
He was standing at my side!
The man himself, a fellow-traveller,
Complete as Adam. From my wondering gaze
He moved away; but his back was not forbidding;
Having seen the family likeness, I read 'Follow'.
He led me down a slope; the way was steep,
For it was on a narrow mountain ridge
We had landed from the air.

　　　　All others I had seen
Were living in their own time, though long since dead;
This timeless man I viewed with curious eyes.
Head and hands were distinct, but body and clothes
Confusingly one. He was neither clothed nor naked,
Or both at once; or was he like a statue
With flesh and drapery all of a piece?
Or was he a ghost? Stamped with the family likeness,
Why else was he silent? It might have been in answer
That, pointing to a mountain across a valley,
He said, 'Mount Gerizim.'

　　　　It took me time
To dig the name out of my memory.
'Mount Gerizim, sir, in Palestine?' I asked;
'And this Mount Ebal,' he replied. These twins
The Samaritan woman saw; this was her land,
A shoal of hills bare to the grey limestone,
Hoary and bald at once, a pallid wilderness,
Yet upheld by golden valleys. 'And that is Shechem,'
He added, pointing downward. The small city lay
Beneath our feet, its streets narrow and crooked,

As though bent out of shape by the stone wall,
That bound it like a belt. A lazy smoke
Hung over it, but men, women and children
Knelt in fields, cutting the short corn with sickles.
I faintly heard their cries. On the terraced hill-slopes
Grew grape-vines; did they watch with small green eyes
That glad corn-killing, the warning of their own
Even merrier death? How strange to know the season
But not the century. But he said Shechem,
Not Neapolis or Nablous, later names;
I was in the time of the Old Testament,
But at which book? Was Dinah yet unravished?
Had Joseph's painted coffin come from Egypt
Or Joshua set up the listening stone?
For this was Samaria. But why was I here?
As though with 'Come and see', my guide moved on.

      Black and tan goats
Lent us a track that crept down by the edge
Of a deep watercourse. Though sullen pools
Fed one another with a grudging trickle,
The tumbled rocks were echo and prophecy
Of winter torrents. Half-way down he stopped:
'You see that man.' Where a long scree of stones
Streamed down the mountain like a silent scream
And broadened at the base, a man stepped over
A vineyard wall. He climbed the slope obliquely
Towards a thrust-out shoulder of the mountain,
Itself a small round hill. To myself I said,
That man did something more than step over a wall,
He stepped out of the Bible.

      Leaving the watercourse
We made our stony way along the slope
To the small round hill. Its green grass a surprise,
It was like the place where the multitude was fed
With loaves and fishes; but how unlike was the feast
That tainted the air with a sweet holy smoke.

A fire greedily fed on the sizzling fat
And entrails of some beast heaped on an altar,
A priest throwing on incense. It burned before a Bull—
Made of gold it was even smaller than a calf—
Set on a pillar. Roofed by shaking trees,
It seemed in the interchange of light and shadow
A living creature. The Baal had his Baalath,
A green-painted Asherah. Husband and wife,
They feasted together on the savoury smoke,
While the worshippers were reclining at a banquet
In a great hall. Though open at one end,
Its other sides bulged out in small annexes,
A sinister spawn. Women glanced at their lovers
Like languid queens, but judged by a silver star
Tattooed on their foreheads, they were sacred slaves.
We had approached the entrance, even stood
Close to the couches, when a woman screamed
And, covering her breasts, ran from the hall.
She had seen him first, the man who climbed the hill.
'Hosea,' whispered my guide.

     Her lover staggered forward,
A wine-cup in his hand, and splashed the wine
Full in the prophet's face. Licking the drops
He spat them out, while the other feasters frowned,
Shaking their heads. His eyes were the first to speak;
Then he lifted up his voice in a wailing cry
As in a funeral dirge. Of his rhapsody
I made out nothing but a repeated word,
A fierce 'Yah-yah'. It was like a hyena's bark,
The 'Yah-yah'. The feasters spread protesting hands
And in the Hebrew gabble they answered back
I heard the same 'Yah-yah'. What was this word
They bandied about, he with accusing finger
Pointing to the Bull, the feasters in defence,
An edge of anger rising in their voices?
Was it their name for God?

Silence fell on the tables,
When a white-robed priest appeared, his piled-up turban
Flashing with angry jewels. But his look was mild,
As equable as the empty pair of scales
Held in his hand. As, stricken by the sight,
Hosea bent his head, I read their meaning:
He had come to buy her back, the screaming woman,
Gomer bath Diblaim, his children's mother,
The wife who had woven her way through paramours
To temple-slave. Slowly lifting his head,
He looked up to the sky with muttering lips,
As though his case were Heaven's. Were they not one,
God's painful case with His adulterous people
And his with Gomer?

It might have been her wedding,
Feasters the guests, the money the priest weighed
Her dowry. Slowly she came down the hall,
A smile carved on her face. He kissed the brow
Tattooed with the star, but with so cold an effort
I felt the prophet disappointed Heaven.

As he led Gomer away,
The feasters sprang to their feet, overturning tables,
And hubbub rose in the hall. The lover ran
And with upthrust thumb gave him the fig. Women laughed
And smiling men plucked kisses from their beards
And flung them after Gomer, as he, God's actor,
Passed on, playing his part in the charade.
But what of Gomer? Would that silver star
Be inauspicious? Was the ascent too sharp
From temple-slave to rigid wife? Not long
I wondered; as I watched them hand in hand
Descend the hill, the sun swooned in the sky,
Rocks thinned in a thickening mist.

10   At Nazareth

            Had the light gone out
As in a theatre when scenes are shifted?
What should I witness next? I blindly turned
To my fellow-traveller; his face was radiant!
It shone with light, not sharp as a spot-light
Flung on a stage, but soft, self-evident
As a glow-worm's torch. 'Are you dead?' I breathed;
He nodded. 'Long dead?' But he shook his head,
Then, as though seeing I misunderstood,
'Here we take no account of time,' he said,
'Nor—look around—of space.' Shadowy shapes
Looming through pallid air, nothing distinct,
Was all I saw, when he caught me in his arms,
Startled, half-frightened. 'I am that dead brother
You never knew,' he said, and added quickly,
Thrusting me off, 'We are in Nazareth;
Watch for a woman; she carries Christ in her womb.'

            That he thrust me off
Impatiently, as though to free himself
From a forced embracement, so took me by surprise
I hardly heard the word about the woman
Till it echoed in my mind. Even then it needed
A sharper 'Look!' to drive away my gaze
From my new dead brother. The stage was being set,
A city building itself before my eyes
On a steep slope. A mist, halving the hills,
Made them look flat-roofed as the boxlike houses.
It was early morning. We stood by the city well,
A pool fed by a spring gushing from grey rocks
Like a special creation. No one came to draw;
Through the loud noises, tossing cypresses,
Scratching palm-leaves, the wind's own naked voice,
The city slept. One of its scavengers,
A tall gaunt hound, slouched down the muddy path,
But stopped; the hair left on its leprous hide
Bristled with fear. Then with a sidelong leap

It fled in a low-backed scamper up the slope.
I had frightened it, a ghost in Nazareth
Two thousand years ago!

      Was it her amulets,
A magic blue, that blinded the old woman,
First at the pool? But I was empty air
To all the others as well, women and children,
Who followed fast. A child strayed picking flowers
Close to my feet; it was the ghost who stared!
I stared at her flowers, crocuses and narcissi.
Why, it was spring. Would Christ be born at Easter?
Or Pentecost?

      But I remembered Korè,
Whose spring is in autumn. It was autumn now,
Thin grass already rising in a green tide
Round rocks, corn sprouting in untidy ranks;
The early rain had fallen, was now falling,
Scores of compasses drawing circles in the pool.
It might even be Advent—without the Advent collect.
The Birthday was approaching. Child or man,
How often had I thought of Christmas coming,
But not in this strange fashion.

      As we watched the women,
Their figures taller for the water-jar
Held by arched arm, go swaying up the slope
With a reedlike motion, one, staggering, stopped,
And, hand clutching her side, leaned on a rock.
My brother bowed, and almost of itself
My head, too, bowed. Not different to the eye
From others, how unlike God's chosen vessel.
She made Christ's coming to the earth seem furtive,
Occult. By Son of Man, ambiguous name,
His nature would be veiled, but to arrive
As though He stole from the paternal shore
A stowaway!

Fingering the door-post,
She disappeared in the darkness of a house.
What had she touched? The 'Hear, O Israel,
The Lord thy God is one Lord'. These were words
Joseph, adopted father, would teach his Son.
The paradox! that He who came as light
Should learn of the darkness. All created things would help,
Birds would be happy omens, and the flowers
Would not stand idly by. For everywhere
He would see the scattered letters of the Word,
And each, a Delphic oracle, would call
Its *'Know thyself'*. Obedient to the call,
Christ would be the first Christian.

The thought grew in my mind,
All I had witnessed in my ghostly travels
Was of the Light, begotten and partaking,
Yet not the Light itself; it was as though,
Moving in time, I startled hues of a crystal,
Red, violet and gold. Instinct with spirit,
Stript almost naked, even of itself,
The amorous earth had an unearthly beauty;
Love, too, though dark and native, bound the minnows,
That darted like a shadow from the stones,
In their mute brotherhood. When the two knights
Fought in the tiltyard, flags and hearts a-flutter,
That summer evening, the sun of earthly love
Was at its meridian; and when I woke,
I saw a church, where pillars, arches, roof,
Had less been built than of themselves had risen,
Drawn up by heavenly love. It was by the Light
Illumined, the two Greek girls saw in the well
A divinity, a favourable Nymph,
And left their pious loaves; while at Eleusis,
Teaching the parable, the Seed of Corn,
It so inspired the mystics that in a symbol
They died to be reborn. If at Mount Ebal
Hosea, his shame so hot, laid a cold kiss

On Gomer's ill-starred brow, yet it prefigured
This kiss the father gave the prodigal son.
In Mary prophecy had reached its end;
The Light Itself was come.

11 The Cave
            My brother nodded,
My sign to follow. The sun was in mid-sky,
As we climbed to Nazareth; in its noon sleep
The city made me feel even more a ghost
Stalking its empty streets. Climbing beyond,
We gazed from a hilltop on a low level land,
That did not need my silent guide to name
The Esdraelon Plain. For how could I mistake
That famous battlefield, flying cloud-shadows
The ghosts of passing armies? But my brother
Drew me with an intimate arm to where a cave
Gaped with wide mouth. Though by a bounding wall,
Heaped stones and thorns, I knew it for a sheepfold,
It was like a sepulchre for the pigmy bodies
Hung from the roof. But we woke memories,
Not sleeping bats.

            That afternoon
Lasted a day. As though held by a hand
The sun hung stationary, filling the cave
With a warm light, while we sat and talked together,
That brother, dead before I was born, and I,
Sharing news of our two worlds. At last I pointed
To where a caravan had long been winding
About Mount Tabor, yet had never moved,
'Those camels, are they stuck in mud or time?'
'We are the Joshuas who halt the sun,'
He said. His light words might have made the sun
Indignant, for time began to make up time;
Rocks grew long shadows; bats one by one awaking
Flew from the cave; the sun, too, its own Phaeton,
Fell into the sea, setting up a conflagration;

Darkness came quickly sowing the stars broadcast.
He broke the silence softly: 'Though I led the way,
Your half-brother at the stepping-stones' — the half-man!
He was smiling at the jest—'your heart was the helm
I followed.' 'And you still will follow!' I cried;
But I cried it because he was already gone.

      The alarm I felt at first
Quickly gave way to wonder, out of nothing
A picture shaping itself. Was it a dream
Such as a ghost might dream? Then how did it come,
By the ivory gate or the horn? Or was it prophetic,
A foresight of the future? He was no shadow
Who stood, a pillar of light, in the sunbeam
That through the open door of a carpenter's shed
Thrust a bright shoulder, no, not Joseph, but
The carpenter's Son. I watched Him at His work,
The eternal Worker, the Word within the word,
'Let there be light'. What was He making now,
Cradle or bier or —?

      But could that be real
Which dreamlike came and went? For He now knelt,
A camel's skeleton for company,
In a land of fire-chewed rocks and gouty shrubs
That spat out spiteful thorns. Heaven had rained stones
On its defiance of the creative Word;
Was He being challenged to change them into bread?
He was near to hell in that weird Jordan gorge,
Where the flat Moab hills, underground mountains,
Rose to earth's surface, and the blue Dead Sea
Glittered beneath them like a fragment of heaven
Dragged down in Lucifer's fall. The pale winding river
Might have been the upturned body of that old Serpent;
But it was not dead; I almost saw the Darkness
With which He wrestled, clutching Himself in prayer.

Stones turned to water,
Not bread. The lake was sparkling in the sun,
A blue sky full of stars. Beside a creek,
Where a brook drowned itself, and a kingfisher
Hovered, I saw Him standing, still, erect,
Watching the brown-sailed boats. When on the road
A circus passed with girls and wrinkled dwarfs
Led by a fat man riding on an ass,
He did not turn; I thought the camels scowled,
Thrusting out the lower lip. The kingfisher flew
And lumps of mud changed to live tortoises,
As a boat raced in and ran aground. Two fishers,
Stepping ashore, busied themselves with their net.
'Two of the Twelve,' I said, knowing the picture,
And added, when they beached their boat so high
It looked abandoned, 'The yeast works in the dough.'

But why did they stand still,
As though hanging back? And then I saw the picture
Was changing; with these two was a third,
St Peter. Shivering mountaineers, they stood
Beneath an immense snowy summit, Hermon.
With fear they shivered, aghast at the enigma,
The familiar Figure in a sphere of light,
A spirit in a crystal. His back was turned
As though He talked with Moses and Elijah.
Was Hermon, outshone, envious? A mist,
That had been agitating its snow-bound brow,
Thickened and, swooping down, darkened the picture.
Or was it by some heavenly jealousy
My sight became extinct?

12 Jerusalem
Would my brother come?
But to what could he return? All was dissolved;
The cave, gaping too wide, had swallowed itself,
The hill was its own mist. Alone and nowhere,
I might have been afraid; but I remembered

His parting jest. I jested with myself:
My loving brother had not so stolen my heart,
He had not left the helm. And the helm was set!
I saw in my mind's eye the little hill,
Where Adam's skull was buried, and Jeremiah
Had sung his Lamentations in a grotto,
Golgotha. No guide, not even the head and shoulders,
It would be my maiden voyage.

    Alighting on a bridge,
I felt it was a symbol of my flight
Across a Limbo. But it spanned a deep hollow,
High over a watercourse, stony and dry,
Shrunk corpse of a stream. Sprinkled with olives,

                                      tombstones,
One slope rose to a ridge, where houses huddled
As though in fear to fall; a battlemented wall,
Blocking the sky, weighed down the other slope,
Climbed by a stair.

    Though all else was clear,
Passers-by on the bridge were strangely blurred;
They might have walked in water. That no one stopped
To stare at the interloping ghost, alarmed me;
I felt I was not there! Was I superstitious
To see in myself a ghost? My apparent body
Mere memory, old clothes, might I not vanish
Like an image from a forgetful mirror, or slowly
Dissolve like a naked toadstool, melting in tears?
Perhaps he came in answer,
Not blurred in an aquatic atmosphere,
But clear as though he carried his own light,
My brother! Greeting and leavetaking one,
The moment might have been forbidden, snatched,
We clung in embrace so warm the passers-by
Looked cold fish in a tank.

I once saw an apparition,
A lady gliding across a lawn to vanish
Through a wall of Ludlow Castle; my brother gone,
It was with the same smooth motion without movement
I glided up the stair, a level road,
To the battlemented wall, built of huge blocks
As long as coffins; passed through a guarded gate
To flutter about in a maze of Corinthian columns,
Perplexed as a bat. That it was Caesar's Cloister
I knew, when through the building's open side
I saw the Temple, saw it with amazement,
Rise like a snowy mountain.

Not criss-cross like a bat,
But with the sure flight of migrating swallow,
I flew towards it. A Babylonian structure,
Less marble than solid light, hung with gold plates
Burning as though in snow, it rose from the rock,
Earth's navel, a place of pilgrimage for angels
Before the man was made without a navel,
Adam. Jews saw their tribes in the painted vine,
That with twelve purple bunches of grapes hung over
The brazen doors. Slowly I floated past
Its frontispiece. 'A lion, broad in front,
Narrow behind', the saying said; I added,
'A porcupine above', the gilded roof
Spiked against Herod's pigeons.

But the little hill, Golgotha!
I had hit the time of year; by the throng of people,
That filled the outer court, hiding the pavement,
And glitter of helmets showing Roman posts,
It was the inflammable Feast of the Passover.
I had even hit the hour; the sun still climbing,
The Shadow of Death crept closer to the Cross,
Though to its own defeat.

But I was fated,
A revenant on earth, an inquisitive ghost,
To miss the hour. For I had hardly passed
Beyond the outer court, when darkness fell
So suddenly, night killed, not followed, day.
Somewhere in the wide precinct I came aground
To grope among carcasses, oxen and sheep,
Laid out in rows. I saw them by a sky
Stars flooded with quicksilver.

What made the earth restless
Was the light of the hidden moon: but soon, a flat orange,
It floated up from the hills. It grew smaller, brighter,
Showing its geography. Objects became plain,
Though less substantial than their crouching shadows.
Safe instinct guiding me, I crossed the precinct
To a guarded gate. Daylight at the Cloister gate
Had blinded the sentry to the gliding ghost:
The sentry here saw nothing, even by moonlight.
Beyond were lanes with houses, shuttered shops,
Bare booths and buildings with carved pots of manna,
The synagogues. My instinct was too blind
To miss the way. Leaving the lanes behind,
I crossed an open space and 'City wall,'
I said, 'and this must be the Damascus Gate.'
Three figures approached. The wind that rose with the
                                                    darkness
Tossed their white mourning weeds: black funeral masks
Covered their faces to reveal their eyes.
One woman's tears were shining in the moonlight
So brightly, they repented they were tears;
'His mother, holy Mary,' I breathed.

Outside the city
The moon was enamoured of the pale tombstones
That paved the level ground; but where the land
Sloped slowly to a valley, it blackened caves,
Rich sepulchres in orchards. Nothing showed

At which the women had wailed, but I knew by its shape
Golgotha, Hill of a Skull. One side declined
To the white Damascus road, but the other ended
Abruptly in a cliff, where I traced the skull,
The brow and broken nose, but how chap-fallen.
The three crosses were gone.

A traveller in time,
Backward, forward, I had but to set my heart!
Why, with Good Friday hardly yesterday
I could wake the sun, sleeping in its sea-bed,
Say it had missed a day. The regress was so short,
It was but a step to the miles of centuries
I had lately journeyed. What then held me back?
That sudden darkness, the night falling at noon,
Had warned me those three crucial hours were private,
Not for ghost-moths, perhaps not even for angels.
I pitied Him who so transcended time
His eternal eye could never escape the sight,
His Son hanging on a cross.

All other loves,
That in my trivial travels I had witnessed
Were thin outcroppings of the primal love
The creative Word imparted to the world
On its six birthdays. They were geologic;
This was Uranian; it fell vertical
Faster than Lucifer, the very Word,
God's Proper Name, creating a new earth,
A kingdom, holy church, all, alas, more veiled
Than the Word made flesh.

13   Back in The Dale

It was still a windy dale,
But not as when I set out from the Shadow.
Trees waved wild arms, grasses rose up like hair
Standing on end; yet I was no more shaken
Than beech-bole or, insubstantial as myself,

Shadow of a flat stone that caught my eye.
But at the stone I stared;
Why, it was there I had seen the strange man sit,
Hair dangling over his book. The hut was gone,
As though it had not been; but I remembered
The rill, a river in its petty rage,
Tugging at the grass. The time was different;
It had advanced, overleaping centuries,
As far as then it slipped back. I should find the castle
A ruin now, gaunt spectre of itself
Or its own tombstones. Had it been my aim?
Or the abbey? No need to follow the track farther:
Here was my journey's end.

    Was the stone magnetic,
Drawing my steps? Its smooth surface said 'Sit',
But it might have been an ant-hill. I sprang up,
My body tingling. Yet the stone was bare.
Sitting again, I felt the prickly heat.
To what was I sensitive? Not ants, but bees;
They were swarming in my breast; they hung from my ribs
A honeycomb, my body effusing the fragrance.
Then I heard birds; was it in my head or heaven
Those sweet birds sang? I rose and looked around;
Heat, bees and birds were gone. Again I sat,
And they were back; they even grew in strength,
Fire, hornets, music. Strange words of themselves
Came to my mind: 'a merry and unknown heat';
'Ghostly electuary'; 'lovely burning';
'The bread of angels'; then, clear as though called out
In rapture, 'O my honey! O my harp!
O my psaltery and song! O my heart's rose!'
But these words I remembered;
The case was clear; here in his hermitage
I was sitting on the stone with Richard Rolle
Writing *The Fire of Love;* we shared the same stone,

Though centuries apart. Or had he risen,
Gone into the heath-thatched hut, no longer there,
For all suddenly ended?

      The autumn dale
Gave a sad welcome to approaching night,
And an owl hooted. Still sitting on the stone,
I watched a small faint feather, blown sky-high,
Change to the moon. No wind stirred the tired trees,
Yet there might have been a hurricane in heaven,
For all at once it was covered by a cloud,
No flying island, but a continent,
Putting out the moon.

      But could it be a cloud
That held my gaze? Its strangeness was familiar.
It had the troubled look of a black diamond,
Blinded by its own light. I knew its name
With a dream's credulity, *Cloud of Unknowing*.
Moses entered that cloud; Plotinus, too,
Flew through it with the flight of a homing pigeon.
Beyond it was the land with no horizon,
The murmuring Solitude and idle Quiet.
Its heat, honey and singing Richard Rolle
Foretasted on the holy stone; I, also,
At a remove. But all God's mystic children.
With sparkling stones, ladders of love, sharp clothing,
Rings of espousals, flaming darts, assaulted
That cloud, an obscure night of loving fire.
Singing with Caterina Serafina
'O love's sweet slavery that sets us free',
Or with God's Goldfinch 'I die because I cannot die',
They escaped the shipwreck of the world and pierced
The lightsome darkness, lost, annihilated,
Their nothing-at-all preserved in the All-in-all,
To a blind and lovely beholding of the Word,
The imperishable 'Is', without where or when,
God in a point.

Infused with grace,
Had their geologic love flown off at a tangent
And touched the Uranian? Was it appointed
I should follow those athletes, cry with Meister Eckhart,
'Up, valiant soul, put on thy jumping-shoes
Of love and understanding'? Soon I should learn;
The ghost must go; the cocoon spun by the worm,
The butterfly would burst. New eyes would see
The invisible world into which my brother vanished.

The Snowdrop

Our Father spun
A little flower with flakes of snow,
That here, unmelted, it might grow
In rain and sun.

And in the skies
He said to it, 'Go, little one!'
And so it came like some sweet nun
From Paradise.

Alas! instead
Of finding earth like its own home,
It grieved that God had bid it come,
And drooped its head.

Winter

Time, like an aged gardener,
Still tends the garden of the year,
And, when the summer sweets are lost,
He weaves the scentless flowers of frost.

When, too, the forest boughs have shed
Their generation of the dead,
Against the stars the sacred trees
Spread out their naked traceries.

And in the night an amorous moon
Sings to the sea a tender tune,
And all the star-encrusted sky
Shivers with silent ecstacy.

For Beauty thus not only glows
Within the wine-cup of the rose,
But like a hermit clad may be
In garment of austerity.

The Bee

I saw a little Golden-thigh
　　Creep in a summer rose,
Which is Our Lady's treasury,
　　As every lover knows.

That this was only thievery
　　Is far from my belief:
I think the little gold-thighed bee
　　Was lover more than thief.

Song

Produis moy du clairet, verre pleurant.

Bring me a weeping glass
　　With teardrops red and bright,
For not fresh leaves, but grass
　　Shall crown my head tonight,—

Wild grass and flowers that fall
　　And winds and rains that weep,
For I am tired of all
　　Sweet things save only sleep.

The Moon

The Night has risen like the sound
Of solemn music from the ground,
And blackens with her dusky hair
The thin, ambiguous air;

And moonlight lies, a pallid pall,
On sombre woods funereal;
The moon-struck leaves speak mystic words;
And rivers flash like swords.

O white and solitary blossom,
Night wears upon her ancient bosom,
Scentless, a flower of silver light
That only glows by night;

The sword of Winter hath no power
To slay thee, O bright Phoenix-flower!
Thy life is as the changing seas,
Changeless through centuries.

The Rose

What subtle power
First fashioned thee a bursting bud,
And filled thy heart with fire and blood,
O bleeding flower?

What hands could spin
The wonder of thy woven flesh?
What scents were captured by thy mesh,
And drawn within?

What flames are these
That clothe thee and thou art not slain;
Smokeless, unquenched by sun or rain,
    Stirred by no breeze?

What lovers knew
The revels of thy rosy bed,
Fragrant with many spices shed,
    And fresh with dew?

O courtezan!
Sweet chamberer with sun and wind!
Art thou not wise in loves unsinned
    By loveless man?

Yet balm of breath
And treasure of thy honey-hoard,
Are only sweet in thee and stored
    Against thy death.

And time shall turn
To ashes pale thy purple fire,
Thy petals red shall be thy pyre,
    And dead, thine urn.

Landscape

Oppressive with its vacant weight,
The moorland stretches desolate,
And like a wound the sunset bleeds
Across a weary waste of weeds.

A tarn is fed by sluggish rills,
Branching like veins across the hills,
And darkened by a wind that flings
The passing shadow of his wings.

Save where one torture-twisted tree
Shrieks out in silent agony,
Oppressive with its vacant weight,
The moorland stretches desolate.

A grey hawk at a dizzy height
Thrills with its sharp suspended flight,
And like a soft, insidious kiss
The snakes within the heather hiss.

To where as in a monstrous birth
The red moon struggles from the earth,
Oppressive with its vacant weight,
The moorland stretches desolate.

Bacchos Chthonios
ὡυτὸς δὲ Ἅιδης καὶ Διόνυσος,
ὅτεω μαίνονται καὶ ληναΐζουσι.
Herakleitos

Lord of the serpent vine,
Thyself the mystic wine
That fills the faint and gives the weary wings;
I also feel the swift
Glad leaping of thy gift,
Wild fire that mayhap was the ancient flame
Of lust and shame
Within fierce lips of courtezans and kings.

Lord of the bright fawn-skin,
Whose kiss is deadly sin,
And gives to Death thy lovers for a spoil:
Yet these red lips are fain

Life's purple cup to drain,
Before I lay my ivy-crownèd head
Where dreamless dead
Are strewn in ashes wet with wine and oil.

Zagreus, twin, sexless, wild,
Bacchos, immortal child
Of mortal mother drawing laboured breath,
No light of star is shed
Above thy lovers dead:
Only lone voices linger like the wails
Of nightingales
In the pale kingdom of the Lord of Death.

Hymn to Zagreus

Zagreus, our Lord,
Who givest a sword,
O Hunter of men who art hunted and slain,
Art thou drunk with the strong
Glad wine-cup's song,
Or with bitter delight of luxurious pain?

Vine-tendrils enmesh
Thy limbs and flesh,
And bite like serpents and bind like thongs;
And we shed dim dust
On the pride and lust
Of thy tigers and women and cymbals and songs.

For our hands and feet
Were fierce with the heat
Of a flame that scorches, a fire that sears;
And we wreaked our will
By hollow and hill
And made thee, O Hunter, the sport of our spears.

Thy wine is a fierce
Sheer sword to pierce
And our hearts were fulfilled with its purple flood,
And we slew our Lord
With that sharp, clear sword,
And the dark earth was bright with the blossom of blood.

But as garlands of flowers,
In the dance of the Hours,
The shreds of thy red-dripping flesh shall be spun;
And god of the Spring,
Afresh shalt thou bring,
Wild honey and vine-leaves and songs of the sun.

A Child's Eyes

When one with torn
Sad heart awakes,
About him breaks
The tender morn.

So, child, I see
Behind and through
Your eyes of blue
Christ look on me.

Sleep

The flowers are ghostly white
Along the dusky lane,
They sleep and turn again
To tender buds at night.

So, tired with all the pain
  Of songs and sins that burn,
  I, too, shall sleep and turn
Into a child again.

Nocturne

Now fall rose-petals in the west,
And dusky flowers are full of sleep;
Dew lies about the roots of hills,
  And Twilight folds her hands.

The Day's sweet pipes and flutes are still;
The Night goes forth in mourning weeds,
Within her hand a broken jar,
  And stars within her hair.

Her eyes are soft as folded flowers,
Or shadowed waters in a wood,
Dim with her dark dishevelled hair,
  And shedding silver tears.

O purple, sombre flower of night,
That from thy petals shakest sleep,
Falling in soft and sable flakes
  On earth and field and flower!

Now fall rose-petals in the west,
And dusky flowers are full of sleep;
Dew lies about the roots of hills,
  And Twilight folds her hands.

City by Night

Each light is like a flashing gem
Within her guilty diadem;
The night is shed on her like hair
That hides a face's dark despair.

The deadly river, too, glides by
Like some swift tiger, stealthily,
Its sinuous back all painted bright
With quivering bars of golden light.

And far above the city's jars
The ancient army of the stars,
That in a quiet, reproachful mood
Keep watch from God's own solitude.

Night Thought

A little while, and I shall be
At one with earth and air and sea:
A little while, and I shall creep
Where none shall waken me from sleep.

A little while, and life shall pass
And lend a greenness to the grass:
A little while, and these dull bones
Shall be companions to the stones.

And yet the Spirit of God's Love
Is more a falcon than a dove;
And can it be that I shall have
No hiding-place within the grave?

O gracious Lips that I have kissed
And tasted in the Eucharist,
With you alone an answer is,
And yet no answer but a kiss.

Vision

    Say not my Lord is dead;
Last night I saw Him in the flesh,
His wounds were red, and fresh
    The thorns about His head.

    'These limbs of ivory,
And precious drops of sacrifice,
Rubies and pearls of price,
    My son, I paid for thee.'

    I saw His pale lips move,
And His bright eyes were like a sword;
I cried, 'Have pity, Lord,
    Thou woundest me with love.'

Daisies

    We often pass,
And never notice as we go
The little flakes of summer snow
    That fleck the grass;

    How everywhere
Their petals white are tipped with red,
And nightly folded overhead
    In evening prayer.

But children do,
Whose feet are fresh from asphodel:
And He who loves the children well,
Loved daisies too.

He may have stood
And seen in them a subtler sense,
Wherein His own white innocence
Was stained with blood.

Danger

Thy wounded lips are like a rose
That sorrows under weeping skies,
Troubled with beauty and the woes
That mar its sweetest ecstacies.

But there is no disaster lies
Within those troubled lips for me;
But that calm beauty of thine eyes
Is like the danger of the sea.

Her Hair

Believe me, Love, that I am tired
Of flowers that blossom on a grave:
All that I thought too sweet to have,
And all that once I most desired.

As one that in dim water dips
His hands, so I would feel the strands
Of thy hair rippling through my hands,
And cool the fever of my lips;

And cease from all the strife and care
   And interchange of song and sin,
   And hide my hands and lips within
The sweet oblivion of thy hair.

The Star in the East

Love, I was but a wanderer,
   And waited for the dawn of love,
Till I beheld the morning-star,
   And saw the shadows break and move.

Now like the star that guided them
   Who bore the gold and myrrh and spice,
And led their feet to Bethlehem,
   Where lay the Lamb of sacrifice,

A purer light within my eyes,
   And on my lips a sweeter song,
O bring me where my Saviour lies
   In weakness that shall make me strong!

At Night

This living darkness is to me
   As thy dim-shadowed hair,
And in my heart the thought of thee
   Is holy as a prayer.

For but to gaze into thine eyes
   Or but to touch thy hand,
Stirs in me deeper mysteries
   Than I can understand.

The sanctity of love is such
　　At thy lips' eucharist,
That other Love I seem to touch,
　　That filled the heart of Christ.

Merchandise

I would not give thy coloured lips
　　That Love has crimsoned with his dyes,
　　For all the pomp of merchandise
That purpled seas in Tyrian ships;

Nor those deep eyes that overflow
　　With love, for all the lights that gem
　　And weave for Death a diadem
About his pale, imperious brow.

No gold-dust out of distant lands
　　Nor all their wealth of woven ware,
　　Could buy this weight of lavish hair,
I hold like water in my hands.

But not thy lips nor languid eyes
　　I love, nor yet thy loosened hair,
　　But that sweet soul that dwelleth where
Stars slumber in wide azure skies.

The Mystic Rose

We grow so weary, Love, for we
　　Have something in us that abides
Of that old sorrow of the sea
　　And hunger of his hoary tides;

The loneliness that breathes and blows
　　With twilight on the dusky ground,
And darkens in the mournful rose
　　That opens out her purple wound;

A heaviness for some far home
　　That makes us mingle, heart on heart,
And lose ourselves til! we become
　　As twain in one, and each a part

Of that eternal Love that glows
　　And blends our lesser loves in one,
As petals of the perfect Rose
　　That makes a shadow of the sun.

Travel

These elements are old and strange
And weary after time and change;
And what is woven into one
Was drawn from earth and sea and sun.

There lingers in thy mournful eyes
The dimness of dew-dropping skies,
And in the eyes that gleam on thee
The greyness of the old grey sea.

Through these sweet-woven limbs there runs
The light of unremembered suns;
And vine-leaves and vine-tendrils were
The dim soft shadows of thy hair.

The sorrow of thy sad red lips
Was sought by men in merchant-ships;
And on the lips that cleave to thine
There cleaves the saltness of sea-brine.

For ere He kneaded dust to men
God wrote it with His golden pen
That what was scattered wide and far
Should blossom in a silver star.

The Sea

In this dim chamber of the sea,
    Where quiet, sunless sea-flowers lift
Tired heads that wave eternally,
    And rootless sea-weeds drift,

Here, like a woman drawing breath,
    The silent tidal waters move,
Rising and falling; but beneath
    There beats no heart of love.

But under earth's wide ways and streets,
    Where all these weary feet have trod,
Oh, somewhere, surely, burns and beats
    The purple heart of God!

The Shadow

They bruised His back with many a rod,
But the bitterest stroke was Thine own, O God.

Girt with Thy glory to earth He came;
They bound His brows with a torturous flame.

The flowers and grass of the garden were wet;
Save us, O God, for His bloody sweat.

They bruised His back with many a rod,
But the bitterest stroke was Thine own, O God.

His flesh was nailed to the naked rood;
Save us, O God, for the price of His blood.

Now pleading before Thy throne He stands;
Save us, O God, for His piercèd hands.

They bruised His back with many a rod,
But the bitterest stroke was Thine own, O God.

Prayer

Have pity on me, Lord!
  Have pity, Lord, for I
  Am broken utterly
And wounded with a sword!

And in Thy pity break
  The barrier of all
  The tears that cannot fall,
The prayers I cannot speak!

O God of Calvary,
  My song is like a bird's,
  A sorrow without words
And half a broken cry!

Have pity on me, Lord!
  Have pity, Lord, for I
  Am broken utterly,
And wounded with a sword!

At His Feet

Here at Thy bleeding feet, O Lord,
  Here at Thy bleeding feet,
I see upon Thy holy rood

Great drops of anguish and of blood;
Such roses, Lord, on such a tree
Are stains of mine iniquity:
Here at Thy bleeding feet, O Lord,
    Here at Thy bleeding feet.

There at Thy blessèd feet, O Lord,
    There at Thy blessèd feet,
Where Thy saints are clad in weeds
Of purity and perfect deeds,
Grant even me, O Lord, a place
Where I may look upon Thy face:
There at Thy blessèd feet, O Lord,
    There at Thy blessèd feet.

The Passion

O most exceeding bitter cry,
From ashen lips in anguish curled!
O body that on Calvary
        The sword of death devours!
        O river red that pours,
And winds a bloody bandage round the wounded world!

O cup they made to overflow,
Whereat our Saviour drinks his fill!
O crown upon that piteous brow,
        With scarlet buds of scorn
        Amid the twisted thorn!
O bloody passion-rose upon the sanguine hill!

Christ with a rod hath broke the bands,
And shattered Death; and lo, the rod
Hath pierced and bruised His holy hands,
        Come hither, ye that mourn,
        And see what He hath borne;
Behold the purple wound within the breast of God.

In Memoriam

Thus she lies, her body frigid
   With the loss of tidal breath;
Every feature stern and rigid,
   Like the iron face of Death.

No faint flicker to enliven
   This pale picture graved in stone,
But a sweetness Death has given
   With a beauty not her own.

Where is all that one remembers,
   Sunny hours and shadowed days?
Silent with the dead Decembers,
   Buried with the leafless Mays.

So we wake her not from sleeping,
   When we gather what remains,
And commit it to the keeping
   Of dim earth and perished rains.

Night her dusky hair is twining,
   And our eyes are filled with death;
But somewhere the sword is shining,
   Drawn from out the empty sheath.

The Ship of Amber

Lutes, laurels, seas of milk, and ships of amber.

Dawn came like a troop of doves that flutter
   With white soft wings in a purple sky;
We heard the voices mix and mutter
   As the flight of prophetic birds swept by.

Together we sailed in a ship of amber
  Through the pallid dawn like a dusky pearl;
Steering by many a rock-roofed chamber,
  We watched the sea-waves whiten and curl.

We looked low down in the sunless spaces,
  Where bloodless sea-flowers float and bloom;
Swaying together with pitiful faces
  They looked on us from the ghostly gloom.

Together we cried, 'O love, O lover,
  Is our sad heart less tired than these;
What palms can the wandering birds discover
  In all the waste of the wide grey seas?'

'What quiet palms with their sombre shadows
  For wings that beat from dawn till noon?
What evening lands with their lotus meadows
  And flower of the honey-coloured moon?'

From the cool, clear depth of her crystal chamber
  The dawn arose like a dusky pearl,
As we sailed away in our ship of amber,
  Watching the sea-waves whiten and curl.

The golden stars in their dim dominions
  Timid at heart took wings to flee;
And the white birds swept with silver pinions,
  Drifting like snow on the lonely sea.

Creation

God plucked a golden quill
  From Michael's wing:
The host that had before been still
  Began to sing.

He spread a sheet of light
  Before Him; then
Deep down into the pot of night
  He dipped His pen.

Earth and the sea and air,
  Sun, moon and stars,
All things of power and beauty were
  His characters.

The mighty word was penned
  Age after age;
And, each age coming to an end,
  He turned a page.

And last, to make all sure,
  (Read it who can!)
He set thereto His signature
  And called it Man.

Here and There

Eyes that are black like bramble-berries
  That lustre with light the rank hedgerows
Are kindly eyes and within them there is
  Love of the land where the bramble grows.

But mine are blue as a far-off distance
  And grey as the water beneath the sea;
Therefore they look with a long insistence
  For things that are not and cannot be.

Sleep

If sleep will muffle up my eyes
   And let me leave things as they are,
Then it may be when I arise
   That I shall find some friendly star
Has made them otherwise.

Or who can say but that there might
   Happen a miracle like this:
That one should come across the night
   And kiss my dreams and make the kiss
A sesame to sight,

So that my feet should rise and run
   Where now they cannot see to creep,
And I should say, That very one
   Brought secret healing to my sleep
Who hurt me in the sun?

Sonnet

Leave me my dreams, I pray, and take all else:
For though ye strip my world I build again
A world where I can have no hurt of men,
But, sitting in a light of asphodels,
Can suck wild honey from their flowery wells,
Sweeter than drips from a dead poet's pen;
And all the noises of your world shall then
Seem as the far-off tinkling of sheep-bells—
So sang the poet: (did ye hear him sing?)
And one came by and looked and with her face
Burnt up his heart, so that he fled the place
And her who looked: and all his dreams took wing,
Changing to bitter birds, and followed on
And troubled him from darkness unto dawn.

Sonnet

When I went back to where the tumbling tide
Lightens the darkness and leaf-dripping dews
Splash on the oyster-beds at Ambleteuse,
Ghosts of dead days came stepping to my side,
Scalding my hands with their chill tears, and cried:
O young proud-hearted master, of what use
To shake us from these shadows where we muse,
Feeding on faded dreams? And I replied:
O shameful things, because the flowers are fled
From your thin faces and night-wasted eyes,
Shall I too live and love no more? And they
Looked at me sideways with long stealth and said:
On you too, brother, shall a sun arise
With no birds singing at the break of day.

Night

Darkness comes unobserved as sleep until
    The daylight has an end;
And I await her coming with goodwill,
    For darkness is my friend.

I love the ways of men and women well
    Who walk the common light;
But more I love the vast impalpable
    God who comes by night.

So I will go a little space from men
    Until I find content:
And it may be that when I come again
    No man shall know I went.

To A—

(On his third birthday)

The Christmas day that you were born
   December snows were far away,
For in the time of flowers and corn
   You made a second Christmas day.

Six times has Christmas come since then,
   To us six times, if to none else;
Three we observed with other men,
   But three came in with no church bells.

We sailed through summer seas and through
   Slant waters, white with wave and wind
And tossing moon; and always you
   Tugged like a little boat behind.

Days pack like autumn clouds: come days
   When your dear feet shall stray from us
To walk in strange and budding ways;
   And we, shall we be envious?

Alas, can summer hope to save
   The sweets her rippling roses shed?
Enough, to know that we shall have
   Long thoughts of love when we are dead.

Morning Hymn of Hebrew Shepherds

When God sets forth His golden scales
And weighs the day against the night
And says again, Let there be light,
And light by the power of His word prevails,
Shaking the drops of night from our hair,
We shepherds make our morning prayer.

We praise Him first for the gift of sleep
That came to beast and surly bee
And the little fishes beneath the sea
And the lamb that lies by the broad-backed sheep,
And came to man to heal and bless
His heart with its mighty gentleness.

We praise Him next for the dews of night
That quenched the embers of dying day
And sprinkled the hot hard earth like spray
And washed the moon to make it bright,
And now when the shades of night are gone
Laugh and dance in the level dawn.

We praise Him last for the morning sky
That blossoms with roses that overrun
The open gate of the out-going sun—
For these we praise the Lord on high;
But he that is wise will praise Him well
For the things his heart can never tell.

Chorus from 'Jephthah'
(on Jephthah's home-coming from the land of Tob)

str. I
They say Sidonian sailors dive for purple and sea-pearls
Where the human-headed fish-god lives and the old
      sea-dragon curls;
And go in ships to Ophir by the wide palm-waving capes
For peacocks, gold and ivory, almug-wood and apes,
And, coming by the Red Sea, bring chalcedonies and beryls
And amethysts for feasting kings to quell the fume of grapes.

ant. I
And traders bring from Tarshish in beaked boats on the
      windy seas
Plates of silver, iron and tin, amber and ambergris;

And camels come from Havilah by the road to Paradise
With mountain gold and cassia, spikenard and sweet spice,
And bring from Sheba silken scarfs and blue-lipped negresses,
Perfumes and dyes and singing dwarfs, incense and golden
     mice.

ep. I
But though one were a tunny to swim through the ribs of
     sunken ships
And gaze on the wavy glimmer of yellow amber and gold,
Or a stone-eating ostrich to fly to the buried cities of old
With their porphyry cups that dyed king Chedorlaomer's lips,
Yet nothing there is could bless the sight of the eye or yield
Such joy as the hidden treasure that lies in a man's own field.

str. II
O Love, that combest the shaggy locks of the mountain
     lion's mane
And filest the teeth of the crocodile's jaws in his nest in the
     water-cane,
Plucking the sting from the banded wasp and the quills from
     the porcupine
And dripping like myrrh from the panther's claws and the
     horns of the Jordan kine;
Sweeter than pipes to the horned asp on the lips of a sweet
     pipe-player
Or Eshcol grapes to the laughing fox or a honey-comb to
     the bear:

ant. II
Love, that bringest the plump-fleshed quails to build on the
     fallow ground
And blowest the cuckoo's call from the wood like a floating
     bubble of sound,
Teaching the crested hoopoe to read where the secret waters
     run
And rousing the bald-headed eagle's blood to plunge headlong
     in the sun,

Making like yellow amber beads the eyes of the cushat-dove
And painting the peacock's outspread tail with a thousand
      eyes of love:

ep. II
Love, O king Love, the conqueror of beasts and the tribes
      of birds
And long-spiked chariots splashed with war, tall crowns and
      wine-dark swords,
Though a king should lead an army south and conquer by
      force or guile
The untameable heart of the many-mouthed dragon of ancient
      Nile
And heap on a thousand ox-hide shields the riches of Mizraïm,
He too would lose the last-fought field, for love would
      conquer him;
Nor could he find in the famous land of the flat-nosed
      Lubim more
Than the Demon holds in his subtle hands that
      crouches beneath his door.

Boaz and Ruth

The scene is the threshing-floor of Boaz outside Bethlehem.
It is night; Boaz sleeps with his head on a sheaf of corn, and
Ruth, lying at his feet, is awake and sings softly.

RUTH: When Jacob came to Bethlehem
He brought his wives and sons and they
Remained a space and went their way;
But Rachel, she went not with them,
For they raised a heap of stones for her
To mark the place of her sepulchre.

And that was the end of all the love
That made him a hind to Laban's hand
To keep his sheep in the Syrian land,
And of all the beauty she had above
All other beauty of womankind
That came before or shall come behind.

BOAZ: Why have I waked? It is not yet the dawn;
The stars still hold the sky, and though the moon
Has dropped from sight its white illumination
Drizzles upon the hilltops.
Did something scare my sleep, making it fly
As when a bird is startled by a stone?
What·shall I think?
Was it a flying mouse? or bright-eyed beast,
Making a shadow richer than the night
Before my threshing-floor? or but a dream
That like an airy bubble burst itself
And left me wide awake?
I am afraid; I do not know at what.
O God!
There is some secret horror in this place,
A soft-pawed creature or a basilisk,
Mingling its loathly being with the darkness:

I feel its eyes upon me and they chill
The marrow in my bones.

RUTH: O!

BOAZ: What art thou?
Art thou some obscene spirit from the desert
Drawn hither by the lust of human blood?
Or rose-lipped Lilith, the snake-woman, who
Sinned with our father by the evil tree?

RUTH: O sir, canst thou not see me?

BOAZ: I can see
Thy shape, but the foul beauty of thy face
I cannot see; it glimmers like a mist,
Lit by the eyes of a flesh-eating bird.

RUTH: Boaz!

BOAZ: What! dost thou know my name?

RUTH: O Boaz,
I am thy handmaid, Ruth.

BOAZ: Ruth!

RUTH: I am Ruth;
The Moabitess, Ruth. Wilt thou be angry?
It was Naomi bade me come, for I
Have shewed her all the kindly words that thou
Hast spoken in the field.

BOAZ: She bade thee come?

RUTH: She bade me come and I did come.

BOAZ: Woman,
Why hast thou come?

RUTH: O Boaz, spread thy skirt
Over thy handmaid, for thou art my kinsman.

BOAZ: What dost thou say?

RUTH: It was Naomi said:
There is our kinsman, Boaz, and he winnows
His barley in the threshing-floor; go therefore,
Wash and anoint thyself and get thee down
And he shall shew thee what to do.

BOAZ: And thou,
Thou then wouldst have me speak of this?

RUTH: With thee
It rests; I, being childless, do my duty
To that dead man, my husband.

BOAZ: And shall I—
What dost thou think?—shall I too do my duty
To thy dead husband? Or if not to him—

RUTH: To whom? what other?

BOAZ: To myself.

RUTH: Thyself?

BOAZ: Would I had all the thunders in my voice
To tell thee how I love thee, Ruth!

RUTH: Alas!

BOAZ: O thou art fair as the night-floating moon,
As the full moon or as the first new moon
That bends her slender bow! Thy eyes are pools,
Fringed with long feathery rushes, where the stars
Splash through the night; thy lips are crimson rosebuds,
Crushed on one spray together, where a bird
Sings to its nested mate.

RUTH: Thou mockest me!

BOAZ: O Ruth, by this vine-scented night I swear,
And by that burning bird, the nightingale,
That hides her head among the dew-drenched leaves
And pours a dizzy song upon the darkness
So sweet, she dies with every note she sings;

By her and that fire-dropping sky I swear
I love thee, Ruth, I love thee, Ruth.

RUTH: O Boaz,
Dost thou not mock me?

BOAZ: O that I could borrow
The sweetness of that bird's heart-hurting song
That I might say again and yet again,
I love thee, Ruth, I love thee, Ruth.

RUTH: Enough!
It is too much.

BOAZ: O night! O dying bird!
Great night, that with thy million eyes lookst down
On all this dull, insensate, sleeping world,
Two dost thou see who are alive, two lovers,
Sweet Ruth and Boaz, Boaz and Ruth, and her,
The bird that, singing of their love, becomes
A disembodied song upon the darkness.

RUTH: I think my heart will die, smothered with flowers.

BOAZ: O that I were that sweet-voiced nightingale,
That, singing with full throat, I could unload
The burden of my heart in song! O Ruth,
Give me thy lips although one little kiss
Will kill me with the sharpness of its joy—
Ah me!

RUTH: Why, what is this?

BOAZ: Alas! alas!
Why have I kissed thee in my madness?

RUTH: Boaz!

BOAZ: It was the glimmering beauty of thy face,
Blurred in the darkness as a misty moon,
And thy pale hands, moving like silent moths,
And the sweet smell of aloes on thy skirts
Beguiled my heart and made me mad.

RUTH: Alas!

BOAZ: I do not fear the living but the dead.

RUTH: The dead? What dost thou fear?

BOAZ: I fear the dead;
For they sit always in a sunless place,
Hanging their faces like pale flowers, and think
Of us who are alive above the earth:
And they are hasty in their minds and if
One wrongs them any way they breathe a curse
That rises upward in a thin blue smoke
And, changing to a scorpion in the sun,
Fastens upon the heart that sinned.

RUTH: What wrong
Is this that thou hast done the dead, thy dead
Or mine?

BOAZ: Why did Naomi send thee here?
I have no power to do this thing she asks;
There is another man, nearer of kin,
Who hath the claim upon thee first.

RUTH: Alas,
What must I do?

BOAZ: Thou, Ruth, shalt go to him
And say what thou hast said to me this night:
And if he takes thee it is well for thee;
But if he takes thee not, why then, O Ruth,
It shall be well for me indeed.

RUTH: Alas,
Was it for this Naomi bade me go
And pluck the mandrakes in the field?

BOAZ: O Ruth,
What dost thou say?

RUTH: Was it for this I broke
Sweet ointment on my head and drew my garments

Out of the sandalwood and set a veil
Before my face and, creeping from the city,
Came to thy threshing-floor this night?

BOAZ: Ruth, Ruth,
Why dost thou torture me?

RUTH: And shall I go
Tomorrow night and, lying at his feet
As I have lain at thine, say unto him
What I have said to thee?

BOAZ: Thou shalt not go,
For I will slay thee first.

RUTH: Nay, let me go!

BOAZ: O Ruth, thy tears are falling on my hands.

RUTH: If thou wilt let me go now, in good time
Thou shalt forget.

BOAZ: I shall forget thee, Ruth,
When dews forget the darkness and the bees
The honey-scented hillside and the doves
The shadow of the window-sill at noon;
When light is severed from the bursting dawn
And heat forsakes the desert and the moon
Withholds her sickle from the harvest fields.

RUTH: Alas, when thou hast long forgotten me
I shall remember thee, O Boaz. Now
Wilt thou not let me go?

BOAZ: I cannot, cannot;
The love that holds us is too strong.

RUTH: Not strong
But weak, if it should overflow and drown
All honour and all duty to the dead
And to that God Who by the stroke of death
Gives us the dead for an eternal gift.

BOAZ: O Ruth, pity me!

RUTH: I do pity thee:
Yet if thou takest me who am not thine,
Thinking that thou shalt have me for thyself,
I am estranged from thee by more than death;
But if thou wilt be kind and let me go,
Then God will take my heart in His own hands
And keep it thine forever.

BOAZ: Go, O Ruth!
The night is fire about me and thy face
Is like a flame upon the darkness. Go;
Before I can repent, go quickly.

RUTH: Yet
There is this sweetness too in love's denial,
The love that goes with honour.

BOAZ: When I die
And wander through the thickest shades of hell
My soul shall hear thee as a nightingale,
Bringing the solace of the former earth
Back to my blood-drained heart.

RUTH: O this is joy!
None knows love's perfect joy who does not know
Love's sacrifice.

BOAZ: And thou shalt sing to me
Out of the myrtle, ivy and nightshade
That drape with their dim foliage and fruit
The dismal forms of the phantasmal trees;
And I shall laugh to hear: and if the dead,
Lifting their faces, ask me with their eyes,
What singing-bird is in the cage of hell?
Then I shall answer them: O foolish ones,
Do ye not know? It is the voice of Ruth,
Singing to me; she sings about the earth,
The colour of the evening on the land,
The shadow of the wind across the corn,

Splashed with the blood of poppies, and the gold
Of shackled sheaves; the running song of larks
And moan of pigeons, stabbed with love; sunset
And rising of the honey-coloured moon
Above the wine-dark hills.

RUTH: Now let me go,
For thou hast given me gladness more
Than all my pain.

BOAZ: No, Ruth, remain till dawn,
And thou shalt be a sister at my side:
For on the morrow I myself will go
And call the elders at the gate to witness
And one way or another this thing shall
Come to an end for both that man and me.

RUTH: Then it is well; for thou shalt keep thy faith
Both to the dead and to the living.

BOAZ: Look!
Dawn is at hand; the little round-eyed birds
Awake each other through the ambiguous air
With interchange of song and the deep hills
Throw off a purple light. Now the Lord God
Takes as a living coal from off His altar
The sun, and, breathing on it with His breath,
Kindles its heat and lifts it in His hand
To hurl its fiery weight across the world.

To a Violet in Autumn

O pilgrim in thy purple hood,
　That strayest late into the year,
When not in meadow or wet wood
　Is one of thy companions here;

The celandine with starry head,
　The cuckoo-flower and cuckoo-pint
Are here no longer, but instead
　The harebell and the grey horsemint.

And now the long convolvulus
　Flings his white trumpets on the hedge,
And saw-wort and blue scabious
　Grow round the rutted stubble edge.

Thou, born again beyond thy time,
　Speakest of woods, dark-leaved and wet,
And brown ploughed earth and silver rime,
　Melting on early grass; and yet

Thou touchest thoughts within my blood
　That make thy coming doubly dear,
O pilgrim in thy purple hood,
　That strayest late into the year.

Youth

Turning away his lovely head
And with a trembling on his lip,
Youth took me by the hand and said,
'Here ends our long companionship;
Though I may walk with other men,
With you I shall not walk again.

'Now when the soft-voiced crickets sing
At sunset, and the evening star
Shines like the first stray flower of spring
Over a sea of lavender,
Now is the solemn moment when
Joy blossoms by the steps of men.

'For you the golden coin is spent;
The singing lark has left the sky;
And you must find a calm content
To turn the leaves of memory,
Where Time wrote with his iron pen
The things that may not come again.'

And then I laughed, 'O not today,
Some other day is time enough;
When little children cease to play
And other men leave off to love,
Then may you say and only then
You shall not walk with me again.'

O Heavenly Love

O Heavenly Love, that in a wind
Didst breathe on One of womankind
In that white town upon the hill,
On womankind Thou breathest still
In such sweet sense that I can say,
I fear not, Lord, Thy darkest will,
If love go with me all the way.

For though my days grow dim as night
And nights seem longer than the light
To sleepless eyes, because hot pain
Touches my flesh or heart or brain,

I smile towards a break of day,
Redder than roses bruised with rain,
If love go with me all the way.

And though the subtle hands of Death
Should interrupt the tides of breath
And set his cobwebs on these eyes,
I, who have looked to other skies
Beyond the night, beyond the day,
Know that the living flame shall rise,
If Love go with me all the way.

Love

In giving love you gave me all,
 Your hand, your heart, your soul;
If other women give in part,
 Yet you have given the whole.

If then you ask me how I know
 We shall not wholly die,
I answer that that love of yours
 Is of too fine a sky.

A love of such dimensions, dear,
 So long, so deep, so broad,
Is such a love as sure must share
 Eternity with God.

Autumn

When light wakes late and early fails;
And where the catkins swung their tails
Like caterpillars on the trees

Nestle the nuts in twos and threes;
A late owl hooting from the wood
Chills my premonitory blood.

And when the hedges, thick with haws,
Are strewn with the loose harvest straws,
And sullen hips upon the brier
Betray the rose's sepulchre,
The stripped fields in the moonlight glow
White with imaginary snow.

How can I know, how can I know
But something of this winter's snow
Shall fall on me till I become
Dumb as the snow-heaped earth is dumb,
And I myself this year shall be
Part of the year's mortality?

Never again to wake at spring
And see the blackthorn blossoming,
And flowers that later days forget,
Primrose and rumpled violet,
Coltsfoot and gold-rayed celandine,
Outspreading with a silvery shine;

And, where the beds of bluebells lie
Like water that reflects a sky,
That white flower veined with lilac blood,
The three-leaved sorrel of the wood,
The same that to St Patrick was
The Godhead in a house of grass.

Flowers are the dull earth's conscious eyes,
Full of sweet hopes and memories,
Making—O Immortality,
Surely thy image here I see!—
A little outspent sun and rain
Mix with the dust and live again.

Song for Autumn

Come, love, for now the night and day
  Play with their pawns of black and white,
And what day loses in her play
  Is won by the encroaching night.

The clematis grows old and clings
  Grey-bearded to the roadside trees
And in the hedge the nightshade strings
  Her berries in bright necklaces.

The fields are bare; the latest sheaf
  Of barley, wheat and rusty rye
Is stacked long since; and every leaf
  Burns like a sunset on the sky.

Come, love, for night and day, alas,
  Are playing for a heavier stake
Than hours of light or leaves or grass;
  Come, love; come, love, for sweet love's sake.

White Violets

The hooded violets of blue
  That drink the rain of April skies,
These I know well; but who are you
  That in white resurrection rise?

These bring us fragrant thoughts of them
  Who sleep beneath the heavy earth;
But you of some white Bethlehem
  Where they are come again to birth.

At Night

Our love is like that broken moon,
    That blossoms on the edge of night,
Holding the fullness of her noon
    In a dim smothered light.

Love, though love's springtime comes and goes,
    We know that summer waits us yet;
It is the sweetness of the rose
    That scents the violet.

Beauty and Love

Beauty and love are all my dream;
    They change not with the changing day;
Love stays forever like a stream
    That flows but never flows away;

And beauty is the bright sun-bow
    That blossoms on the spray that showers
Where the loud water falls below,
    Making a wind among the flowers.

The Death of Eli

The scene is the courtyard of the Temple outside Shiloh.
Eli is seated by the door. Having waited all day for tidings
of the battle to which his sons, Hophni and Phinehas, have
gone with the Ark of God, he has fallen asleep. Priests are
offering a sacrifice in the Temple.

SACRIFICE-SONG OF PRIESTS *(from the Temple)*

Crash the brazen cymbals on high
And leap, ye priests, on a nimble foot;
Strike sackbut, harp and psaltery;
And, O ye sweet flute-players, put
Lips to the flute and the double flute.

Take flowers, take flowers in your hands,
Flowers and a white cart-rope to throw
On the young horn-budded steer that stands,
Lowing as votive oxen low,
When the loud ram-horns and sheep-horns blow.

Go forth, go forth, ye priests, and guide
The flower-crowned victim in; and slay
The sacred victim and flay the hide,
Leaving the priests the hide ye flay,
While the pipes and the shrill-voiced bagpipes play.

Piece by piece give the entire
Victim; let no portion fall
Apart from the fire; give to the fire
Liver and heart and caul and all
The fat of the liver and heart and caul.

Crash, cymbals, crash; higher and higher
Leap, ye priests, from the holy ground;
Sound, O lute, and, loud-voiced lyre,
Sound and, O sweet pipes, resound,
As the dancing priests go round and round.

ELI *(waking):*   Where is my staff?
For I would judge by the sweet smell of flowers
It is the hour of sacrifice. Alas,
They go their ways and I am left alone.
O that it might be with me as it was
With Jacob, when, an old old man and blind,
His children gave him in the cave at Dothan
The coat of little Joseph, and the smell
Brought back the light of day to his dead eyes.

(NURSE *enters.*)

NURSE: There sits the old blind priest upon his stone,
As drowsy as a serpent in the sun,
Sucking the heat into his withered blood.

ELI: Who speaks? Is it some woman from the town,
Come to the Temple carrying in her basket
A pigeon or a little raisin cake?

NURSE: Eli, Eli—

ELI: Good nurse, reach me thy hand;
For I too will arise, I, the old priest,
And weaving almond blossom on my staff
Join in the holy dance.

NURSE: Be still, O priest;
Is it a seemly thing for one so old
To dance with the young men? But tell me rather,
For I am come to learn, if any tidings
Has reached the city.

ELI: One who came at noon
Reports that when the priests brought down the Ark
To Ebenezer, where the people lay,
So great a shout went up that the bright air
Writhed as in pain and singing larks fell dead
Around the camp; and when it touched the ground
The whole earth shook like an unsteady sea,
And clouds of smoke poured forth and through the smoke
Men saw the eyes of the twin Cherubim,
Shining like stars on water.

NURSE: Is God's voice
Dumb in thy heart, O priest? or wilt thou speak
And, speaking, call some blessing on the land?

ELI: God's voice has long since perished from the land.

NURSE: God's voice may speak again if thou wilt speak.

ELI: Who knows if, speaking, it will bless or curse?

NURSE: No word can speak against the holy Ark.

ELI: The Ark! Ah me, I tremble.

NURSE: Speak, O priest;
The word of God is hanging on thy lips.

ELI: Alas, what evil ecstasy is this?
My head is light as air; my blood is fire;
A spirit rushes on me with black wings,
And old dead murders bleed before my eyes.

NURSE: What mad moonbeam has slipped into his mind?

ELI: O dawn that rose in blood upon the door!
She stooped upon the threshold but the priest,
Cutting the body of the concubine,
Sent out the bleeding flesh through all the land.

NURSE: Why dost thou speak of old unwholesome things?

ELI: Well of Labonah, where the woman danced,
Crushing the crocus with their naked feet
And tossing on the wind their hair like smoke
That flies behind a torch, a bitter draught
Thou gavest unto Shiloh on the day
When through the vine-leaves rushed the ambushed men
And seized each man a maiden with his hands.

NURSE: His mind is like a dismal cave of bats.
O priest, hast thou no softer word to speak,
With her, thy daughter-in-law, brought to her bed,
And with the Philistines this day—

ELI: Ah me,
I see that dragon rising from the sea;
He strikes his claws in the Judean hills
And gapes with empty hunger on the land.
O land of Judah! O the Ark of God!
My head swims round and round; I fall, I fall.

(ELI *faints*.)

NURSE: Alas, these words of cursing will destroy us.
It is a piteous thing indeed—O God,
What is that dreadful crying from the city
Like the shrill wailing of dishevelled women?
What do they cry? The Ark of God is taken!
The priests are slain! The priests are slain! I fear
The sword that slew them is a two-edged sword,
That slaying them will slay my mistress too.

(NURSE *goes out*.)

INCENSE-SONG OF PRIESTS *(from the Temple)*

When God drove out from Paradise
That Root of Life, our Parent Man,
He gave him for his sacrifice
The seed of every precious spice
Mixed by priests in the incense-pan.

And the sons of Joktan took them thence
And planted Mount Arabia
Beside the sacred Pison; whence
The merchants bring sweet frankincense
And myrrh and cassia-lignea;

And cistus yielding labdanum
That shepherds pluck from the beards of goats;
Almug-wood and galbanum
And sap of the opobalsamum,
Brought on the seas in wind-blown boats;

And mastic-gum that overflows
When the bark is cut by a sharpened stone;
Spikenard, mace and lign-aloes
That make the desert a Syrian rose
Where the scowling camels journey on.

All that comes by labouring seas
Or sky-encircled caravan,
Barks and gums and powders—these
With salt and oil and ambergris
We burn in the golden incense-pan.

ELI *(waking):*   I smell the scent of flowers, not like the scent
Of vines of almond blossom in the spring
Or the white crocus, but a strange sweet scent
Like honey in the wind; and that they say
Is sign that one is on the point to die.

Then let them not do with me as they did
With Joseph, when they tore his entrails out
And filled the dark red hollow of his ribs
With honey and sweet spice; for that is why
More than all other gifts the Lord abhors
The gift of honey in His sacrifice.

(NURSE *enters.*)

NURSE: Ichabod, Ichabod, O Ichabod,
She called him Ichabod before she died.

ELI: Ah me, is it the nurse's voice I hear?

NURSE: She shuddered on the bed and, Ichabod,
She cried, O Ichabod, O Ichabod.

ELI: O bed, hast thou brought forth these ill-matched twins,
Birth to the child but to the mother death?

NURSE: Together these two fought, mother and child;
They fought together, she with bitter cries,
He plucking at the blood about her heart
Blindly; and when we stooped and drew apart
The child, she lifted up her head and cried,
Ichabod, Ichabod, O Ichabod.

ELI: And I, the priest of God, cry, Ichabod;
The glory is departed from the land.

NURSE: Too surely did this raven croak before.

ELI: O ye who lift your robes to tread the grapes,
Stamping the bubbled clusters till the blood
Rushes in rosy foam about your feet,
Are not the vats yet full and full enough
And ye not weary of exultant sin?

NURSE: Who can run after this unbridled tongue?

ELI: And thou, O Shiloh, where the short-legged ox,
Goring the flowery garland with his horns,
Is led by white-robed priests along the streets,

Can the rich slaughter of a thousand bulls
Or all the snowy pigeons of the land
Drown the shrill cry of blood beneath thy stones?

NURSE: He comes, he comes, the messenger of death.
The death of his two sons will slay the priest;
I cannot bear to see the blind man die.

(NURSE *goes out.*)

ELI: The blind are in a living dream; but God
Has blessed their blindness with one gift of sight,
To know that all, the seeing and the blind,
Alike are in a dream; for some men rise
To follow in a dream a track of blood;
Others to dig for treasure in a dream;
Others to dream they go upon a journey
By land or sea; others to seek the love
Of wife or child, though that too is a dream;
All struggling on by strange and devious ways
Of good or evil to the hidden end,
None knowing that the end is not in man
Himself, but in the mind of God alone.

(MESSENGER *enters.*)

MESSENGER: What man art thou staring with these dead eyes?

ELI: Eli, the priest of God, and thou—

MESSENGER: O priest,
I bear a load of tidings on my tongue—

ELI: My sons—

MESSENGER: Thy sons are slain in battle.

ELI: Ah!
My sons are slain. Why then, my sons are dead.

MESSENGER: The Ark of God is taken.

ELI: The Ark, the Ark!
Alas, why wilt thou murder an old man?
Dost thou not see that I am old and blind,
An old old man almost as old as God?
My sons are slain—the Ark of God is taken—

(ELI *falls back and dies.*)

MESSENGER: The priest is dead; the voice of God is dead.

(MESSENGER *goes out.*)

LIBATION-SONG OF PRIESTS *(from the Temple.)*

When father Noah smelt the rain,
He built his ark of gopher-wood;
And the ark rose up like a trumpeting crane
And sailed over city, hill and plain
And seas beneath the Flood.

And the year went by him where he sat
And watched the floating rains prevail
Over the world; and after that
He saw the back of Ararat
Rise like a heaving whale.

And he planted grapes, and stem and bud
Sprang up and began to overrun
The holy ship; and banks of mud
Like wallowing monsters of the Flood
Reeked in the crimson sun.

And Noah was first to set his foot
To tread the grapes and fill the vat;
For every vine that yields her fruit
Is child to that ancestral root
That grew on Ararat.

And this, the crowning gift of the feast,
We splash on the double-horned shrine;
For first the hyssop-waving priest
Offers the blood of the votive beast
And last the blood of the vine.

Dedication
J.Y., A.J.Y., R.A.Y.

Dears, take this little book;
   Taking it make it ours;
Here runs a thin-voiced brook
   Enskying some few flowers.

And when from the last hill
   Fades the flame-coloured light
Dears, will you hear it still
   Singing across the night?

If Passion-Haunted Nightingale

If passion-haunted nightingale
   Sing from my lips no more,
Think not his song should ever fail
   Seeking an alien shore.

If brook that went with talking sound
   Under thy blossoming tree
Is silent, think not it is drowned
   In an estranging sea.

From celandine that stars the spring
   To orchid's twisted flame,
In every changing flower I sing
   Thy variable name.

Epitaph
M.F.H.

A flower herself to flowers she went,
Sharer of Beauty's banishment;
She left us winter, but to her
It was the springtime of the year.

Spring Song

Lark sings to sky,
   Thrush sings to tree;
O love, my love, to whom should I
   Sing but to thee?

Blackbird dips beak
   In faery gold;
Knew I where such gold to seek
   Seek it I would.

Ivy clings to bole,
   Moss clings to stone;
Two hearts make one perfect whole,
   One heart none.

The Cherry Tree

Walking in dim wood
   Where hides the daytime night,
Rooted to ground I stood
   Seeing a sudden light.

Is it the sun I see
   Or a white cloud? Ah no,
It is a cherry tree
   Laden with laughing snow.

To see that foaming bough
   Think you I was glad?
Glad, O yes, glad enough,
   Glad and a little sad.

For to my mind appeared
   (I did but look behind)
Just such a tree but bared
   Not by earth's rain or wind.

Yet at the spring's sweet breath
   Laughs this light-laden tree;
And I stared hard at Death;
   And did Death stare at me?

Moschatel

When spring fires with sweet rage
   The breast of singing bird
And with faint gold of saxifrage
   The dim woods are blurred,

Grows the green moschatel,
   Five heads square-set as one
Like to that city whereof doth tell
   That saint of God, St John.

Where are those streets of gold?
   And who doth walk in them?
He that can see one stem uphold
   The New Jerusalem.

Absence

Where last night there walked two
Tonight there walks but one.
You ask, am I alone;
Alone, love, but for you;
Yes, you and that sweet Venus star
That signals where you absent are.

Your absent presence here
Is like this thronging night
That throws a whiter light
On each increasing star
And those white campions that hover
Mothlike about the night-turned clover.

A mystery? Ah, no;
Love has no periods,
Your love, my love, nor God's;
Is it not always so,
Love's absence makes us conscious of
More than could ever present love?

Downs

The weald is well and well enough
    And roads lead everywhere;
But when I walk this wind-cropt turf
    I walk three feet in air.

There houses nestle neat as nuts
    And folk like beetles go,
And grandly the church steeple struts;
    I hear its wind-cock crow;

But on these slopes cloud-shadows gloom,
  As over windy Troy
God-shapes swept by with hastening doom
  For one weak lovesick boy.

There hollyhocks hang out their plates
  And sunflowers with brown eye
Stare hard across the painted gates
  At every passer-by;

Here orchids growing free in grass
  And burnet's blossoming stem
Low curtsey to me as I pass
  And I curtsey to them.

Now God be thanked for these great downs,
  Calm, comfortable, broad,
Where free from men's thought-tainted towns
  I think God's thoughts with God.

The Dark Night

That night was brighter than the day
Though no moon showed to show my way;
  Moon's watery beam did I
  Need? No, nor star-grey sky.

The trees were black as visible death,
Heavy and black, lacking all breath;
  No trees I ever saw
  Filled night with so deep awe.

Islanded were they in sea-mist
Where Love could keep her sacred tryst;
  Love with no second one,
  But with sweet self alone.

A Child Sleeping

She is like the sorrel's white bud
That grows in a sun-watered wood
In springtime, opening with brief sun;
But whenever the day is done
Or sky is overcast by cloud
Quickly her slender head is bowed.

But birds are busy in that wood;
They have no time to seek for food;
And sluggish and enormous trees
Pull their green smocks down to their knees;
And even the sun, centuries old,
Renewing youth shakes off the cold.

The Snail

I praise the solemn snail
    For when he walks abroad
He drags a slow and glistening trail
    Behind him on the road.

Clock ticks for him in vain;
    Tick tick tick—will he run?
He hankers not to share men's pain
    Of losing to the sun.

Snail keeps a steady pace,
    Therefore I honour snail;
For if none saw him win a race
    None ever saw him fail.

You say, But in the end
    He fills a thrush's throat.
A life, how could one better spend
    Than for a song's top-note?

Flesh, sinew, blood and bone,
    All that of me is strong,
Blithely would I bury in one
    Short-lived immortal song.

On the Hill

One, two, three, four—eleven,
    Slowly the church clock beat;
I laughed knowing the slope of heaven
    Rolled around my feet.

A thousand flowers were there,
    Rock-rose and tormentil,
Blue rampion that claws the air
    And rubied pimpernel;

Great downy-leaved mullein
    Tall as a man can walk,
Heavy with blobs of gold that climb
    Blossoming his thick stalk;

Rest-harrow, sage, self-heal,
    Eyebright, squinancy-wort,
Marjoram that grows too tall
    And thyme that grows too short.

God, as these grasses are,
    (I prayed there) so be I;
For them no sad presaging star
    Darkens a flawless sky.

Of death they have no heed;
    Fruitfully they die,
Coining in dead living seed
    Their immortality.

Childhood

Listen! As I walked forth tonight
A strange thing struck my wondering sight;
I saw white evening campions blot
The darkness of the fields with light.

Now seeing these could I not tell
That, night-diminished, grew as well
A host of flowers, forget-me-not,
Foxglove, rose, poppy, pimpernel?

Flowers of full summer, could such grow
In budding springtime? For I vow
Today in my own garden-plot
Snowdrops were sleeping in their snow.

To A—

Son, fill thy heart with praise;
    To praise be added prayer;
Irreverent heart makes summer days
    Wintry and cold and bare.

Be thou thy father's son
    True to thy blood and birth
Not in one single thing but one,
    The love of God's sweet earth.

For when as of one dead
    Men speak my good and ill,
Yet he could walk, let it be said,
    An Enoch on the hill.

Child Love

Love once but not again,
  Love once and love forever;
Twice netted by that trembling pain?
  Never, O never, never!

This to myself I said,
  And so might well believe;
For if all other hopes are dead,
  What hope remains to live?

Yet love is still my song;
  And, love, am I to blame
If love I call on all day long
  But by another name?

For this new love of mine,
  She is not lightly won;
Speak I to her, she makes no sign
  When the last word is done.

Love, love, all day I cry;
  O love, my love, I plead;
She looks at me with silent eye
  And gives no pleasant heed.

But, love, I say to her
  Taking her by the hand;
But will she smile? or will she stir?—
  She does not understand.

The Wind

Who hath marked the wind,
  Insubstantial, sightless,
Bodiless, unlimbed,
  Colourless and lightless?

We hear her flapping cloak
  Caught in a trammelling tree;
See we an undimmed smoke
  Or a tempestuous sea?

Rivers lie in bed
  Like sick men all day long;
Blackbird hides his head
  Hushing too rapid song;

Steadfast stands green hill;
  Sea drags her tidal chain;
But wind will never be still
  Nor in one place remain.

Sea-waves run after her
  With a white gift of flowers;
And when she is not there
  They wait on her for hours.

She sings so low that scarce
  We hear her or so loud,
Frightened the moon and stars
  Scurry behind a cloud.

When rushing like a river
  She flows through unbanked air,
Ecstatic aspens quiver
  And flowers kneel down in prayer.

The wind blows where it lists
  Over this world of ours,
Sluggish in clinging mists,
  Sudden in kneeling flowers.

The Dead Sparrow

Today I saw a bird
  Lie upturned on the ground;
It seemed as though I found a word
  That had no sound.

Quickly once that sparrow
  Flew rising through the air;
But quicker flew the flying arrow
  That laid it there.

O strange to see it now
  Lying with sidelong head;
Stranger to think it does not know
  Where it lies dead.

That sparrow asks no man
  To dig for it a grave;
Gentle is death, I thought, that can
  Both slay and save.

Summer Night

Speaks now the silence of the moon,
  A white, silent and lovely speech;
With few faint stars the sky is strewn
  Remote and out of reach.

Soft winds that seem born from nowhere
   Pursue the day's last ardent heat;
Thin scents stalk lightly on the air
   Setting on flowers their feet.

Black trees stir in their massive sleep;
   The grass sighs with a great content
And hawthorn hedges that breathe deep
   Breathe a bewildering scent.

Now, soul, go forth, thou art alone,
   Free at last from day's busy sloth;
Moon, stars and flowers, all are thy own;
   Go forth, night-loving moth.

Moth Mullein

What are those fairy folk
   That fight with spears of grass
And hang on thy tall stalk
   Stained shields of palest brass?

A dream! And what art thou?
   Burns thy pale-petalled flower
So ghostly, who can know
   If thou thyself art more?

To a Child

There is a sea between our lips and eyes;
No dawn trembles across its star-swept skies,
And no sharp wing of fork-tailed swallow flies
   With spring's assurance to our homeland birds.

When I take your two hands in my two hands
And speak to you, you are as one who stands
A traveller in new-discovered lands
    That cannot break to meaning native words.

My warmest kiss falls coldly on your brow;
Yet, O my love, kissing you even now
I saw a half-smile flicker and I know
    Surely a sail draws within sight of shore.

Love, when I go beyond your sight and speech,
Make a lengthening water from the beach,
Will you reach hands, stretching beyond your reach,
    To touch my hands, drooping upon the oar?

At Owley

Dear, I wished you had been there;
It was almost a pain to bear
The beauty of that place alone;
One needed a companion.

You know the hour one trembling star
Anchors off a black belt of fir;
I trembled too, like him unshod
Who saw the flowering of his God.

And I remember came the thought,
Should God by act of death be brought
Nearer than now, might I not die
Slain by my immortality?

Song

With every sweet apostle,
  That spread the news of spring,
Linnet, lark and throstle,
  Blackcap and redwing,
  I too began to sing.

Though summer days draw over
  And half the seeds are flown
And flower by flower the clover
  Drops her dead florets down,
  Withered and dead and brown,

My spring outlasts their summer
  And I am singing still:
Let birds grow dumb and dumber,
  Of song I take my fill
  By each hedge and hill.

Ploughman, Ploughman

Ploughman, ploughman, hold thy hand,
  Lead back to stall thy clanging team;
When poppies nod, leave thou the land
  To sleep awhile and dream.

When apple-scented chamomile
  Strains with her gold breast to the sun,
Gather thy apples, leave awhile
  The earth to slumber on.

By thriftless thrift men do not thrive;
  With autumn heat thy horses steam;
And O take heed how thou dost drive
  Thy plough across earth's dream.

Autumnal

Hangeth the blue-skinned sloe
   Where blossomed blackthorn once;
Thinning their leaves trees show
   Outspreading skeletons.

Foot doth through reaped field stray
   Breaking the sharp brief straw;
Hip coffins rose and may
   Smoulders in sullen haw.

Flowers few, too few, remain:
   Of these pink centaury,
Small flax, lean-stalked vervain
   And blue-wheeled chicory,

Lucerne and melilot
   And the grey-whorled mints
Mainly I love, but not
   As that ripe cuckoo-pint's

Red-berried stem; for I
   Seeing those berries clear
Stand under new May sky
   And Cuckoo, cuckoo! hear.

Sand Strapwort

When colour lifting from the earth
Catches from trees a dying birth
And in the ivy's yellow bloom
Wasps and blue flies make angry hum,

Here, twenty paces from house-door
Where men so strangely rich live poor,
Where few sea-poppies still unfurl
I set my foot in budding pearl.

Strange joy is mine to know I stand
Here in one spot of our England
Where God and the small strapwort strive
To keep one English flower alive.

Late Autumn

The blue flax fades upon the wall;
Ripen her seeds in hollow ball;
Fade too the long-sunned flaxen skies
And leaf-lit woods full of gold eyes.

Loosestrife bleeds purple in the sedge;
Hemp-agrimony topping hedge
Waves grey and tawdry; firm and stiff
Clings the hoar samphire to sea-cliff.

The bindweed that with open bell
Twined thorn and twined my heart as well,
Withered and dead now will depart
Neither from thorn nor from my heart.

Flockwise the delicate swallows sit
Musing on telegraph wires; they flit
Seaward already on the wing
Tireless of vague imagining.

And I but half-sad turn away
From this year's faded yesterday
To kindlier flowers than grow on earth,
God-planted on my winter hearth.

Go Now, My Song

Go now, my song,
Let your wing be strong;
Fly and dart and dip
With a chip-chip,
A wren among the thorn
Of the world's scorn.

Never have a fear
Of thorn that would tear
Or the cold stare of men;
O my chitty-wren,
Let not courage fail
Your upturned tail.

Rooks

In a high wood
Where great trees on their tree-trunks stood,
I seemed as one
Lost with the giants of an age bygone.

A small bird sung
And those old trees were once more young,
Their upper wood
Renewing spring with a faint flush of blood.

I lifted eyes
And saw their tangled tributaries
That to earth sunk
Condensed in the broad river of tree-trunk.

High in those trees
Rooks built their storm-bound villages,
Nest on dark nest
Swaying at rest on the trees' frail unrest.

They cawed and cawed
Till I felt stricken like a man outlawed,
And ill at ease
I sheltered under tempest of those trees.

Then I went out
Where silent grass gave a loud shout;
Looking behind
I saw them like black crosses on the wind.

The Moon

Tread not the chambers of my mind;
See, moon, I draw this sightless blind;
    Dust lies on table, chair and shelf,
    Dust that was once myself.

Enough to bear on this day's road
The faggots of tomorrow's load;
    Why should the dust of yesterday
    Blind the eyes of today?

A man lies murdered in a wood
Where thieves have stript him of small good;
    Let no armed conscience enter in
    On half-corrupted sin.

Today I saw the sunlight splash
Its silver on black-budded ash;
    Soon black nor silver will be seen,
    But an immortal green.

Look, moon, where the dark ivy clambers
Screening the windows of my chambers;
    All listless dust of memory
    Let it in its dust die.

Spring

I never noticed, till I saw today
How budding birches stand in their green spray
And bracken like a snake from earth upheaves,
How many in this wood are last year's leaves.

The Wood-Cutter

The white mist made the hanger dim,
   Else I had never heeded
   The spider-webs mist-seeded;
That clinging mist showed me the slim
Shine of each gossamer
That hanging from nowhere hung there,
But hid from sight the sorry wood-cutter.

The preacher stood in his pulpit,
   But not one word was heard
   By any sort of bird,
Wren, sparrow, linnet, finch or tit;
They sang in the wood's fire,
The smoke that thinned out rising higher
To sky as blue as man's farthest desire.

'The spring is come that was to come,'
   So preached the cuckoo-pint,
   But the birds would not stint
Their song that preached the preacher dumb,
Though still that axe rang out
With shout that followed fast on shout;
Whether from axe or tree played with my doubt.

Pasque-Flower

Dear, ask no song tonight,
My heart is heavy with sad delight;
　Beauty's have been these hours
　And yours and the pasque-flower's,
　That having gone are now forever ours.

Forever ours indeed,
Blown away to be memory's seed
　And like the pasque-flower still
　To haunt on Streatley Hill
　Dark with juniper above Streatley mill.

The Old Man

Strange how it all came back to me,
The small clear cottage looking out to the blue sea
Over the bents, loose-sanded and thick-grassed,
(O white-scratched bare brown legs that passed
To tread the cockle path with tender feet!)
And seated on the rustic seat
The old, old man (grandpa) with thick
Fingers bunched on his varnished walking-stick;
But he looked out on nothing—he was blind,
Blind to all but the sunny wind
That whirled the two jack-tars on the tall pole;
Round and round those wooden tars would roll
In their blue jackets and white trousers,
For those two sailors were no drowsers
Whichever way the wind went,
Though he would sleep sometimes in the hot scent
Of stocks, moss-roses, majoram, southern-wood and sweet-
　　　　　　　　　　　　　　　　　　　williAM
And other flowers with a sweet name;
But when he raised a listening finger

Each bird-note in the silence seemed to linger
Till to each one he gave a name;
Though he was blind he knew them all the same.

Today it all came back to me
While I leaned on the wrinkled bark of an elm-tree;
Around me was the spring, the yellow celandines
The sun outshines to silver, and the bines
Green-leafed already of honeysuckles,
Drooping wood-sorrel and gold-blobbed archangels,
Anemones white as the Magi's star
And ash-buds brushed with shining tar.
And why? Because the spring was crossed
By one lank and outlandish ghost,
A last year's tarnished thistle,
And among many bird-notes there was one clear whistle
That sounded like a man's,
A young man swinging with milk-cans
Across a court and out into a lane
Whistling the same tune over and over again.

June – To Alison

Rain drizzling in the high blue pines,
A misty tangle of loose lines,
Here in the hollow wood had ceased,
Except when by the wind released
From broad leaves and the bent tree-tops
Rattled a shower of thunder-drops;
Then sudden shafts of light shot through
As the sky dried to pools of blue.

I idled while the hot sun toiled
And thick with steam the moist wood boiled,
Watching on the wet-blackened boughs
Raindrops dark and mysterious
Shining along their silver rows

(Strange as the level eye looked close
Small trees in each to see outlined)
And hazel buds, green, soft and blind.

Four years ago this day of June,
Clear in the sky, a thread-thin moon
I saw you first, you weak, I strong,
As small tit's chip and thrush's song;
Still with increase of strength we grow
Like nut or raindrop in a row,
You fattening in your fringed sheath,
I gathering strength to drop beneath.

Hill-Mist

Down where mown hay in swirling waves was tedded
    Light seemed to stare;
Half up the hill the honeysuckle wedded
    To bush of briar,
Breathing desire from neck and arms, was bedded
    High in clear air.

But from the hilltop trees dim smoke was growing
    And vaguely forth
Rising and never rising but still slowing,
    Tree-trammelled growth,
Failing desires from earth to heaven flowing
    And mingling both.

The Butterfly

This butterfly I see stumbling about
    Is tossed with doubt;
It cannot make with choice of flowers so many

Sure choice of any;
Soon will it flatten its tired wings upon
   Some stick or stone.

Lord, who has made the love of Thy earth's beauty
   My lovely duty,
Let not my spirit's moments so be spent
   In uncontent,
Till tired it ask no more to rest upon
   Than a cold stone.

The Young Martins

None but the mouse-brown wren
That runs and hides from men—
Though for a moment now
Clinging with fine claws to a bough
One watches me askance,
Who dimly sit where the loose sunbeams dance—
Trills in these trees today;
All other birds seem flown away,
Though when I scrambled up
Through the thick covert of the combe's wide cup
Shaking down the last dog-rose petals,
My hand kissed by the angry nettles
And clawed by the lean thistles,
Blackbird and thrush flew off with startled whistles.

I see the hillside crossed
By a black flying ghost,
Rook's passing shadow, and beyond
Like skaters cutting figures on a pond
High swifts that curve on tilted wings are drawing
Vanishing circles; but save for the rooks' cawing
And trill of the small wren
Lost in the green again
No birds are singing anywhere,

As though the hot midsummer air
Hanging like blue smoke through the holt
Had driven all birds to sit apart and moult.

Yet when I came up through the farm
Where the stacked hay smelt keen and warm
Heads of young martins, one or two,
Black and white-cheeked, were peeping through
The small holes of their houses;
There where all day the sunlight drowses
They looked out from the cool
Dark shade of eaves and saw the pool
Where white duck feathers raised a storm of foam,
The cock that stood with crimson comb
Among his scraping hens,
The short-legged bull behind the fence,
The line-hung sheets that cracked and curled,
All the sun-laden dusty world;
And nodding each to each
They kept up a small twittering speech,
As though they ready were
To launch out on the air
And from their nests of clay
Like disembodied spirits suddenly fly away.

Findon

This unforgettable place, dear love,
These falling hills, O clear enough;
My memory fits it like a glove.

So stood that one lean row of trees,
So on this slope busy with bees
Frail rock-rose spread its golden fleece.

There in that hollow henbane grew;
Seeing it first I called to you,
Its sluggish beauty to both new.

Calling you now I call in vain;
Your absence works in me like pain
More poisonous than dull henbane.

Now thinking how I stand alone
I ask, Am I the selfsame one
Who made two with you in that sun?

They say these flakes of flesh depart
Till of quick brain and the slow heart
No part remains the selfsame part.

Yet love remains and memory
Of God and you, of earth and sky,
All that is intimately I.

So when it hurts the heart to think
Of that most bitter, abrupt brink
Where the low-shouldered coffins sink,

I ask, should spirit be aghast
That slipt slow bodies in the past
To fling off the whole flesh at last?

You absent from me are most near;
It is such presence with me here
That sanctifies this solemn air.

The Prayer

I stopped short in my walk
  I knelt on silent knee;
  A flower shook azure claws at me,
A moth clung to its stalk.

I knelt to see that flower,
  Strange flower and stranger moth;
  Knee clung to earth with strangest sloth,
To rise I had no power.

I knelt, but I was blind,
  For flower nor moth I saw;
  Moth swung on stalk and the flower's claw
Clutched empty at the wind.

Why was I kneeling there,
  Eyes closed and lips apart?
  Why had that slogging slave, my heart,
Turned from its work to prayer?

Had I not seen them both
  Together, rampion
  Unsheathing blue claws in the sun
And the cinnabar moth?

The Sand Martins

The sand martins were flying,
Flying around and crying;
Till late in the grey light
I watched their twisted flight;
Then with the last light gone
They housed in holes that riddled the sandstone.

I rose and passing by
One thin contented cry,
Chirp of sleep-settling bird,
I heard, and no more heard
Save the late gulls that cried
Down by the wave-lit darkness of ebb-tide.

Night-Flowering Campion

Close on the bat-crossed hour
I waited for a flower
By light grown visible
Burning the vivid hill.

Pimpernel in night-bud
Showed like small drops of blood;
It was no common flower
I kept late vigil for.

I watched by falling light
Till I saw how with white
And patient petals shone
Night-flowering campion.

So white those petals showed
And such a rich scent flowed,
I said, 'Are we not one,
I and this campion?'

Seeing how for us both
Sweetness followed on sloth
I felt my own song's power
In that night-flowering flower.

But when I came that way
In the clear light of day
I noticed a mean plant
Sticky and small and scant.

The Hawk

I watch the tree-tops stir
  Not with the wind but motion of their height;
Two throaty pigeons purr,
  Till one bursts forth baring his breast in flight.

Why is it no bird sings,
  But all birds sit silent as pine-perched cones,
And only stonechat flings
  Monotonous succession of sharp stones?

Oh, I too see that tense
  Hawk rest on flicking wings high in the air
And in a deep suspense
  Keep silence with those singers here and there.

Already throstle thieves
  The ripening astringent haws, and now
Among fly-bitten leaves
  Fatten the fringed twin nuts on hazel bough.

But when that bird drops down
  Tearing those leafy trees bare to the bone,
What shall of us far-flown
  Be left? One silver bird-splash on a stone?

Ghosts

When purple on the hill
Struggles the dwarf thistle—
A hand that grips below
Forbids its stem to grow—
From the spear thistle's crown
Shakes loose the thistledown.

Silver against blue sky
These ghosts of day float by,
Fitful, irregular,
Each one a silk-haired star
Blown by the wind at will
O'er the flower-nodding hill.

Vaguely like butterflies
Flowerwards they fall and rise,
Till by a trammelling bush
Caught on their onward rush
And from the wind's aid freed
They settle on their seed.

Not by the famished light
Of a moon-ridden night
But by clear sunny hours
Go these white ghosts of flowers,
Taking from the glad earth
Their burial and their birth.

The Burdocks

No one ever comes here—
Not since last April when the gamekeeper
Choked with lopt boughs this coppice-track
Scarcely distinguished from the black
Tangle of thorn, these autumn gusts

Are stripping cinder-bare,
For only here and there
A last leaf rusts.

So all along this track
Whose length I wander aimlessly and back
With leaf-clogged footsteps that fall dumb
The burdock-leaves hang in foul scum;
But oh those gummy burs are sly,
For brushing by a stem
My coat is thick with them
Withered and dry.

But glad am I to think
Those brown eyes saw in me a badger slink
Back to its earth or the high brush
Of fox dangle from bush to bush
Though none has for an age at least,
Spaniel nor gamekeeper
Nor any walking here,
Seen either beast.

The Track

There, there! I see it now,
Deep down and distant, a stone's throw
Lengthened by its long fall, the track
That runs from edge to edge and back
Round this old tree-grown quarry. Oh,
How strange, buried in air so far below.

I draw it through my glasses;
No one is there, for no one passes
That way; though one morning I guessed
Seeing a bed of grass downpressed
Of lovers who from heart to heart
The day's taut distance drew too far apart.

I hate that jay's guffaw;
Each time I leap the wood's ha-ha
I hear it. There, crash! and it's gone,
As though my hand stooped to a stone.
Young saplings swing and heavier limbs
Of trees where matrimonial ivy climbs.

Come next April or May
The tangled thorn will cry, No way!
And blackthorn, bramble, rose will choke it;
Then autumn's rotting rains will soak it,
And birds only sing through the lazy
Winter to come to the unwithered daisy.

The Shot

'Hast thou found me, O mine enemy?'
  Where the blue sky was wrinkled
  With twig on twig that tinkled
  And stem that clacked on stem,
  While wind swept over them,
  And yellow-blue tomtits
  Chipped stones in little bits,
'Hast thou found me, O mine enemy?' cried I.

For standing in my shady cover,
  There on the other side
  With the rich sunlight dyed
  As bright as old church brasses
  I saw them through my glasses,
  Thin-legginged gamekeeper
  And his dog with him there
The black spaniel—was his name not Rover?

Crack, crack! gun's loud double report;
  And as the silence grew
  I stood still for I knew

Awkward death for someone
Noised from that sudden gun.
Pigeon, woodpecker, jay,
Which of us fell today
Of all who favour this high wood's resort?

The Turkeys

The wind shakes on the grass
    Water the horse-trough carries,
As I watch the ruffled turkeys pass
    As stately as dromedaries.

They call this Mary Farm,
    And here sunlight will sprawl
On coldest winter day and keep warm
    Behind the grey-mossed wall.

Have they named it after her
    Who often wondered whence
Those tall kings came, carrying myrrh
    And gold and frankincense?

She laughed; but quite contrary
    The Child woke up and cried,
Seeing those strangers enter, till Mary
    Clutched Him to her heart's side;

As thousands of women will do,
    When the merry carols are sung
And those high-stepping turkeys are due
    To have their proud necks wrung.

They'll strain to their heart again
    The Child who cries, How murk is
This Christmas eve on the window-pane
    And those cold naked turkeys.

The Long Man of Wilmington

What figure, drawn in chalk, strides with his pole
Across the Downs, as naked as a soul?
Odin or Balder? Time will solve the doubt
And mail-clad robots look on a Boy Scout.

The Moon

'What gars Garskadden luk sae gash?'
    Kilmardinny said to one,
While late into the early morn
    They sat drinking on.

'Garskadden's been wi' his Maker
    These twa hours,' said he;
'I saw him step awa, but, faith,
    Why spoil gude company?'

Kilnaughton Bay

From the black rocks
    Whose shadow with the waving water swings
A heron squawks
    And floats away on widely-flapping wings.

Lighthouses wink,
    One winking slowly with a blood-shot eye;
Stars rise and sink
    As, seeking light, earth whirls from sky to sky.

Dead Leaves in Spring

These beech leaves in their courses
Are like withered sea-horses;
They do not change at once
To fibrous skeletons;
Brown and brittle and thin
They keep a sun-tanned skin.

Stuck at a rabbit's bury
They peer a moment and scurry,
As though they frightened were
And loved the sunny air
And glistening grass that waves
More than dark gaping graves.

So they rattle and run
Before the wind and the sun
And when, as dancers do,
They pause a minute or two
It is the wind falls slack,
Not any breath they lack.

Good Friday

How often have I peered
    In that dark forest,
That thou, my mind, hast feared,
    Thou, flesh, abhorrest.

All autumn leaves that flee
    Fall from that forest;
Ah life, tree after tree
    With death thou scorest.

Even one fallen leaf
  Makes all that forest,
And then I think thy grief,
  O heart, is sorest.

But once on the chief tree
  Of that dark forest
There hung, O my soul, He
  Whom thou adorest.

The Old Tombs

What are those tables for,
Stone table set by stone table
Under the east gable
Of this old church, Saxon and Norman,
With Death always the foreman?

Do the dead at Bishopstone
Rise from the ground like moths
And sit at white table-cloths,
The moon at Easter spreads for them
Or the Star of Bethlehem?

In Balcombe Forest

Earth wakes again stretching thin arms of bracken,
From sleepy fists the silken fingers slacken;
These and that purring rattle of nightjar
Hint age, as children do, so young they are.

Osea Island

I came in sight of Osea Island
  Walking the turfed sea-wall;
To right mud-banks chirped like a cricket,
  To left I heard sedge-warblers call.

I never went to Osea Island,
  Perhaps I never shall
More than those crabs with sun-bleached bodies
  That through the grey sea-purslane crawl.

I took the road to Osea Island
  Soft to my feet and green
As any road that through a wood-ride
  Vivid with summer grass is seen.

Before I came to Osea Island
  The seaweed on the road
Rose in the tide that from the mud-flats
  Flowed through culverts and overflowed.

Why do I think of Osea Island?
  Perhaps I am afraid
Some foaming tide may overtake me
  Walking a blossom-dropping glade.

The Ant-Hill

I stand here like the sun
  And look down on this vast metropolis
Where the small emmets run;
  I almost think it is
The same sun that looks down
On London now or any other English town.

Yet I know well enough
   That clapping dove is no dove but a culver
And under the sheen bough
   Of—no, not holly, hulver,
These heavy cows that lurch
Call with a hollow bell to some lost pagan church.

But matters it so much
   If like those kissing brimstone butterflies
We too a moment touch,
   And whither each one flies
We do not know nor whence;
Just so to touch our first and final prescience?

The Birds

What do you know?
   What is it that you do not know,
O birds, singing as years ago
   Behind the elder-bushes' balls of snow?

I would not ask
   The mocking cuckoo or a jay that laughed
Nor would I call to task
   The nightingale in the moon's hollow shaft.

Such a moonbeam
   A ghost drifts in these trackways now
Recovering his dream—
   Am I not broken by each bough?

O birds, be dumb!
   I do not question the jay's laughter;
A revenant I come
   Today as I might come fifty years after.

Why do you sing?
    What is it that you do not know?
Do you not feel my weight upon your wing?
    What do you know?

The Old Man

I listened to the grasshoppers
    Like small machines mowing the hay,
Hot and content to think myself
    As busy and idle as they.

A woman sat under a tree
    Cursing the flies that tormented her;
I did not stop with 'Which is the way
    By Herbert's Hole to Ballinger?'

I thought of that old man I asked
    Who saw each meadow, stile and lane
Clear as pebbles washed by the Chess
    And never shall see them again.

Wicken Fen

Nothing is here but sedge-cut skies,
Azure of darting dragon-flies
And horse-flies settling on my flesh
Soft as the touch of spider's mesh.

A plunging pike rocks with a wave
The white-spoked nenuphars that pave
With smooth round leaves the loose-mired lode
That through the fen drives its straight road.

And as the wind blows back the stream
Shaking the buckthorns from their dream,
Time flows back here at Wicken Fen
To swine-steads and blue-woaded men.

Small shaggy men that plunge again
Through sedge and the black rotting rain;
And I too shudder as I feel
The whole earth shake under my heel.

Loch Nell

She won me by a tress,
By one white ringlet washed up on the shore,
She who lived here once
And keeps her youth for evermore,
Naisi's mistress,
Deirdre, by the Loch of Swans.

Who was Naisi
Who with that exiled queen at the chessboard sat?
I wonder was it I
Or he who leered at me between his fingers,
The tramp who robbed the garden for his hat,
Or someone else of earth's poor singers.

Ben More

Two ravens from the summit rise and croak
Sailing in circles over the hill-smoke;
Why do their raucous cries strike on my ear
Less than those motor-horns I cannot hear?

Eriska

Eriska was an island,
A little tree-clad highland
With heather and rhododendrons
And whaups crying over the stones.

Clouds on Morven behind
Were bluer than the wind
On which the cottage reek
Flowed with a vanishing streak.

From blue they deepened to black,
Negroid as a wet peat-stack;
I wondered, 'Does she wonder
What tryst there could be yonder?'

We looked between the boughs;
From Appin a lighthouse
Opening a gold eye
Winked twice and thrice Good-bye.

Denholm Dene

Chaffinches dropping on the oats
Toss up and down like little boats
And blue geraniums with their bill
Peck at the winds from cleuch and hill.

The winds blow down from Rubers Law
And sweeping over holm and shaw
The Teviot and its white townships
Break on that crag-perched tower, Fatlips.

Audley End

It's raining now; without a doubt
Here is an end to the long drought.
How often from the shade of trees
I thought of that rich man, Dives,
And how no diamond drop was given
To his or earth's cracked lips from heaven;
     It's raining now at Audley End.

The oxlips flowered in Ugley Wood
When by this sunken wall we stood
And saw the neck of the flying swan
Stretched out over the smooth-shaved lawn
And blue-capped turrets of the house
As white as dusty scabious;
     It's raining now at Audley End.

Then may was budding in the hedges,
But now they've reaped even the sedges
And Time that was the trickling thread
Of an old hour-glass is outspread
To a quicksand; high on the air
A peacock screams (though none is there);
     It's raining now at Audley End.

The Hanger

Stubble the ploughshare narrowed
Lies as bare earth, seeded and harrowed,
Loose clods and upturned stones
And flints scattered like pigmies' bones.

Crisp leaves across it roll;
A sun-greened jacket on a pole
Guarding the seeds from harm
Salutes the wind with broken arm.

Black eyes in elder bushes
Are half picked out by thieving thrushes;
No green save ivy lingers
That crawls and climbs with small webbed fingers.

Why do I grieve at fears
And make these falling leaves my tears?
These trees do but undress
To wrestlers clad in nakedness.

Half of the wood is blue
Where in wide rents the sky falls through;
A second Adam, I
Walk in the compass of its eye.

Frith Wood

The rain steadily falls
And in the muddy lakes and canals,
Where timber-wains rutted the road,
Bubbles rise, float and explode
Like St Sophia's domes
Where Christian saints had once their homes.

A mist not cold or warm
Dims the white cowls at Furnace Farm,
That smelted iron and grows hops,
And sunset on the chestnut copse,
Not this day's, could it come,
But sunset of the late autumn.

When this rain drowns the earth,
The whole earth from Land's End to Perth,
And anything that lies beyond,
Star or mountain or bracken frond,
Dear, shall we know for certain
What lay behind this drifting curtain?

In Westerham Woods

Two lovers here once carved their name,
A heart between them like a flame;
Now these two lovers' names depart
From either side a broken heart.

On the Ridgeway

Thinking of those who walked here long ago
On this greenway in summer and in snow
She said, 'This is the oldest road we tread,
The oldest in the world?' 'Yes, love,' I said.

Castle Rocks

Look! on Fin Cop a castle stands
Guarding the dale, not made with hands;
The wind that built himself a house
Could only build it ruinous.

Now when young ashpoles rise and twist
Thin flames in the amethystine mist,
What is the silence listening for—
The falling of that wind-built tower?

Kinderscout

O heart, why did you knock
So loudly on that sky-bound wall of rock?
Was it to see again
Behind the weeping rain
No, not the Edge of Kinderscout,
But visionary hills long since burnt out?

Here is nothing but black peat-hags
Where a slow Lethe drags;
Peat-hags pitted and pitted by frost
As though a flock were lost
Or in the mist
With shepherd kept a hidden tryst.

The Hill-Wood

Who was it laughed just now?
Or was it but a creaking bough
Or wind-blown rook
That tosses like a black Satanic book?

Why should they laugh at me,
An old, old man who with bent knee
And doubled back
Creeps under boughs that overlean his track?

I stand upright again
Where caterpillars drop like rain
From hazel boughs
Whose mealy leaves hang bare and ruinous.

Let a light gust go by,
A rabbit dive—I turn my eye
At every sound
Alert as a bright light-spot on the ground.

Who is it that I fear
Shall one day crash down on me here
Loud as some beast
Or blackbird stepping through dead leaves at least?

The Sea

I ever feared the sea;
Ah, false and fawning even as he,
That Greek, who with his fishing-rod
And two cross-sticks makes a tripod;
Then waits till bass or ling too late
Finds the sly bait.

Now as I walk away,
Across the flats of Pevensey Bay,
My footsteps keep so harsh a speech
With these loose miles and miles of beach
I think that it is still the sea
That follows me.

The French Coast

Across the sea what lovers walk,
    And what sweet things are planned and vowed;
But what to them is solid chalk
    To me appears a low white cloud.

In the Wood

Where trees were sloping on the hill
I stood and wondered where
All this that I now saw and heard
I saw and heard before;
Beyond the path as through a door
The busy light of open day
That seemed so far away,
The silence broken by a bird,
A restless bird among the boughs,
The idle sunlight in the gloom;
And then I knew;

We stood and sat around the room
With sunlight falling on the floor,
Black silent figures listening to
Those stealthy noises here and there,
Those slow steps on the stair,
The day the dead man left his house;
Yes, there I waited still
Musing that all was now the same,
Silence and gloom and sun's sick flame,
As when the dead man went his way.

A Windy Day

What is your haste
To heap the wood with leafy waste
Confusing to the eye
Starlings and leaves that fly?

Whoever you are,
You made one wind-poised leaf a star
That still lingers behind
The leaf that went on the wind.

The Tree-Trunks

How often were these trees
With multipartite vaults and traceries
Pillars of a cathedral
Aisled like Abingdon Church on Thames;
Now rusty gold crowns fall
From heads of old gods and their dames.

Here I am young again,
Young with the youth of Saturn's reign,
So young or old I feel that awe,

324

Spark in their night of nescience,
Men felt before they raised a saw
Or lying Homer passed his hat for pence.

The Teasels

How could I feel a stranger here
Who know all changing seasons of the year
    From buds that speak in hints
    To frost that sets the flints
    As fast as precious stones?
    I know them all at once,
For when on thinning boughs the birds are dumber
My memory can make a full-leaved summer.

But now today out of the trees
Flies and falls down a flock of greenfinches
    And on some teasels lighting
    Cling with crying and biting,
    Till tugged and torn by them
    Each fringed brown-headed stem
Shakes like the wand tossed by a thyrsus-bearer
And I stand looking on, a strayed wayfarer.

The Long-Tailed Tits

I stopped to hear it clear,
The sound of water tinkling near,
Although I knew no dowser could
Turn hazel-fork in that beech-wood.

Then on the high tree-tops
With rising runs and jerks and stops
Like water stones break into bits
Flowed the cascade of long-tailed tits.

Restalrig

Now maist o' us maun sleep in earth
  Until the Judgment Day,
But wi' that traitor Restalrig
  God wot it wasna sae.

Whiles he was sleepin' in the earth,
  Weel-happit wi' the grass,
Word cam unto the Lords o' Council
  He a foul traitor was.

He didna bide the angel's trump
  Nor twinklin' o' an e'e;
They howkit him oot o' his grave,
  A three-year corp was he.

They brocht him into Edinboro court,
  'Fause traitor,' cried they a';
Now God preser's lest sic a thing
  Should ever us befa'.'

To Anthony

To you, my little Gallio,
Who care for none of these things (tho,
She will not mind it is not hers),
To you I give this book of verse,
Dearest, take it and make it yours
So it shall be most surely ours.

I know you care for none of these things,
Hidden motion of angry bee's wings,
Slow staggering flight of butterfly
(Blue wings that bear the whole blue sky)
Flowers, birds, stars brighten for no moon
Or night born with that silver spoon.

You care for none of these things; tho,
From the pink almond blossom's snow
(You know these two trees in our garden
That drop green nuts before they harden)
To summer's blue-stacked wheat. Enough,
Where we once loved, you too may love.

Cowslips

Where is St Peter gone,
That trusty fisherman?
Runs he as once he ran
On the sweet Easter Morn,
Leaving his bunch of Golden Keys
Here by the paler primroses?

Alas, to seek his Master,
In empty sepulchre?
No foot of mine shall stir,
Yet shall I run the faster,
Who find these flowery keys unlock
Paths where the risen feet still walk.

The Sheep-Dog

The dog leapt over the hurdle—
I did but stare at sheep
Sharing the God-like languor
Those solemn heads did keep.

I stared and the sheep stared,
Each twitching a soft nose,
Moist to strange airs that flowed
From my face, hands and clothes.

Wagged tails of thick-legged lambs
Wild in their milky pleasure
Impatient sheep moved on
Scouting their full measure.

Then that dog leaping hurdle
Rolled on me like a log
O that my guardian angel
Were a shaggy sheep-dog.

Gypsies

I saw those white and brown and brown-white kine
Among the gold-fleeced gorse. Ah, friends of mine,
The gypsies, said I. Did I fancy those
Coloured kine were the quaint coloured clothes
That gypsies hung out, using for clothes'-horse
Jove, Danaë's lover, golden on the gorse?

Last week I stayed my steps in rusty heather
Talking with one who talked about the weather;
'A fine rain this, Sir, right thing for the land,'
He said, waving his blue tea-cup in hand.
I wondered what the weather meant to him,
That blue-chinned gypsy, both unkempt and trim.

'This rain will do the land a world of good,'
He said to me, while I impatient stood,
Watching his ponies on the hill-grass browse.
(Or for neat ponies had I taken cows?)
I answered him but did not answer her
And 'Spare a shilling for the kiddies, Sir.'

No, they were gone. But where their camp had been
Straw, rags and blue enamelled pot were seen.
Elsewhere lounging beneath their tented sheet

They lent some other earth their bodies' heat.
Only a coat, limp and wet-heavy, lay
As though a man had melted clean away.

Rain

The rain softly sings
   On the light beech-wood,
Branches shake greenwings
   For the sweet food.

A hoarse dove calls,
   Cuckoo says Cuckoo;
No more the rain falls,
   Sky gapes blue.

Toss the trees rough,
   Shower begins again,
As now from my song's bough
   Shakes a brief rain.

Lightning

O serpent-tongue of lightning,
That with a sudden brightening
Darts on my dark way
A phosphorescent day,
Thou blushest and art gone
And no direction
Of east or west thou knowest
But equally thou flowest.

What is thy silent scream,
The momentary gleam
Waking magnificence
Of earth's dead conscience?

Or in that dazzle-rift
Saw I an eye-lid lift
An instantaneous eye
Bright with eternity?

Anemones

White stars flew through the wood
  Along the ground, under the trees,
Till with the wind blown by there stood
  Starry anemones,
That looked up through tree-latticed sky
With bare exposure of gold eye.

Once more the rising wind
  Those flowers to starry tempest roused
Till my thought lifted from my mind
  Saw the night-sky, star-soused,
That signals with her secret fires
While heart in dusty heart suspires.

More than I understand
  Is here, I said; on reverent knee
I bent and with a sheltering hand
  Held one anemone;
As star of night that star by day
Seemed lonely, and as far away.

The Hill

Bird-like I perched on the tree-tops
  Climbing that slope behind
A slope so falling-steep it seemed
  That standing I reclined
Before me swung the bright beech-wood
  Speaking to a soft wind.

Tree-tops and foaming hedge below
   Made height where height was none
So that standing on that sharp hill
   I hung high and alone
Like a still hawk before it drops
   Turned to a sudden stone.

Far over wood the patterned weald
   Stretched with diminishing square
Till distance flying out of sight
   Made visible blue air
The earth fell from me as I rose—
   I stood no longer there.

Pointed at me each village spire
   When I flew out beyond
Rivers darted like snakes away
   And silver gleamed duck-pond
Farms, orchards, copses, villages
   Lay painted on the ground.

Then pigeon crashing from that wood
   Flew by in swift alarm,
And I fell back to earth again
   Taking no sudden harm.
I stood as flightless as those eggs
   She left there blue and warm.

The Wood

The birds were loud as when a man
   Breaks stones by a road-side;
Chap, chap, chap — you know the sound,
   Sound not to be denied.

I know not whether their sweet labour
   Of nest-building was done,
I know the song those loud birds sang
   Was louder than the sun.

Fresh leaves were smoothing out their creases,
   Anemones starred the wind,
Pale hyacinths had broken earth,
   With buds, blue-stained and blind.

A stream was flowing through that wood,
   Holding the entranced trees
(So shine you on my flowing mind)
   Shaken by its smooth breeze.

My song was loud, loud as the birds,
   Too loud for pleasant ear;
Love, can you hear it still who have
   The silent ear to hear?

Sleep

Tread softly lest ye tread on sleep;
   O faint the breath
She borrows from those flowers that heap
   Her silent form with a white death.

Speak not or let the head be bowed;
   Empty of speech
Her hands be silent as a cloud
   And as removed from our hands' reach.

Lift her lightly lest she awake;
   Her soul may go
Walking in dream where white stars wake,
   Shedding their never-falling snow.

Too rude, alas! her sleep is shed.
  Broken and gone;
Nay, let her be; around her head
  Birds sing in the star-dimming dawn.

The Fly-Orchis

Not of the earth or of this earth's sky,
  Nor of any rash and common hour
Is this brown-winged immortal fly,
  This flower-like fly upon a flower.

Kings sleep in scribbled pyramid
  Like small babes swaddled at their birth
This fly embalmed in fly-orchid
  Sleeps fast on the spring-haunted earth.

The Sheep-Track

I know a sheep-track green with grass,
Rutted by rocking carts that pass
When shepherd sits backed by a heap
Of round-sliced turnips sweet for sheep;
By that broad track I sought the hill
And lay in blowing wind stone-still.

Searching the sky for hidden lark
I closed my eyes with light grown dark
And heard their sheep-bells ring as though
Wide flock of sheep did dancing go
And near at hand noise of loud trees
That from their prayer would never cease.

All round me from the busy ground
Rose an infinite tiny sound
Where green grass hid green grass-hopper

Weaving his shuttle with shrill stir.
And by my eyes light-lit and blind
Hoarse bees swung by with singing wind.

There with bees, birds and praying trees
I slept awake, sharing their peace,
Then opened eyes in a light dim;
That dim light was my prayer to Him,
Who by a hill-track broad for sheep
Led my feet to the fold of sleep.

Peace

Peace on those owl-brown eyes that see the light
      But not the sun;
Peace on those soft-fleshed legs that never walk
      Save when they run;

Peace on pale hair that barters with the light
      Its original gold;
Peace on this mouth where earliest kisses are
      Bought but not sold;

Peace on small hands sturdy to grasp loose food
      That mouth to feed;
Peace on the sprouting rows of first-born teeth
      As small as seed;

Peace on those ears that listen with quick ear
      Fresh words to speak;
Peace on that face that ruddy apple slit
      Half for each cheek.

But bird of peace, build not as obvious birds
     Hard by road edge
Venture on darkness and sharp thorn to nest
     Deep in thick hedge.

Spiked Rampion

1.40 was my time of train
At Uckfield; three good miles to walk,
Watch creeping close on one o'clock;
Why did I linger in that lane?

Ask old Gerard or Culpeper,
Bartholomaeus Anglicus,
Tho. Kynge or Parkinson, why thus
My steps so long delayed me there.

But what with hours had I to do
Or any Anno Domini
Who saw against forgotten sky
Those hooded monks walk to and fro.

The gold-billed blackbird was less loud
Than clanging sound of chapel bell
For Vespers or departing knell
Of monk that moulded sheltering shroud.

I saw their plots of healing herbs,
Spiked rampion and blue bugloss,
Golden moth-wort and pigeon's grass
Clearer than cockney flowers on kerbs.

Scores of such sweet-named herbs were there,
Chervil, strong-seeded caraway,
Marigold, rue and rosemary,
Fennel and spittled lavender.

Screamed in my ear a distant train
Both hooded monks and herbs were gone,
Save one the white spiked rampion
That lingered with me in that lane.

Groundsel

(Senecio Vulgaris)

Jack-by-the-hedge loves a green shade
    Where he shoots straight and tall
But pimpernel a sun-baked field
    Where she creeps small.

Thrift matting turf on the sea-rocks
    Sucks honey from the sea;
Grey mistletoe builds like a bird
    On blue-mossed tree.

Lily from pool lifts a gold fist
    That to curved star uncurls
Dodder on furze spreads ruddy shawl
    Clasped by pink pearls.

But groundsel goes by any ground,
    An old man with bald head
None but the finch loves this poor man
    Who gives her bread.

Rain at Night

First fell a warning drop
    And the dim grass said, Hush;
Then raindrops without stop
    Spattered in a loose rush.

Raindrops chilled on my face
    Melting as fast again
And soon each listening place
    Muttered with a loud rain.

Darkened the road, but trees
    Flung shade of a brown light;
Hedges and vague grasses
    Were voices on the night.

The moon had gone to cloud
    And no stars were sight-seers;
Sky to the earth was bowed
    As night shed thoughtless tears.

'If night sheds thoughtless tears
    Night never laughed nor could
As that girl close to fears,
    Who talks in the lone wood.'

Motherwort

I stood beside the vicar's house;
A man came up the road with cows:
'You little devil' — this to a cur
That helped at them. To me, 'Well, Sir,
Have you found what you was looking for?'
I answered that I had. 'A flower
Was it?' Yes I replied. 'That one?'
This passed at Heanton Punchardon.

He told me that his father had
Shown him this flower when he was a lad
As doubtless he his son. He knew
Nothing but in his village grew
A rare flower that flower-hunters seek

(There was a man who came last week)
He felt it gave a place in the sun
To little Heanton Punchardon.

We talked as friends and then good-bye
He called harsh to his cows; for me
The austere beauty of that flower
Held all my lesser thoughts in power
For finding it I found the pain
Of other things I sought in vain
And shall not find by light of sun
That shines on Heanton Punchardon.

The Coombe

Across the coombe cloud-shadows were light fliers,
   The trees were red with autumn tints of spring,
Larks, furious in the sun, were loudest criers,
   Flashed the green-gold of yellow-hammer's wing.

My open path made mountains of mole-mounds
   Like shag-heaps graced with grass above dead mines,
An undistinguished track, kept within bounds
   By carts that staggered in its deep-delved lines.

Delight had stayed my steps at long stand-still
   Since cuckoo called Cuckoo from close behind
And from the dwarfed trees on the other hill
   Straggled an echoing call across the wind.

There silent, I moved on; two cuckoos swept
   This way and that with plaintive cuckoo-call
They came together while my footsteps slept
   But parted at my wakening footfall.

Strange things a man may do for ill or good
   Whether he stay at home or range abroad
But that for half-an-hour I should intrude
   On casual love of cuckoos seemed so odd.

Bog Pimpernel

Sets her white sail the moon
Trailing one dinghy star
Before brown cock-chafer
Drones from his faint bassoon,

By moon and star I sit
But blind as bat to both
For like night-going moth
Still among flowers I flit,

Where in a starving land
In loud sound of the sea
That booms like angry bee
Behind high mountainous sand

And where tall dye-rockets
Writhe in the wind like snakes
Pink bog pimpernel makes
Sunset that never sets.

Behind this heathy hill
Day's sunset drains away
But in full light of day
That pink sunset lies still.

Sea-Birds

With a thin earth for crown
The rising cliff falls down
Bathing her rocky knees
In the foam-netted seas.

Sea with slow waves a-crawl
Marbled round this rock-wall
Roars with the thoughtless voice
Of dull incessant noise.

When to this cliff I come
Sound of the sea dies dumb
Drowned by the shriller cries
From bird-disordered skies.

Foam of the foam are they
Tossed up like a white spray
Bright on the cliff below
Dim in the air as snow.

Though with these birds I share
Sea, cliff, nor hollow air
At my appearing form
Awakes this white sea-storm.

The Farm

When I came down out of the wood
　　Where shade was light that I walked by,
I blinked to see that farmstead stand
　　Snow-bound in the blue burning sky.

Carved out of silence stood a bull
    Basking in shadow of tree-bough;
He looked at me with a slow wrath
    Jutting in horns from his broad brow.

A cock among his scraping hens
    Stared with jewelled eye from blood-red comb;
Ducks shaking tails waddled to pond
    Where white plumes raised a storm of foam.

Sheets cracked along a tugging line
    And blue smoke from a chimney can
Flowed fast and leaned upon the wind;
    No other sign saw I of man.

Then somewhere in that silent house
    I heard a clock stirring with pain
It waked and struck the longest hour
    And settled back to sleep again.

And I looked up and I looked down
    From sun to shadow at my feet
And looked round where the rolling wood
    Moistened with green the sky-blue heat.

By sunrise I had seen that sun
    Rise like a gold mine from the ground,
By sunset I had seen it set
    Smiting the hills with a loud sound

And now, I said, should that same sun
    That all men's clocks are measured by
Strike any hour from one to twelve
    God would cast it out of the sky.

Amberley

At Houghton Bridge by Amberley
The men were dancing at mid-day
A one-step as I heard them say

One step or two steps I took seven
And from the bridge looked down on Heaven
Floating on water smooth and even

Danced maze of may-flies to my eye
In air and on that river sky.
Which was fly-shadow and which fly?

With slow and heavy step I crept
Through Amberley while all men slept
Sound as the dead and shadows wept.

I saw the broad-browed hills look down
On Amberley no earthly town,
My own brows knitted in slow frown.

Then seeing a dust-cloud advance
I stood rooted in sudden trance
To see dead men in their dust-dance

I watched them with long leaps and hops
Skim like sun-gleam through grassy crops
From church-year on to Hacket's Copse,

That horse-shoe hollow on the hill
Where the blue heat is never still,
Flies buzzing on fly-honey-suckle.

As I came back by the hill-ridge
My heart was dancing like a midge
While anglers slept at Houghton Bridge.

Private

Trespassers will be prosecuted—
    How? By whom? Who has the right?—
Hush, go your way; let lip be muted
    With finger; trees will screen from sight—

Then who has placed this notice-board?—
    No one; myself; what matter who?
The one who claims to be landlord
    Of this hill coppice and path through,

Each cracking stick loose flint and all
    Wild flowers, untenanted snail shell.
White butterflies that rise and fall,
    Round holes of rabbits and all else.

But why dispute? Thick crowd the leaves;
    Deeper sleeps moss across the trunk;
Wayfarer notes on thorn-stabbed sleeves
    Green caterpillar's arching back.

Ten years from now at most a score
    This tangled pathway will be lost,
And where its owner walked before
    Moonlight will stumble like a ghost.

Late Summer

Old? No I am not old nor young
I am like honey-suckle swung
    Midway the wild flowers' year
    From March to October.

With violets I felt the smart
Of murmuring rain on my near heart,
    Felt too the ravishment
    Of rain-delivered scent.

Now loose on the least breezes blown
The seeded silk of thistle-down
    And bird's-foot trefoil shows
    The black print of her toes;

And the round-headed rampion
Unsheathes her blue claws in the sun
    Clutching at every wind
    That leaves her still behind.

I know that I am no self-heal
But oh, dear God, give me to feel
    One small chill drop again
    Of primrose-lightened rain.

The Bird

Last week, last night; tonight's the third
Time I have startled the same bird
    Here by field path she has
    Her nest, close in long grass.

Flutter of wings and she is gone;
I mark the place by a white stone;
    Each time I say tomorrow
    Sight of those eggs I'll borrow,

Or nestlings as they now must be;
Broad mouths outstretched shall gape at me
    And in my god-like form
    See hope of a red worm.

At Rossetti's Grave

Saturday night—
Noise and light of the square
Outfacing the star-light
Remote and mild in the upper air.

Noise nor light joins
Dust that is sleeping by
Remoter than those stars
Whose brighter dust sprinkles the sky.

What is the dust
That dark shrub-sheltered grave,
Holding in treasured trust,
Cannot with all close striving save?

Has hidden death
After twoscore slow years
Made of that mouth's sweet breath
A song too pitiful for tears?

O my song, hush!
Forgetful dust forget;
That cloud you saw—his brush
Dipped in the colours of sunset.

Cuckmere Haven

Heavy with a sea-falling flood
    The grey stream flowed through the banked plain
Echoing frosted sea-wormwood
    And olive-grey purslane.

Sea-weed and sticks and dusty froth
    Floated on the smooth current by
Drifting with dull indifferent sloth
    Against a dove-grey sky.

Deep in its bed of sluggish chalk
    A crab from waking sleep awoke
Speeding away with side-long walk
    In a thick cloudy smoke.

Sea-mist creeping up from the sea
    Dimmed sky and the white watery sun
And dimmed my eyes as close by me
    I watched the stream-drift run.

The Fields

Once as I did labour
    Working on my own farm
I looked across the hedge to see how things fared with my
                             neighbour
    And oh my eyes were warm.

Yes, warm with stinging tears
    His fields were harvest-swept
One year for him was sufficient, but after all these years—
    I hid my face and wept.

At the End

Lord, I but praise in part
Thy love maintains the start
For time makes more and more
All I would thank thee for.

I praise thee Lord and yet
I am the more in debt
For praise brings blessedness
Makes praise seem less and less.

So, fast as I may run,
I am the losing one;
Still behind Thee I fall
By lengthening interval.

And thus do I conceive
More than I might believe
Praise that can live for ever
Lost in its vain endeavour.

Morning Moon

The moon rose late and large
Hung in the sky her golden targe
Seeing her limp on shrivelled thigh
A dying moon, said I.

That moon in morning air
Will seem a cloud that is not there
And my night's song will linger on
Echo of what has gone.

Friston Church

From Friston Church down to the Tiger
    Path through the field runs to and fro,
Scorèd with the feet of happy children
    Dead men and women long ago

Church Field, the field; the scented orchis
   Shoots from the grass in rosy spire
Such odour of sanctity was wafted
   Never from stone church with white choir.

Ruin summoned me to church's shelter;
   Baring my head I entered in
And from last pew kneeling on hassock
   Waited for service to begin.

No priest was there, nor any people
   Nor rows of washed white-surpliced boys
The Book left open on the lectern
   Read with no aid of human voice.

I sat and listened to the lesson
   Till through the roof beamed with black oak
Old and worm-eaten, spaced with plaster,
   The rain of Heaven began to soak.

It fell through roof and sturdy rafter
   On hands and on hand-hidden face
Never knew I such shower of blessing
   As dropped on me in that same place.

I left the church; a swinging gateway
   Led my steps to the road beyond
Surprised I noticed how the raindrops
   Winked in circles on Friston pond.

Freda

Why did they lay her down so deep,
   I wondered at the time;
One foot of earth from that lost utter sleep

Were hill too hard to climb
If she would take our air by noon
Or steal to us by thievish light of moon.

Child for whom day was swifter than
    Sleep's sudden flight of hours
If she lay nearer to the wind that ran
    Shaking grass seeds and flowers,
She would lie closer to the thoughts
That seek her in our blue forget-me-nots.

Today I stooped to pluck a flower,
    A strange and rare orchis
But found my hand half-way had lost its power,
    For scarce from chrysalis
Increased, I saw a butterfly
Bear on its wings the weight of the blue sky.

Steyning

'Sir John Gough's house, 1771'
Who was Sir John? What had he done?
Surely that knight has changed abode,
And some way down, across the road
I'd find his house, if I should search,
There, near to Steyning's Norman church.

Well, here I tread the same hill-track
Sheltered by trees, where small sticks crack
Like sound of distant machine-gun;
On hanging spider's thread the sun
Glides to and fro like one who walks
A tight-rope, and last cuckoo mocks.

Tree leaning back whispers to tree
And sky-blue fly and fussy bee
Make the air hum; whistles of birds,
Recognised airs, are close to words;
All is so still, tick-tick I catch,
No, not my heart, it is my watch.

Then, questioned by some thought, I press
Hand on my knocking heart; o yes,
You, heart, my joy, you too as well
Like nestling trampling on its shell
Shall break to freedom; soon enough
Too soon; remember Sir John Gough.

Back to the Land

Last night we talked of this and that
Pullets that lay pigs that grow fat
Bees, fire-alarmed by a smoke puff
That gorge on honey, more than enough
And cows that carry sweet milk kegs
Swinging at ease between hind legs.

O how our talk was sweet and warm
As manure heap close by a farm
Deeper in colour, richer, hotter
Than Rembrandt, Ruysdael or Paul Potter;
Then at the gate, hand clasped in hand
Laughing we roared, Back to the land.

Today one works in motor-shop
And one on tall chair perched atop
Shifts her neat piles of numbered money;
Pullets, pigs, cows, bees and their honey
All gone, save one bee left alive
That swift with sweetness drives for hive.

O how this sun of blue-skyed June
Bores through the trees bright as the moon;
How silently four-winged grey moth
Flits in dim shadow, blessing sloth;
Even this nettle, stinging my hand
Hisses angrily, Back to the land.

BIBLIOGRAPHICAL NOTE

Andrew Young's first *Collected Poems* (Cape, 1936) consisted of the forty-five poems from *Winter Harvest* (Nonesuch Press, 1933), forty-four from *The White Blackbird* (Cape, 1935), one poem 'The Nest', transferred from *The New Shepherd* (J. E. Bumpus, 1931), eight revisions from *The Bird-Cage* (1926), *The Cuckoo Clock* (1929), and *The New Shepherd* (J. E. Bumpus, 1931), and eight new poems. There were a hundred and six poems in all.

His second book of *Collected Poems* (Cape, 1950) had wood engravings by Joan Hassall. This was a compilation of *Collected Poems* 1936, the forty-three poems of *Speak to the Earth* (Cape, 1939), the thirty-eight poems of *The Green Man* (Cape, 1947) — one hundred and eighty-seven poems in all — together with the verse play *Nicodemus: A Mystery* (Cape, 1936). 'The House Martins', revised for *Speak to the Earth,* was re-named 'The Swallows', 'Autumn' from *Winter Harvest,* was re-named 'Penelope', 'By the Erme' was a re-writing — but very much more than a revision — of a much earlier poem 'On Dartmoor', which had first appeared in *The New Shepherd.*

Andrew Young's *Collected Poems* (Hart-Davis, 1960) consisted of *Collected Poems* 1950, *Nicodemus,* and twenty-two additional poems, a total of two hundred and nine poems; the poems, for the first time in a collected edition, were arranged chronologically.

Of the twenty-two additional poems, seventeen were resurrected from the pre-1933 books. They were 'The Leaf' from *Songs of Night,* 'On the Cliff' from *Boaz and Ruth,* 'The Bee-Orchis' from *The Death of Eli,* 'Islands', 'Cuckoo', 'Waiting' and 'A Child's Voice' from *Thirty-One Poems,* 'The Tumulus', 'The Gate' and 'Green Hellebore' from *The Bird-Cage,* 'Rother in Flood', 'At Oxford', 'On the Beaulieu Road', 'The Oak-Wood', 'Sunbeams' and 'Kingley Bottom' from *The Cuckoo Clock,* and 'Round Barrows' and 'The Flint Breaker' from *The New Shepherd.* To these were added 'In the Dingle' from Andrew Young's prose book *A Prospect of Britain* (Hutchinson, 1956), and revisions of three poems from the earlier books: 'Hymn', now in the *BBC Hymn Book* (1951), which appeared in its first form in *The Adversary,* 'July' from *The Bird-Cage,* and 'At Grime's Graves' which, in its revised form, was first included in *A Prospect of Britain.* One poem, 'By a British Barrow in War-time', had been previously contributed to *The Nineteenth Century,* and had never before appeared in book form. The *Collected Poems* of 1960 also had a bibliographical note and the Joan Hassall wood-engravings. A special edition, consisting of sixty-five copies, of which fifty were for sale, was also produced at the time; the fifteen presentation copies were signed by poet and illustrator.

The present edition is properly called *Complete Poems.* Unlike the earlier *Collected Poems* it contains every poem known to have been written by Andrew Young, together with the play *Nicodemus.* It must, therefore, be considered the definitive edition.

However, one wonders how many poems Andrew Young wrote and destroyed. Knowing how much of the original 'Into Hades' he destroyed, and something of the character of the poet himself, it is safe to assume that he was equally severe with the short poems, though he did not speak of this to anyone. For so long a life, a final total of under four hundred poems, does suggest that the wastepaper basket was much in evidence during Andrew Young's writing life.

Complete Poems consists of the whole of *Collected Poems* (1960) which had the imprimatur of the poet himself, *Out of the World and Back, Songs of Night* (1910), all the poems in the 'Wilson' books which did not appear in *Collected Poems* 1960, and thirty-four unpublished poems, all of which were written between 1920 and 1926.

Not included here are three early plays, one still in manuscript, and two, *The Adversary* and *Rizpah,* first published in *The Adversary* (1923), one of the 'Wilson' books. These have been excluded, not only because of their length, but also because they do not strictly belong to a volume of poems. *Nicodemus* is included because the poet himself regarded it as belonging to his corpus of poetry, and it also appeared in *Collected Poems* 1950 and 1960. The two poems from *Out of the World and Back* were not included in *Collected Poems* 1960 because the former was still in print at the time and, for obvious reasons, its publisher did not wish for two copies of the poems to be in print at the same time. 'Into Hades' was extensively revised for *Out of the World and Back.* Of this volume, Andrew Young said, in a brief introductory note: 'When the spring of short Nature poems ran dry, I was not sorry; for while my interest in nature was intense, it was not as deep as the underlying interest that prompted me to change my style and write 'Into Hades'. That poem was published in 1952; it has now been much amended, sufficiently, I hope, to justify its re-appearance along with the sequel, 'A Traveller in Time'.

The poems previously published in the 'Wilson' books, but not included in *Collected Poems* 1960, are placed in the present volume at the end of the book with *Songs of Night* both to respect the wishes of the poet who did not consider them good enough for any of the books published in his life-time, and also because this is a volume called *Complete Poems* and they should be made available for the scholars and critics who wish to study Andrew Young's whole body of work, as well as for the general reader. Such an arrangement should go some way to placate those who believe that poems, previously published, but discarded by the poet in his lifetime, or, for other reasons, by the editor of *Collected Poems* 1960, should not be included in any edition of the poet's work. Nevertheless, there may well be poems in this section of the book which some may consider to be of sufficient merit to find a place in the earlier part of the present volume, in spite of what the poet himself thought of them. This explanation having been made, it is not considered that Andrew Young's reputation is in any way damaged, for it is not necessary for him to be judged by the poems which appear in this final section. A study of these poems, in fact, will give positive evidence of how Andrew Young developed, and also show that the signs of his genius were already present in many of them. There are one hundred and thirty-two of these poems from the seven 'earlier' books.

But there are also poems included in this section which have never before been published in book form. There exist two small books, in manuscript, of fifty-two poems by her husband copied out by Mrs Young. Eighteen of these manuscript poems originally appeared in *The Bird-Cage*, and some of these were later revised for *Collected Poems* 1936 and included also in *Collected Poems* 1950 and 1960. The remaining thirty-four poems in manuscript are now included in the later section of the present volume.

One poem, 'At Arley', was found among Andrew Young's papers following his death and was probably written towards the end of his life while he was at work on 'Into Hades'.

To summarise, therefore, *Complete Poems* consists of the two hundred and nine poems from *Collected Poems* 1960, the two long peoms which constituted *Out of the World and Back*, the hundred and thirty-two poems from *Songs of Night* and the 'Wilson' books, and the thirty-four poems in manuscript, making a total of three hundred and seventy-seven poems.

This is not a large body of work for a poet whose first book of poems was published in 1910 and his last in 1958, but it is a distinguished corpus by a poet of remarkable consistency. As far as the 'nature' poems are concerned, Andrew Young's prolific years appear to have been from 1930 to 1947. From then onwards he turned to prose, though prose of a lyrical nature, with the exception of the two long eschatological poems with their marked change of style.

'Wiltshire Downs', a much anthologised poem, is a very interesting example in this matter of revision. This first appeared in its present form in *Speak to the Earth*. It is the result of merging portions of two separate poems, 'Cuckoo-Bottom' and 'Downland Shepherd', which first appeared in *The Cuckoo Clock*.

First Versions:

Cuckoo-Bottom

The tunnelling mould-warps
Build their fresh barrows on a kicking corpse;
Where the old barrows linger
This winter sun points no long-shadowed finger.

The thudding race-horse hooves
Print on the sodden soil their lucky grooves,
But wethers chime a bell
Where Briton warriors sleep who sleep too well.

The cuckoo's double note
Loosened like bubbles from a drowning throat
Those Britons do not hear—
Cuckoos in Egypt call this time of year.

Downland Shepherd

While stable-boys go thundering by
Slinging dark divots at the sky,
Like a windhover he stands still
Beside the sun, late on the hill,
And chin on hands, hands on his crook;
Tegs, shearlings, yoes cons like a book
Or sees them pass slow as a cloud,
Four hundred heads with one prayer bowed.

Final Version:

Wiltshire Downs

The cuckoo's double note
Loosened like bubbles from a drowning throat
Floats through the air
In mockery of pipit, lark and stare.

The stable-boys thud by
Their horses slinging divots at the sky
And with bright hooves
Printing the sodden turf with lucky grooves.

As still as a windhover
A shepherd in his flapping coat leans over
His tall sheep-crook
And shearlings, tegs and yoes cons like a book.

And one tree-crowned long barrow
Stretched like a sow that has brought forth her
farrow
Hides a king's bones
Lying like broken sticks among the stones.

'At Formby' also shows considerable revision. There was a poem with this title in *The New Shepherd*. It appeared again, sixteen years later, in *The Green Man*:—

First Version:

How strange to walk that shore
No foot had ever trod before
Or since the sea drew back the tide;
It seemed so vast, lonely and wide
As though God were not there
To mitigate that empty sea and air.

Strange too on the coastland
Those pines no higher than my hand;
Though as I walked the trees grew taller
And I myself grew small and smaller,
Till in a high dark wood
I seemed to find again my lost childhood.

Final Version:

From that wide empty shore,
No foot had ever trod before
(Or since the sea drew back the tide),

I climbed the dune's soft slide
To where no higher than my hand
Wind-bitten pines grew in the clogging sand.

But farther from the beath
The trees rose up beyond my reach,
And as I walked, they still grew taller
And I myself smaller and smaller,
Till gazing up at a high wood
I felt that I had found my lost childhood.

It is perhaps of interest to students to note that the poems listed below appeared in their first published versions as follows: in *Thirty-One Poems* (1922): 'In Moonlight' (as 'Full Moon') (page 187); in *The Adversary* (1923): 'Hymn'; in *The Bird-Cage* (1926): 'The Spider', 'The Wood', 'The Rain', 'The Beech', 'The Evening Star', 'The Feather', 'The Loddon', 'The Cuckoo', 'The Chalk-Cliff', 'The Ventriloquists', 'August', 'Autumn Seeds', 'Snow', 'The Swallows' (as 'The Housemartins'), 'The Thunderstorm', 'A Wet Day', 'The Blind Children', 'On the Hillside', 'The Day Ends', 'The Gate' (as 'Gossip'), 'July'; in *The Cuckoo Clock* (1929): 'The Roman Wall', 'Loch Luichart', 'February' (as 'January'), 'The Oak Wood', 'The Missel-Thrush', 'Wiltshire Downs' (as two poems: 'Downland Shepherd' and 'Cuckoo-Bottom'), 'Christmas Day' (as 'Christmas Eve'), 'The Shower'; in *The New Shepherd* (1931): 'Winter Morning', 'Penelope' (as 'Autumn'), 'Illic Jacet', 'The Shadow', 'The Secret Wood', 'Stay, Spring', 'The Slow Race', 'Sea Wormwood' (as 'Evening Walk'), 'The Fallen Tree', 'The River Dove', 'The Chalk-Quarry', 'South Downs', 'The Gramophone', 'At Formby', 'In Avebury Circle', 'At Grime's Graves'.

Leonard Clark

Index of First Lines